I'M JUST
HAPPY
TO BE HERE

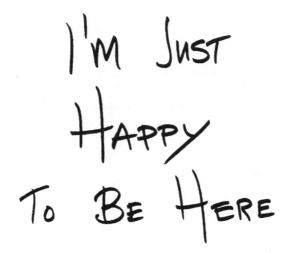

I'M JUST
HAPPY
TO BE HERE

A MEMOIR OF
RENEGADE MOTHERING

JANELLE HANCHETT

hachette
BOOKS

NEW YORK   BOSTON

Copyright © 2018 by Janelle Hanchett
Jacket design by Amanda Kain
Jacket photograph © plainpicture/Readymade-Images/Franck Juery
Cover copyright © 2018 by Hachette Book Group, Inc.

Hachette Books
Hachette Book Group
1290 Avenue of the Americas
New York, NY 10104
hachettebooks.com
twitter.com/hachettebooks

First Edition: May 2018

Hachette Books is a division of Hachette Book Group, Inc.
The Hachette Books name and logo are trademarks of Hachette Book Group, Inc.

The publisher is not responsible for websites (or their content) that are not owned by the publisher.

The Hachette Speakers Bureau provides a wide range of authors for speaking events. To find out more, go to www.hachettespeakersbureau.com or call (866) 376-6591.

Library of Congress Control Number: 2017952977

ISBNs: 978-0-316-50377-8 (hardcover), 978-0-316-54943-1 (ebook)

Printed in the United States of America

LSC-H

10 9 8 7 6 5 4 3 2 1

Hey, Mom. Look. We did it.

CONTENTS

PART ONE

1

FAMILY PLANNING ON ECSTASY

The first thing I did when I found out I was pregnant with my first child was head out to the balcony of our one-bedroom apartment and smoke a cigarette. It wasn't even a real balcony. It was a gray stoop barely big enough for one unwatered plant, a dusty mat, and a twenty-one-year-old in vague denial. I would have preferred outright denial but found it impossible, having just peed on two sticks offering no ambiguity.

My plan was to formulate a plan out there on the balcony before informing the father, who was my boyfriend of three full months. We shared the apartment, but I made sure I was alone that afternoon, protected in isolation, so nobody would see me cry, or rage, or decide to handle the situation silently. I was never the kind of person who wanted company in moments of vulnerability. I never wanted a concerned friend to pat my head and smooth the hair off my forehead while I puked or cried. I wanted to lie in bed in solitude, where I could turn my head to the wall, stretch my legs out, and rise again smiling, while the world slept soundly in its room.

The last thing I needed was a loving and emotional man celebrating the seed in my womb before I knew how I felt about it.

Moments before, I had stared at those double lines with detached curiosity, a sort of numbed awe, as they popped up without hesitation in what seemed like a "fuck you" pink. I figured there could still be some mistake, so I took another test, and upon the second neon positive, pulled up my jeans, walked through the living room and onto the balcony, grabbing my Camel Lights and lighter on the way. I allowed my condition to sink one inch into my brain, where it hovered like a storm cloud creeping toward me. I knew it would shower me in panic, and soon I would feel it pouring down my arms and into my shoes, but those first moments felt liminal, half-real. I emboldened them with a cigarette. One more cigarette in the line of a thousand before it, a meaningless action of my same old life. An action of the nonpregnant.

Nothing to see here, folks. Just another woman on a balcony having a smoke.

That February afternoon was cool and bright, and as I watched the cars do nothing in the parking lot of our apartment complex, I thought about being a senior in college, my job as a waitress, and the few months Mac and I had been together, most of it grayed and hazy from alcohol, fast and romantic and possibly fake. I thought about how he would respond if he were there.

He would smile a soft smile. "Wow," he would say, "I love you so much," and his eyes would fill with grateful tears as more supportive words crossed his lips. He would study my reaction with his huge brown eyes. He would look as if he had waited his whole life to hear those three words.

I am pregnant.

I took a drag, inhaling *I could have an abortion*, but exhaled the startling realization that I would not.

And with the thought, the cigarette grew foul between my fingers. I stamped it out beneath my foot and wondered how the fuck I had ended up here again. I understood the physiology of pregnancy. I did not understand how that wasn't enough.

In my defense, the first one was an honest mistake. I was eighteen, in my first semester of college, and had spontaneous, unprotected make-up sex with my long-term boyfriend. I knew immediately I would not have that baby, and I did not feel guilty about that decision, though I suspected this made me something of a monster. I felt sadness, but at that age, in that life, I mostly felt relief. We had sex, and *yes* I happen to have a uterus and ovaries hell-bent on reproduction, and our act was neither smart nor mature, but *it was his fault too.* My defense was that of a petulant child, but I had no interest in spending my whole life paying for a five-minute interval of questionable sex with a man who could walk away if he felt like it.

As I stood on the balcony, I wondered again, *Who the hell gets pregnant accidentally more than once?*

I stared at the horizon and shook my head in disgust as I traveled the recesses of my brain looking for answers, recalling only a woman in my freshman comparative literature class. She had told me, "Getting an abortion is like getting your teeth cleaned." When I raised an eyebrow, she explained, "It's just something you have to do." She was in her thirties and married to a local rock star. She had bad teeth, three children, tattoos, and that haircut of the '90s where bangs were cut stupidly short in a band right against the forehead. I respected her.

Her teeth cleaning theory sounded erroneous if not downright depraved, but her nonchalance convinced me I would be alright, and that I was even perhaps not quite as foul as I had believed during my trip to the clinic that week, feeling like a slut and regretting with my whole heart those minutes in the dorms.

Apparently this is a thing women do.

That seemed true. I did it.

But I would not do it now.

And it didn't feel like the fucking dentist.

Back inside, I stretched out on our quilt-covered couch, clicking my tongue at Fatboy, the giant black-and-white cat we inherited from Mac's childhood. When feeling particularly affectionate, Fatboy would turn his head and glance at you from across the room. But that day, he folded up in the crook of my knees and stared up at me, as if he knew things were heavy.

I took a deep breath, looking around the apartment, the carpet so bland I couldn't tell what color it was, the kitchen and bathroom floors a yellowed linoleum with pastel blue squares, ripped up and black at the corners. The cabinets were a 1970s brown with gold handles, and metal mini-blinds hung above a box air conditioner in the window that would sputter along against California's Central Valley heat. That summer, we moved our mattress beneath the little box, creating a pocket of decency between the white walls. Our television sat on boards and cinder blocks. It was the kind of apartment that never felt alive or permanent, but Mac and I were kids and in love, and it was ours.

He was nineteen and I was twenty-one.

• • •

I was right about Mac. He did smile through tears and say all the lovely things I suspected he'd say when I told him I was pregnant, but the next day he added, "If you don't have our baby, I can't stay with you." I considered telling him about the moment I knew I wouldn't have an abortion, but instead I merely nodded. I wasn't ready to speak the words, "I am having a baby." I was stretching the liminal gray a few days longer.

When he spoke those words, he didn't read my face to adjust his tone. He was not afraid of my response, or conflict, and there was no subtext. It was merely data to inform a decision. If his statement had been a threat, an attempted entrapment, I would have left immediately on those grounds alone. *Fuck you for even trying to get me to stay*, I'd have thought.

But that's not what he said, and I knew it, because he said it with warm acceptance in his eyes and mouth and forehead—the way he looked at me when he said everything, even when he yelled and postured and I thought maybe I hated him. Or, perhaps that's why I hated him, because he seemed capable of only adoration, and even in his anger he was devoted and irrationally loyal. It made me feel a little sick.

I get it, man. You can't withstand the resentment you'd feel toward me if I didn't have our baby.

But he is not why I had her. I was always going to have her and I knew it, though I didn't know how to explain that I knew. I didn't understand yet that motherhood is a lot of knowing without knowing.

But I knew *her*. She was already made.

I was afraid of having a baby. I was afraid of committing to him like that. I was afraid of what my parents would say, but Mac misread this fear as indecision. I had her because she was meant to be here and I was meant to be her mother, and I believed that in the same way I know the sun will rise. I had her because the moment I knew of her, she existed, like a strange new friend who moved in and wouldn't leave.

I told myself I was about to graduate from college, that I wasn't *that* young, that Mac was going to be a good father—and I loved him, or thought I did. In this way, I rearranged the facts, the furniture of my life, to accommodate my new friend.

Two weeks later, Mac peeked his head over the curtain while I showered and said, "It's going to be a girl."

"I know," I said, and laughed. *How weird we are*, I thought. *Clairvoyant. So in love she's already shining through—through the blood and walls of my body.*

We thought of names. We thought of Aurora and Leah and Althea, but one day while I waited for customers to arrive for dinner in the restaurant where I waitressed, I flipped through a magazine and found an article about Ava Gardner.

We settled on Ava Grace, as if anything could be more beautiful.

• • •

I told my mother I knew she was a girl; she didn't think that was strange at all. When I asked her what the hell I was going to do with my life now, she said, "Well, honey, you're going to have a baby." Her simplicity and perky use of the word "honey" shot red annoyance down my spine.

My mother's perpetual optimism made me wonder if she existed in some sort of sociopathic love cloud. As a young girl, I joined in her optimism, jumped on the "it's going to be great!" train with glee, but over the years, as each new beginning almost never turned out "great," I realized her outlook was as much fantasy as it was hope. It was a story to justify rushing headlong into another disaster, the same thing we'd done for years. Businesses. Marriages. Personality improvements. Diets. It was always going to be different this time.

It was an old, raw burn, and her sweetness still stung.

The moment she mentioned relationships, mine or hers, somewhere in me the memory of my former stepfather stirred, the way we moved in and out of his house like a vacation rental. But mostly, I remembered her suffering and how I thought I could fix it, how the solution was perfectly clear to me, how everybody said I was "very mature for my age." My mother used to say, "I don't know how you see the things you see, Janelle."

I didn't either, but I wished she'd see them too, because I was tired. And even at twenty-one, I was still tired, perhaps more tired than I'd ever been, and I had long since stopped believing in her dreams.

And yet, I always called her first, to bathe in the optimism she turned toward me, too, toward the person she believed I could become. I needed that. I needed to believe things were going to be different *right around the corner.* That sick hope was infectious, seeping into me whether I wanted it or not, and as much as I distrusted it in her, I clung to it like a drowning woman, because at least it was something.

"But how do you *know,* Mom?" I didn't mask my irritation.

"Because you are going to be fine, sweetie." I wanted to throw up.

She must have told her mother right away, because the next day Grandma Joan called and said, "You know you don't have to marry this guy just because you're pregnant," and my jaw hit my flip phone. I wasn't anywhere near marrying Mac. I barely knew him. *I am merely going to have his baby, Grandma.*

Being a woman born in 1930, Grandma Joan of course assumed marriage, and I assumed she would push marriage. She was in her seventies and a Mormon woman who had made her husband dinner every night since they were married at eighteen, and if she was not home in the evening, she prepared the food and put it on the counter so all he had to do was heat it up. He had been the quarterback of the high school football team and she had been the new girl in town—and a cheerleader. It was a movie, and yet true. They still held hands when they sat on the couch together, and they flirted like teenagers. He was sure old Benny at the post office was waiting for him to "kick the bucket" so he could swoop in on Grandma.

She would smack his leg, roll her eyes, and say, "Oh, Bob," with exasperation and a kiss in her eye.

At family functions in her home, all the women would bustle around the kitchen for hours preparing dinner for thirty while the kids played in the basement and the men watched football in the living room. After dinner, all the women would bustle around in the kitchen for hours doing dishes while the men watched football in the living room, and the kids ran around in the basement. By the time I was a teenager, I wondered what the hell was wrong with these people. But I loved being in the kitchen, where my mother and three aunts talked and cooked with the chatter and laughter of a lifetime of sisterhood, occasionally popping out to rescue a screaming baby, talking of report cards and breastfeeding and wayward teens, of Grandma's silly ways and how she really should sit down, *she's tired*, but she never would. When she finally did, my uncles had begun barbequing on the deck outside and nobody played in the basement anymore.

I sat with the men, too, as babies crawled around their laps, each of their faces illuminated with the television screen as they watched sports, speaking of things I didn't understand, like "downs" and "bad calls" and "finals." I felt honored when they spoke to me, a little nod to my sport-less existence. I understood their acknowledgment of me was a quick trip beneath themselves, a little jaunt to a place less sacred. They were, after all, the ones who got to do nothing while groups of women worked on their behalf.

Although the kitchen was warmer, and had better conversation, sometimes I would sit at the dining table between the living room and kitchen, so I could watch both ends and refuse to commit.

At twenty-one, I joined the women in the kitchen for good, though I had always promised I'd never be like them. "I'm not going to get married until I'm thirty," I'd say as a teenager at our annual Christmas party, "and I won't have a baby until thirty-five."

"Good job," my aunt would nod. "Just don't rush it."

"Of course not," I'd answer, irritated that she'd even consider the possibility of me ruining my life with an unplanned pregnancy at a young age.

I was the youngest of my cousins to have a baby.

People surprise you, though, especially when they're old and sick of the bullshit, and I saw Joan anew the day she called me, after fifty-five years spent with my grandfather. While she spoke, I wondered how many women of her generation married terrible men because of unexpected pregnancies, and then stayed because of more. I felt myself, for an instant, counted among them.

"Thank you for your concern, Grandma, but it's different with us," I said.

I may be in the kitchen like the rest of you broads, but I am different. I could not articulate how, exactly, but I knew I wouldn't end up washing dishes while the men watched other men slam into each other on brightly lit screens. It seemed archaic and absurd. I would demand freedom, even within the confines of pregnancy. I suppose that, too, is something women "just have to do."

If I had to guess, I would have said my future would unfold more along the lines of my paternal grandmother, Bonny Jean. She was an intellectual, a fiery Christian Scientist, and natural skeptic who believed in God but not doctors, grassroots journalism, and stockpiling mayonnaise in case there was another Great Depression.

She grew up behind the stage with her parents, who were traveling actors. I once attempted to explain "gay people" to her because, *you know, as a relic she wouldn't understand such things.* She spun around to face me in her house robe and said, "I grew up behind a vaudeville stage in the twenties. You think any of those people were straight?" I never tried that shit again.

She had five children from 1945 to 1955. They were raised largely by her father-in-law while she ran her newspaper, which she and my grandfather purchased in 1956. Bonny Jean would attend every local city council meeting, critiquing what she saw in scathing weekly editorials, which she would often dictate over the pay phone in the city council hallway. She once fought the head of the San Francisco plumbers' union, a man with rumored Mafia ties, who was trying to take over her small town's water council. When she broke the story and refused to back down, he threatened her. I once asked how she managed to fight a man like him as a woman in the 1960s. She said, "Oh, that was easy, honey. I was not afraid of him. The truth is a strong defense."

When I told her about the pregnancy, I thought I heard a touch of sadness in her voice, despite her congratulations, because for a split second, they sounded like condolences.

The hardest person to tell was my father. I was barely old enough to handle him knowing I had sex, and yet I had to tell him there was an actual human growing in my body, deposited there by the sperm of a man. Telling him felt something like bra shopping with my mother at fourteen: uncomfortable in a deeply shameful, yet unknown way. Everybody has sex. Everybody gets boobs.

Still, somebody please kill me.

I had always felt my father saw me as a kid who was going to do something impressive in life, who was going to become a lawyer or doctor or at least make a lot of money. Instead, I was joining the Mormons in the kitchen. I knew he wouldn't say it, but he would be disappointed in me. He knew how many times I had stood at family functions declaring my plan, and he knew I never consciously abandoned that.

It's hardest to fall in front of those you've convinced, through years of tone moderation and personality suppression, that you are not the type to falter.

•   •   •

I stopped smoking and drinking immediately after my balcony denial, which felt wholesome and deeply mature, despite Mac's and my decision to move out of our apartment and into his parents' house on their ranch. They lived in a dome-shaped house about ten miles outside of Davis, California, the clean, well-manicured town where I went to college and met Mac.

Davis boasts the second-highest per capita number of PhDs in any city in the nation, and a special tunnel for frogs so they don't get killed on the road. The town is teeming with students, artists, and intellectuals on bicycles, but also suffers from an epidemic of highly educated, splendid liberals. I learned to spot and avoid the latter from a distance of approximately one hundred feet, having had many years' practice. The problem is not that they're liberal—surely one can learn to live with that—it's that they can't quite understand why a person wouldn't dress her child in only organic cotton, or shop solely at the co-op, where they sell nineteen dollar olive oil pressed from olives grown on blessed trees in sacred Native American valleys.

These are the kind of people who call gentrification "restoring the neighborhood" and spend four years on a waiting list for a $1,500 a month preschool while claiming to deeply understand the plight of the underprivileged. Davis is the kind of town where *everyone breathes social justice* via diversity stickers on their Priuses, but many citizens request that the kids from the Mexican enclaves surrounding the town simply stay in *their* schools. *It's not about race. It's just . . . you know . . . let's talk about public radio. Do you support it? It's kind of my cause. That, and the ACLU.*

Most of the mothers in Davis were married, in their late thirties, and living in $700,000 houses when I showed up at age twenty-one, unmarried and pregnant. When I realized nobody would talk to me at the park, having dismissed me immediately as some sort of teen-pregnancy situation, Mac and I bought a pink diaper bag with a giant rhinestone Playboy bunny on the front. It was my subtle "fuck you" to everyone who wouldn't talk to me anyway, and it almost convinced me I didn't care.

I turned twenty-two that March and finished my last semester of college in September of 2001, two months before our baby was due. Mac worked at his father's slaughterhouse on the ranch, and our bedroom was where Mac had played with Hot Wheels and G.I. Joes as a boy, and hid his weed at fifteen. We shared the home with five other people: his parents, two sisters, and his sister's boyfriend. All the bedrooms were upstairs and opened into a shared center hallway, kind of like Foucault's panopticon only without the glass. His family was kind and relaxed and pretended we weren't kids about to have a kid, but I felt exposed and watched—too close to people who weren't quite mine, humans I knew but didn't understand, and whom I was still trying to impress. They were family, but I didn't want them to see me naked, or notice I stunk up the bathroom or yelled at their son. I self-regulated, even though there was no guard in the watchtower.

We bought a crib and an oak dresser, which we wedged together in a corner of the bedroom. I lined each drawer in lavender-scented paper with tiny pastel pink flowers on it, and I bought clothes from Baby Gap and Gymboree and Marshalls. I bought most of them in "newborn" size because they were the cutest and least expensive. I didn't know they were discounted because babies outgrow them in twelve minutes.

We had a keg of beer at our baby shower, and Mac came because we were "too in love to be apart." I received about seventy-five various bath items because when my stepmother asked, "What do you need for the baby?" I answered, "Bath items." I didn't know you were supposed to "register." I didn't have any friends telling me about pregnancy or babies because only losers had babies this young. And I never hung out with losers.

My pregnancy was like living in a dream, a sort of ethereal fantasy ticking by in nebulous form. While my belly grew, I spent my days petting hand-smocked outfits with embroidered ducks and imagining our little threesome. Mac and I played pool at my local university's student union, and I wasn't even embarrassed of my belly. I wasn't embarrassed of my age, or Mac's lack of career, or that we lived in a room in his parents' house. Those things weren't in the dream.

But I couldn't help but feel inklings of shame as I walked to class during that last semester, when I barely fit in the desks, because the sidewalks and grass and offices on campus were the places where women like me rarely succeeded, and nobody was impressed with expanding uteri. These were PhDs and MAs and lovers of Derrida. They could see right through me: I was the kid who lost, the girl who failed. As I walked I remembered maybe I was going to be more than this, but then I thought of Mac and the baby girl to come. I thought of that love and squared my shoulders.

We went to peaceful birthing classes and breathed together and when Ava came it was fast and insane and Mac sat by me and held my hands and never broke my gaze. The nurses said we were the most beautiful birthing couple they had ever seen.

I wasn't surprised. It was the only way it could be.

• • •

I met Mac for the first time in my living room the night before Halloween, thirteen months before Ava was born. I was living in a converted garage in a house I shared with four eighteen- and nineteen-year-old males I had found in a newspaper. Three months before I responded to their "roommate wanted" ad, I returned home from a year studying abroad in Spain. I tried living with my mother up north in Mendocino, California, and found a job waitressing, but got fired after two weeks for counseling the owner on how she could improve her business. I found myself bored, embarrassed, and broke, so I moved back to Davis in the fall and began waitressing at an "Asian fusion" restaurant and drinking too much.

I had long before decided I could not live with women. They were too complicated. They needed things like talking and support and genuineness. I needed things like rum and Coke and silence. So I asked those boys looking for a roommate if I could move in, and they said yes immediately upon hearing I could legally buy alcohol.

Three months later, a man I had never seen before sat stoned against our living room wall, next to the television. He had a beard that stuck out in every direction and a head of hair that looked exactly the same. It was as if somebody had taken a donut of three-inch-long black curly hair and popped a face into the center of it. He was a high school friend of my roommates', a newcomer, thin and tall and quiet, and I would not have noticed him at all had he not said something witty. In our house of drunk eighteen- and nineteen-year-old man-boys, nobody was saying anything witty. I beamed my eyes at him from across the room in curious surprise and locked them with his. They were the kindest eyes I had ever seen. I remember that moment exactly as it happened, in slow motion, as if it were a scene in a Meg Ryan movie. The Eye Lock. His were deep brown with eyelashes that carried on ridiculously, but it was their gentleness, their steady calm, that made me want to know more.

So naturally, I decided to get him drunk and shave his beard off to assess his jawline. He drank Bacardi out of the bottle until we ended up in my roommate's bathroom. I borrowed a razor and went to work on the facial hair while he called me "Mary," eventually passing out facedown on my futon. He woke up the next day at dawn to go work at the ranch, hungover, after just a few hours' sleep. I had never seen anybody get up that early and go to work in that condition. Except me.

Mac was a worker, I learned, and highly attractive without the hair donut. I was intrigued, and since that day happened to be Halloween, I figured we should probably head over to Chico to take some drugs and fall in love. Before he could get out of my room that morning, I said, "Hey. Want to go to Chico tonight? It's crazy on Halloween. Everybody's loaded in the streets."

"Yeah," he said, smiling. "Let's do that."

I remember the way the gray morning light fell on his face as he buckled his belt and pulled on his shirt, and I wondered if he'd kiss me. He didn't. We hadn't touched at all other than my fingers against his face and my shoulder pressed against his chest as I shaved. He seemed indifferent to me, which made me wonder if perhaps I was already in love. It wasn't until he walked out my bedroom door that I realized I had just committed, in the heat of mad passion, to dressing up in a goddamned costume.

I barely knew how to dress myself as *myself*. As a child, my idea of fashion was pairing a green print with a green solid and brushing my hair. In high school, I wore jeans, Doc Martens, and tight white v-necks intended for boys, until my father suggested I "try a little harder." After that, I'd walk into Gap or J. Crew and buy an outfit featured on a mannequin, figuring that must mean the clothes matched.

Dressing as *somebody else* was an unbearable enhancement of an already agonizing lifelong struggle. But for Mac I wanted to appear confident and cool, so I cradled my hangover, drove thirty minutes to a costume store in Sacramento, and eventually selected an ensemble that could only be described as "slut Egyptian."

On my way to Sacramento, my former boyfriend of three years called to ask if I wanted to see him that night. He and I used to hang out together in Chico, but we hadn't seen each other in a year. I was struck by the synchronicity, and strangely sensed that the choice I made in that moment would alter the course of my life, but I dismissed the thought as ridiculous. *It's just a Halloween.* I suppose somewhere I knew if I saw my old boyfriend I would return to him, because he was safe and comfortable, and the sound of his voice said, "I'll still have you if you'll have me." But there was something about Mac, his quiet strength, the way he cinched his faded leather belt that morning.

I told my old boyfriend, "I'm sorry, I already made plans," and then turned up the Grateful Dead on the stereo and rolled the windows down as the October sunset called from across the farmlands.

• • •

My costume consisted of a beaded headdress and beaded crop top that highlighted my impossibly flat midsection, which I believed needed toning. I paired the beaded top with blue silk pants—because I had blue silk pants—and then I ate some ecstasy. That pill was the key accessory to my outfit, for mine was always a problem of perception. I knew I'd look exquisite as soon as I was high. No longer a scared girl without sartorial confidence, I would be a devastatingly attractive woman prancing in beads.

While sitting on a park bench that night in Chico, watching drunken masses of college students flop down the streets, I told Mac's buddy, "I think I'm in love with your friend," but I said it loud enough for Mac to hear, because it had been 24 hours and I was tired of the bullshit. *Let's do this.* Mac was shy. I was not shy. I had no problem barging into your life and demanding a fixed place in it. Right now. *Step aside, assholes. Slut Egyptian has arrived.*

At my house later that night, and after taking more ecstasy, I dropped my head onto Mac's chest while we lay on the floor and planned our lives together. I suggested we have four children: two biological and two adopted. (I was going to save all the children.) He told me about his two sisters and a pot-bellied pig on their ranch who couldn't fit through a fence. He chuckled so hard my head bounced on his chest and I looked up to see him grinning while he described the pig balancing on his belly trying to push himself through.

I remember thinking only an excellent and loving man would tell a story about a pot-bellied pig getting stuck in a fence. It made him laugh. It made me want his babies.

"Mom, I think I met my future husband," I told her the next morning while circling the lawn, possibly still high, definitely smoking a cigarette and squinting under the morning sun.

"He's from a ranch around here. Really kind. I think his parents might be Republicans. He gets up and works every day at five a.m."

"I like the sound of him," she said, and I took a stunned drag off my smoke, because my parents hadn't liked the sound of most of what I'd been saying for the previous eight to twelve years. "He really sounds like a good man for you."

Within a few days I was bringing Mac meatball sandwiches while he worked—chasing unruly chickens with goat blood in his ear, butchering animals and cutting meat, smelling of lanolin and yesterday's Captain Morgan. He wore thick canvas pants or overalls with rubber boots over them, and ripped, bloodstained T-shirts and old button-down flannels, layered up to keep him from the cold or block him from the sun. After work, he smelled so intensely of animal guts and lanolin I could hardly be near him, but I watched him from afar and thought, *My God, he's tough.* Still, it was some ineffable tenderness that made me wonder if he was even human. He was a ranchman with tattoos and piercings, and he wasn't even a Republican.

I had never met a man like him. A man so classically macho without the machismo, a country boy without the puffed-out chest of country boys. Where was the posturing? The guns? The huge truck with a "Piss on Chevy" bumper sticker?

Mac didn't even watch sports. He drove a small, dented red truck, sang songs from Broadway musicals, and whistled to himself in the shower. But he could punch the hide off a sheep in three minutes and work eight hours without a break in a frigid slaughterhouse. He would fall asleep every night ten seconds after his head touched the pillow, and I would watch him. He was always so, so tired.

My roommates told me I had somehow landed the best man in the world, and the only person they were ever truly afraid of in high school—not because he was mean, or a fighter, but because he was the kind of person who would break a bottle over someone's head if necessary. He wouldn't like it, but he would do it.

I saw that. I saw loyalty that defied reason and ignored facts. I saw loyalty that was decided. Etched. Right there in the bones, and that was what I needed. I needed a love that couldn't see me.

We were never a decision. We were already made.

In January, three months after we met, we rented our apartment together. A few weeks later, on Valentine's Day, he pulled out a ring as we returned home from dinner. He killed the engine and opened a little box. I smiled, knowing what was about to happen. "I'll marry you," I said, "but put that thing away and ask me again. This is not romantic. This is a parking lot. And you have to ask my dad first." I was a real stickler for tradition.

So he asked again, after we knew I was pregnant, this time in the middle of the restaurant where I waitressed. He walked in with flowers, wearing a dress shirt and tie. The restaurant was packed with a Friday night dinner crowd when he got down on one knee and asked. I said yes, and everybody cheered. We were engaged and I was pregnant with our love child and in the movies this was all going to be quite perfect.

And it was. Even the nurses said so.

•   •   •

For two days in the birthing center the dream went on. Our baby girl slept in my arms and nursed while our friends came and went. We took a thousand pictures. Mac slept in that chair "bed" and I dressed my baby girl in outfit after outfit, all scented, all carefully chosen, while I wondered what the fuck happened to my vagina and how I'd ever pee again. One of the outfits was pink and fuzzy on the inside with a white bear on the front. It made me think of the nine months and several days of perfection I had just experienced—until I stepped outside the birthing center as a mother, and the rest began.

My story wasn't untrue. It was simply unsustainable.

2

STOP DRINKING WHEN YOUR LIPS
GO NUMB

I did not start on that balcony. I did not wake up one day dropped into a life of pregnancy, cigarettes, a three-month-old relationship, and an almost college degree. I built that, one moment at a time, while I thought I was building something else.

I probably began on a two-week trip to Honduras when I was sixteen years old, which I heard about one day in my public speaking class. I attended an all-girls Catholic school in Santa Rosa, California, in the middle of vineyards, where winery owners and their offspring lived. The trip was "an opportunity to learn about the rainforest and conservation," but more accurately it was a chance to send privileged kids to a "third world" country to learn guilt, American exceptionalism, and how local ignorance caused the destruction of the rainforest (as opposed to, say, global capitalism).

I did not know this, nor did I care. I was simply aching for something new.

My mother worked in the school's kitchen for my discounted

tuition, so the trip made little sense in the financial context of our lives, but I presented it to her as a situation deciding my continued survival, as only a sophomore with a vision can. My mother leapt in my support as she had always done, my grandparents donated to the cause, and, somehow, a few months later, I was stepping off a plane into a wall of humidity.

In the Tegucigalpa airport, I watched men in green camouflage uniforms pace the halls with machine guns in their arms. They were terrifying, but my teachers explained they were "protecting us." As we approached the yellow school bus that would cart us around for the next week, my friend Gloria asked, "Are those bullet holes?" and I looked up with delight at the black spider punctures around the bus. They were indeed bullet holes. *My God*, I thought, *how exotic!*

Sweaty and giddy and wearing fanny packs, we shuffled into the bus and drove in what appeared to be the wrong direction on a highway into thick vegetation. We spent the next week hiking in the wet, green rainforest behind a man with a machete, who whacked a path in front of us while teaching us about local plants, animals, and indigenous populations. We dove into glistening swimming holes below warm, white waterfalls until we broke for naps on shaded rocks. We ate lychee nuts, beans, rice, and tortillas at every meal, every day. The other girls complained of the monotony, but I loved watching the Honduran woman who made our tortillas in a clay oven. I would wave at her and smile and she would wave back, but never move from the oven's face. I felt we were experiencing something sacred when we ate her food, something old and vital. It never occurred to me that she never seemed to leave that spot in front of the roaring oven, cooking for a bunch of wine country kids.

Nearly every day we would take an excursion in the bullet-hole bus, and every time we did, we would for reasons unknown pick up a lady with a cage of chickens. If our bus got stuck in the sand, the driver shoved palm fronds in front of the tires while we lined up behind the rear bumper and pushed with all our might. When our bus broke down completely, the driver walked down the road a few hundred feet, bought a Coca-Cola in a tall glass bottle, reclined against a bus tire, and took a nap. We just sort of waited there, dumbly, while he snoozed, wondering what our next move was. *Drink a Coca-Cola*, I thought, *that's the next move*. So I did. The other kids refused, for fear the bottle was washed in unclean water.

We drove by people living on cardboard, sweeping dirt floors, riding ten to twenty in backs of trucks. I saw a young girl taking a shit in the street. I felt enlightened. I watched the poverty with a distant gaze, as if it were occurring in a fishbowl on the shelf. I was too young to see real suffering, too ignorant to understand my country's contributions.

One day on a hike in the rainforest, I accepted our guide's suggestion that we try eating termites out of a tree "for protein." I stuck a stick into a small hole in the bark just as he had done and ate the few unlucky bugs that wandered up. He was correct; they were crunchy and tasted like sap. I was the only girl who did it, and I was disgusted as their little bodies crunched between my teeth, but I wanted the other girls to wonder at my bravery. I wanted to shock them with my valor. But mostly, I wanted to not be bored. At sixteen, I was already bored: with school, church, my family, my little job at a local pool's snack bar. I needed some damn escapades.

We spent the second week on Roatán, an island in the

Caribbean with dirt roads, a plumber who stopped by occasionally from the mainland (whether or not your shower was broken), and where the mail came every two weeks by way of Florida. We spent our days there snorkeling above the Mesoamerican Barrier Reef, learning about its fish and destruction, and how urine soothes the burn of jellyfish stings.

Before we left the United States, we attended ominous meetings with our parents in which the teachers described in somber tones how dangerous Honduras could be for American children.

"They will steal you, and then they will kill you because your passports are worth more than you are."

"They will steal you, and they will rape you, and you will not come back."

"There have been many accounts of tourists getting kidnapped. You must never leave the teachers' sides, and you must never stray from the group."

In the rainforest, men with machine guns paced outside our sleeping quarters and occasionally fired their weapons into the night sky "to ward off guerrillas."

I was so terrified by all this I decided I needed to sneak out in the middle of the night with my friend Stacy. I was tall, slender, and very tan, with blonde hair that fell past my waist. Stacy looked absolutely identical but with larger breasts. We crawled out the back window of our motel room in the middle of the night, and while Stacy was chatting with some locals down the beach, I met a wandering American hippie with unwashed dreads, patchwork pants, and a heavily pregnant girlfriend. We bantered with each other until the man asked, "Hey, do you want some acid?"

"Yes," I answered. "Yes, I do."

I was an expert on acid because my mother had told me about dropping it with my father at the Fillmore in the 1960s. The man handed me three hits and said, "These are strong. Share them with your friends."

So I tore off two tabs and gave Stacy one, telling her he only gave us two, and set the remaining hits on my tongue. Without hesitation or thought, in the middle of the night, on a remote island in Honduras, I took a drug most people live their whole lives without taking, and I did it with a lie.

• • •

Two months before the acid hit my hungry tongue, I sat in our Mormon bishop's office confessing my mistake of smoking weed, once, in a moment of weakness, because Satan had overcome me.

"I will never, ever do it again," I told the bishop. "I think I had to try it once to get it out of my system." I looked at him from across the wooden desk and tried to show my sincerity with my eyes. He told me to repent, and ask the Holy Ghost to come back to me. At home that night, I got on my knees and repented and vowed to stay on the straight and narrow.

Four months before the acid soaked my blood in Technicolor, I stood at a high school lunch table proselytizing to my classmates how drugs ruin lives. At that age, I was staunchly opposed to anything that would ruin my life.

I knew in my heart I would never be so misguided. I believed myself lucky to have been shown a better way than the foolish teenagers around me smoking weed out of peer pressure and insecurity.

"My father is an alcoholic," I preached. "It is the reason for my parents' divorce! I know where that life leads!"

Six months before I ministered at the lunch table, I stood behind a podium in a blue tank dress with a jean jacket to cover my shoulders, "bearing my testimony" to an entire Mormon congregation. With tears in my eyes and a quiver in my voice, I explained how I knew the church was true, and the Holy Spirit was in me, and I would never do anything that would make my body—my temple—unclean, and therefore uninhabitable for the spirit of God. I rose voluntarily almost every month to get behind that podium.

And I meant it every time.

Eight years before I stood at the podium, my mother took us to the Mormon church for the first time. I was eight years old and wore puff-sleeved dresses with shoulder pads and big, innocent flowers to the chapel. We went every Sunday and Tuesday, and possibly Saturday, but in between these meetings, we would leave completely, in body and mind. Or at least that's how it felt.

We listened to "How Great Thou Art" on Sunday and Grace Slick on Monday. We snuck into high school football games we couldn't afford by passing ticket stubs through the fence, a form of stealing my mother explained was "small stealing" that didn't harm anyone, and therefore, need not make us feel bad. It was not a real sin. And if we could pay, we would.

My brother and I heard stories of Joseph Smith and "the fullness of the gospel" after my mother's stories of drinking Southern Comfort with Janis Joplin in the Haight. I was intrigued by both, though I found Joseph Smith something of a bore compared to, say, watching Ginger Baker play drums in Golden Gate Park during the Summer of Love. Salvation is divine, but it's tough to compete with bra burning and Jefferson Airplane.

When a song she loved came on, my mother would turn it up and sing loud and tell us what the song was about, even if it was weed or acid or free love. She'd tell us where she heard it first—maybe the Polo Fields at Golden Gate Park, or the Berkeley Hills, or the Avalon Ballroom. My favorite story was the first time she heard Dylan's "The Times They Are A-Changin'" on the radio, how she pulled her car over and cried because she never knew music could be like that, and how San Francisco in the sixties was electric with hope and change and none of the parents understood. In fact, Grandma Joan said Dylan sounded like "a dying cow."

I always thought he sounded like God.

I knew that feeling, the one my mother had when she first heard that Dylan song, because it happened to me the first time I heard Jerry Garcia sing "Ripple," and I dropped my head against the giant 1980s boom box on the shelf in my closet, closed my eyes, and cried. It was the saddest, most jagged and piercing sound I'd ever heard.

And it felt true, truer than the gospel, truer than Jesus. But still, on Sunday, I got up and bore my testimony, reverently.

•   •   •

The next thing I remember after dropping the acid in Honduras was rolling around in the gentle surf in front of a local bar about a quarter of a mile away from our motel. Stacy and I were in bathing suits now, and we laughed and sang and let the sand and water move across our bodies and hair. We were on earth, yet severed from it entirely. I looked up from the ground and observed the silhouette of a young, skinny white man with bleached, wavy hair standing above us. And then he was with us.

Acid trips are like that. Things appear, disappear. Technicolor flashes.

Stacy and I swam and walked and ran along the shore. He watched us while we played in the ocean. I asked him why he was there. He said, "Well, I can't really leave you like this, can I?"

I dove back into the surf.

•   •   •

My mother was a "convert" to the church, meaning she was "not born into it," and since I was baptized at nine instead of seven, I was a convert, too. This placed us figuratively just outside the church hall. My mother was also a single mother, divorced at thirty-six, with two children and a non-Mormon boyfriend, who later became her husband. This placed us more literally just outside the church hall—we lived differently from the true, better Mormons, and weren't allowed into all the rooms of their temple.

My mother converted to the church as a young girl after missionaries showed up at her family's door. Her sisters and mother were also baptized, but my grandfather preferred to stick with his evening gin and tonic. At eighteen, she met my father, a non-Mormon, and for the eighteen years of their marriage, she didn't attend church. So she carried with her, whether she wanted it or not, a history of falling in love in a bar at eighteen, of rock and roll, of working for Francis Ford Coppola in San Francisco as the girl who brought him lunch and snacks, of playing the Stones so loud you broke woofers, of alcohol, and a touch, I heard, of the harder stuff.

Maybe she found God in all of that. I had trouble seeing it so seamlessly. By fifteen, I had persistent questions about the Mormon church, but mostly I wondered whether I was good or evil. I felt like I was good. I meant well. I was not particularly mean and I didn't seem evil (I was sure as hell nicer than some of the delinquents I went to school with). I didn't cheat and I didn't steal. When bored on summer days with my best friend Elizabeth, I wanted to break into the house down the road *to see if we could do it* (but not hurt anything, of course), and spray the stucco of Elizabeth's house with hair spray and light it on fire, *to see what would happen.* In junior high, we wanted to steal her grandmother's Cadillac for a quick trip around town, because *who wouldn't want to drive a Cadillac down Main Street on a summer night?*

I was sure I loved my family more than most people loved their families, and yet I wanted to masturbate occasionally. I wanted to do things my church told me were sins. I could ask forgiveness all I wanted, but then I'd just want to do them again.

I was never holy enough. I could never purge myself of the impure thoughts, and I could never shake the sound of Jerry Garcia's black-tar beauty from my mind.

I wondered why my non-Mormon father was not going to the "highest degree of glory." I only saw him a few times a year since he lived on the northern end of California, but he struck me as morally sound. And Grandma Bonny, too. She had her own deeply held religious principles. In fact, that whole side of my family seemed decently wholesome. I wondered why, if you had to be Mormon to get to the Most Excellent Heaven, God had people born into remote parts of the Amazon where they never met missionaries. I wondered how there could only be "one true church." What about all those other people on the planet? Were they simply wrong? When I asked these questions, the church leaders said, "There are some things we just don't understand," and that felt to me like a cop-out. How could you possibly know the plan of salvation but not know how everybody can get there? Later, they explained that people wait in the spirit world until somebody on earth is baptized for them. But then why the hell would I obey the rules if somebody could just do it for me when I die?

"Because you've already been shown the plan of salvation. You can't go back now."

Well, fuck. So I would have been better off born somewhere where the church never was so I could live without all these goddamn rules and still get to heaven.

And there were so many rules. Don't date until age sixteen. Once you date, only kiss, but not with the tongue. Don't have sex until marriage. Don't drink coffee or black tea. Dr Pepper is a gray area. Don't buy things on Sunday. Don't wear tank tops.

I liked tank tops. I liked my shoulders. I wanted to show them without shame.

But really, it didn't matter how many times I showed up on Sunday in my "modest dress" and paced the halls with the stoic face of holiness, I still got angry sometimes and chased my brother around the house with a butcher knife, explaining to my mother and brother that a person named "Margaret" lived inside me, and she was a real psychopath. We all laughed because it was such an innocent name and they thought I was joking, but I knew I was not.

Nobody named Margaret would chase people with knives.

But I would.

And it didn't matter how many prayers I whispered at night, I still couldn't sleep with my hair flipped over my pillow, even though it was more comfortable and I wanted it off my neck. I couldn't do it because I feared there was a man under my bed who wanted to cut it off, and though I knew intellectually this was not true, my fear was untouched by rationality. Or whispers to my Father in Heaven.

And even though the church elders praised how eloquently I spoke of the truth God had revealed to me, telling me I was a leader among young women, I was still unable to say the thing that would help my mother see that my stepfather was never going to change, and that we couldn't move again, because it wouldn't be different across town or in Texas. It didn't matter how brightly I shined on Sundays, I yelled and screamed and chased with knives and masturbated when nobody was looking.

I couldn't even muster the Holy Ghost's presence when un-speakable tragedies came, like when my mother told me she had three miscarriages before my brother was born, or when kids made fun of my brother's acne, or when my stepfather mocked my mother, again. Or when my brother and I would go fishing, and even though I always wanted him to catch a fish more than I wanted to, *I always did*, and he did not, until once when we were camping in the summer, and he and I went down to the pier at dusk, threw our lines in, and caught fish after fish after fish without even trying. Big, fancy trout. We couldn't believe our luck, the way we'd cast a line and immediately catch one. As the sun went down, we filled the stringer until every spot was taken. We only stopped because there was no more room.

We caught them together and nobody had to go back to tell our mother who caught more. But when I untied the stringer of fish, our faces beaming at the mass of them, the bottom fish pulled and the wet string slipped through my fingers, back into the lake. In an instant, they were gone, strung together through the gills, to die.

We were going to show them to our mother and eat them for dinner. I can't remember if we tried to catch them again, or who hurt worse, or even how long I cried or apologized.

Where was God then?

The one time we both caught fish, I let them all go, and I couldn't find Him there, in my guilt and pain, in my "irrational reaction" I couldn't seem to quell, in the desperate sadness of my mother's miscarriages and the way she told me so matter-of-factly, saying we would "see them in heaven." But my siblings were dead. I had dead siblings. *Who let them go?* I raged and wept, and my brother and mother looked at me like I was deranged. I knew I was crazy, but I couldn't stop. They said I was "just too much," but I couldn't be less.

Maybe it was Margaret. Maybe I was evil.

It didn't matter how eloquently I testified, I couldn't get my mother to stay when she wanted to leave for the night, even though I was convinced she wasn't coming back alive. I would rock and cry on the couch, getting herded by our border collie, who seemed to think, *If we can just get this one home, she'll be fine.*

Nobody seemed to know how to get me home, not even God.

It didn't matter how clear the world seemed when I sat in the church room listening to very kind women explain the way to heaven, I still walked around the playground at school eyeing the other kids with fascinated skepticism, a twenty-foot invisible wall between us, wondering how they knew how to be kids on a playground. *How do they know how to play tetherball? What is happening with these people?* I wanted so badly to join them; I wanted so badly for the ball to smack them in their adorable little faces. I figured God had handed out a Playground Manual before he sent us all down here, and I, unfortunately, was absent that day.

But I couldn't tell you that, and I couldn't ask, "Hey, could you teach me how to play tetherball?" I couldn't let you know how much I wished you'd sit with me at the lunch table, so I squared my shoulders and straightened my backpack and walked somewhere very important, like the library, to prove I had a place to go. There's a chance you didn't notice me leaving. There's a chance I was proving it to me.

When I got home, I would go straight to my bedroom, and make myself the smartest and most capable person in the room by lining up my Cabbage Patch dolls and playing "school" with the door shut. I did this for definitely too many years. My favorite book to teach was *The Miracle of Life*, because it involved new life and vaginas, even new life *exiting* vaginas, so it was educational *plus dirty*. Nobody bothered me in there, not even my mother when she got home from work. I felt better after a couple of hours of solitude and fantasy, sometimes even good enough to see what the crazy kids were doing on their bikes out on the street.

I had no idea how to join them.

Maybe I didn't even know I wanted to join them, that I wanted to feel a sense of unity with the people around me, that I wanted to not feel fear, that I wanted to feel better inside. I tried the church for many years, and it almost worked, but all that Mormon preaching and black-and-white Truth was a pathetic substitute for what I really wanted: relief. A deep exhale. A sigh in my guts that let me rest, fully, completely, secure and unafraid. And whole.

I yearned for that acid in Honduras with my whole self, with every single moment I lived before that day, but I didn't know it until I saw the tiny tabs in front of me, and God became the ability to feel different. To feel free.

• • •

When the acid began wearing off, I was lying on the edge of the man from the beach's bed, aware of the movement next to me. Stacy was in the middle. He was on the other side of her. I was terrified of men and sex, so when they started kissing, I panicked and headed to the bathroom (if I'd had a backpack, I would have straightened it). I figured I'd take a shower to wash off the evening, but this turned out to be a questionable idea. The black mold spots on the white tile refused to stop shaking. My eyes told me they were bugs. My mind told me it was the acid. There was no hot water, and no plumber to fix it.

I got dressed and sat on his couch until he and Stacy joined me. It never occurred to me that it would have been rape if he slept with her. I was merely grateful to be alive and out of that bed. He explained he was a graduate student from San Francisco studying marine biology, and that he was from Sebastopol, a tiny town about fifteen minutes from our city of Santa Rosa. I could not believe it. He said he saw us rolling in the surf in front of a bar and knew we were high and not safe, so he stayed with us. He left out the part about hoping he could take advantage of a couple of young, dosed girls.

I had no idea where I was or how to get back to the motel. He said, "Walk straight down the beach, that way," and dismissed me with a hint of disgust in his voice, probably because I wouldn't fuck him. I was useless to him now.

I thanked him and laughed, thinking how his directions reminded me of the "straight and narrow." How far I had strayed from the iron rod now.

As I walked back to the motel alone in the heavy morning air, I worried about Stacy, who had refused to leave the man's house with me, but I walked faster and faster, running to get away from him, from the night, thinking of the silent motel room, and of getting there before the teachers woke up. I thought about rolling in the surf on acid and how I wasn't raped or mauled or dragged into a cave for my passport or any other reason. As I unlocked the motel room door, I thought, *Wow, I can do really stupid shit and not get in trouble for it.*

But mostly, I thought about the weed I had smoked a couple of months before, and how I was absolutely convinced something spectacular would happen in that moment. I thought the sky would crack or shatter, or clouds would gather or part. I didn't know what would happen exactly, but I knew it would be mighty. Surely, I would be punished somehow.

And yet, nothing.

I began to suspect my aunts, my mother, and the entire Mormon church were lying. They all but *promised* a volcanic eruption on the day I blackened my temple, and here I had quite clearly at least grayed it out with intentional marijuana, and not one single fucking thing happened. Nothing fell out of the sky. No lightning. Not a word from the creator.

I didn't even feel different.

But still, I wanted to believe. I wanted to be a holy person, and for them to be right. I wanted to reach my potential—*and there was so much, you know?* I was a shining star at school! I would be the first person in my family to graduate from college! I would do better than my parents! My father moved in and out of drinking. I heard stories of their friends shooting up heroin in their necks, of junkies burning up in their own houses, of drunken fights and limb-crushing car accidents. *I knew better.*

But I couldn't shake the feeling of having been lied to, of being hoodwinked. And I wondered what else they were wrong about. I suspected *everything.* So I set that acid on my tongue, and gave up trying.

It was my last sacrament, my last communion. I had spent so many years believing that if I could figure out how to be good enough, I wouldn't be the person who chased loved ones with knives or craved Jerry's cracked desperation as a salve greater than salvation. I thought *any minute now* my external reverence would manifest in internal peace, and all the darkness would be cast out through my grand gestures of morality. The sinner, the darkness, gone, and me, unified in good.

But it never worked.

And if there was a God, he knew the truth about me, so fuck it.

I'm tired.

• • •

Later that day on the island, after a short half-hallucinatory sleep, I talked to Stacy, who told me "everything went fine" with the marine biologist after I left. I was never quite sure what that meant. I told myself to believe her.

I walked outside my motel room that day as the sun was going down across the water, casting orange light on my face and shadows in long, peaceful strokes across dusty roads.

I went snorkeling with the other students that evening as usual, but for some reason this time I got going way out there in the ocean, kicking along for what seemed like twenty miles. I don't know why, I just kept going. I was scared I'd get eaten by a shark, but I kept kicking anyway because it was too damn beautiful to stop and the fear made me kick harder.

I was entirely alone now but I kept kicking. The reef was down below me and then farther and farther away until it came to an end. I kept kicking past that, but it was just blue and blue and blue in every direction, so I turned around. When I did, I saw a wall of black before me, but a little below me, the reef stretched in every direction in front of me, and the crystal blue water above it. And me, hovering there like a speck of flesh in nothingness, a mass of dark that stretched forever into the bottom, though no bottom. I felt like I was looking at God and death and I shuddered. I felt like I was hovering above an abyss that would swallow me at any moment, as if I were taunting it with my squirming little body. The water above the black looked like a sliver too shallow to hold me, and I thought I could not cross back over. My eyes darted down, right, left until the terror of the black overtook me, and I threw my head up and ripped my snorkel off to suck in the air and stare at a spot on the beach—to swim back, and remember I was still alive.

I didn't look down again.

Until I got home, and began my descent into the black.

• • •

Two months later, my friend handed me a bottle of peppermint schnapps and said, "Stop drinking when your lips go numb."

But I never did. I had found what I was looking for.

3

SYLVIA PLATH PUT HER HEAD IN THE OVEN OVER THIS SHIT

On our first day home as a family of three, Mac woke at dawn and went to work at his father's slaughterhouse, just like every other Thursday, Friday, Saturday, and Sunday since he was ten years old. This particular day, the day I walked around in pajama pants over a bulging hospital diaper with a colostrum-sucking newborn in my arms, happened to be Thanksgiving. Twelve hours before, we had walked into the dome through the pouring rain, with Ava in her car seat, and everybody cheered for us. For some reason, they clapped when we made it home. Perhaps it was the rain.

After dinner, Mac went to sleep. I did not.

In the morning, Mac left.

I did not.

Leaving for work was not something Mac thought about, but rather something he simply *did*, no matter what day it was, or who was just born, or how sick he was. Only absolute incapacitation would keep him from that slaughterhouse. I did not grasp the magnitude of this commitment until the first time we tried to take a vacation beginning on a workday. This was evidently the first workday he had missed for something as frivolous as "rest." He spent the first nine hours physically ill in the bathroom of our San Francisco hotel room while I sat on the bed wondering how he could possibly ruin my experience in such a selfish manner.

"Mac, I don't understand. People are allowed to take vacations," I said, as he crouched against the wall near the toilet. "What the hell is wrong with you?"

"I don't know," he said, and I believed him even through my fury. I never understood how a person could grow so intricately entwined with a job. On the day I told his mother I was pregnant, she said, "You can take the man off the ranch, but you can't take the ranch out of the man." Her words seemed true, but still, I wanted to extricate him from whatever sickness festered between him and his work, or whatever it was that gutted him for taking a day off, but he couldn't explain it, and I soon learned the source was invisible. It tore through him years before we existed together, and planted itself beyond reason's reach.

But on that day, the Thanksgiving he went to work leaving a two-day-old newborn and mother, it did not occur to me to be angry. Luckily, my mother was there, and she didn't tell me a father shouldn't leave the mother of his child two days after she gives birth, especially if it's Thanksgiving. I wonder if she knew and withheld that information, or, slightly more awkwardly, didn't realize it was weird either. Maybe she craved time with just the baby and me, or maybe my father would have done the same to her, or maybe we were all so fucking overjoyed by the baby we didn't notice his absence. I think it was the latter.

Perhaps it would have been nice for somebody to say, "Hey, Janelle. You should ask Mac to stick around a bit." Then again, logically, something we don't know must be benign. Unless it burns under the surface, like a wound growing larger right beneath our nerves, where we didn't even know we had nerves or needed help at all, until one day we find ourselves doubled over a toilet for taking a day off work. Maybe that's what happened to Mac. Maybe that's what happened to me.

Maybe that's what happened to me three days after we brought Ava home, and I sat in a rocking chair in the middle of the November night under our bedroom window, out there in the country, where the sky is so clear it makes the cold seem colder. Light shone onto my face and Ava's, and I guess it was moonlight. I tried to nurse her. My nipples cracked against her petal mouth, but I nursed her anyway, because she was tiny and just right, and I refused to not breastfeed. I closed my eyes and gritted my teeth through the rush of fire in my breast. The nurse had told me, "If she is latched correctly, it won't hurt," so I figured I was doing it wrong, but the milk spilled out around the edges of her little mouth. Seemed to me something was working.

I was drunk at the sight of her, almost too much for my eyes, swaddled in my arms as my mother had taught me with my dolls years before. *You put the baby's head a little below one corner, and then you pull up the bottom corner, pull the right one over the chest and then the left, and then tuck it in tight like a little burrito.* But as we rocked, and as I glanced at her and back at her snoring father, maybe I rocked one, two, three too many times, and nudged some pain I couldn't see right up to the last layer of my skin, where the moonlight touched and her newborn head met my flesh. Because on the final glance at Mac, a truth settled into me like a sheet of ice.

I had made an irreversible mistake. Not any mistake. The greatest mistake.

Her. Him. The love. The pregnancy. It was all a horrifying error. I looked at him and her and back again and hated them both.

No. Not her.

Him. Him, there, free, alone on the bed while I sit spitting milk and pain and blood with the beautiful tucked-in bundle. His body his own. His dick his own. His future his own. And me, decimated.

I don't want this, I thought. *I don't want him or motherhood and I don't want this body or man or house but now I am stuck, dragged and chained through a lie.*

My own, or yours? Did I do this? How did I do this? I was conned. I was wronged. I was betrayed.

I knew I had only myself to blame, but it was too cold to stay in that knowing. So I blamed him.

You wanted this, Mac. Now you've got it, and I'm gone.

• • •

My jealousy of people without children, of people I viewed as still free, became a living, breathing entity. My rage palpable, dizzying, smoldering always in my chest, and yet it was not alone. If it were, I could have walked coolly away from him, that life. If all I felt were sorrow and rage, the kind that engulfs you like a warm black cloud, seeping into every pore until even your breath feels leaden and ugly and wrong, I could have simply walked out on the bastards. In the dark of midnight, I imagined doing exactly that, but every day, at every moment, alongside my frantic desperation, was a love and fixation and pull to that baby more powerful than anything I'd ever known. Beyond me and utterly nonnegotiable.

I could never commit to anything in life, except her. Fully, undeniably, against my every desire, her. It was a love that had me checking her ten times a night. A love that had me burying my nose in her mouth to inhale her milky breath, bathing, nursing, and holding her with arms that ached if she were not in them. When apart, I missed her the way we hunger for food: immediately, physically, and for survival.

But while I drove into town and she slept in the car seat, or screamed as if the devil himself were gouging her in the eye, I felt the weight of my sagging belly and tits and thought about Mac working at his going-nowhere job, and our little corner of the big ranch house, and how it all had become sad and heavy and boring. I would think about where I was supposed to go with my life instead of the car, and I would get lost. My grief drove me around in circles. I'd drive as long as I could, as long as Ava slept, because at least the time was mine, some solitude, some untouched mental space. Sometimes I drove by places I used to frequent in college, old bars and friends' houses, to remember my former life as some sort of masochistic lamentation. Sometimes I drove by my old boyfriend's house, the one who called that Halloween, and pondered what it would have been like if I had made the decision to meet him that night instead of Mac.

He was with somebody new. I hated her too, even though she was a former high school friend and I was the one who broke up with him. I hated the childless happiness they occupied in my imagination. I fantasized about running off to some Midwestern motel, where I would change my name to Charlotte and bartend for a living, simply pretending *none of this had ever happened.*

For I always had a next move, a way out, a backdoor exit plan. Another man, another drug, another town. Another job or friend or lie. I always had a posture or scheme to get out of a life that wasn't working. But motherhood, motherhood is a trap. It's like the goddamn "Hotel California": *You can check out, but you can never leave.*

If I stayed, I faced a ruined life. If I left, I faced taking care of Ava alone, and sharing her with Mac and whatever slut he ended up with. The thought alone made my stomach flip. I couldn't stay and I couldn't leave, and when the permanence of motherhood dropped onto me, when I understood that *no matter where I physically went* I would not escape it, my panic was indescribable. I was a feral cat in the first moments of capture, scrambling and clawing and screaming as she realizes there's no exit to her cage.

So I married him, as I said I would, because it was the only thing I could think of.

•   •   •

We took our vows on a cold, gray December day under a tree outside a courthouse in a town called Woodland, which is probably the nicest part of the town. My mother wore four-week-old Ava in a black sling across her chest. Our plan was to get married "technically," then have a fantastic wedding a year later.

I wore all black. I was planning on wearing jeans and a hooded sweatshirt, but my mother-in-law said, "Oh you can't do that. You're getting married!" and kindly took me to a boutique clothing store the same day, but I had recently given birth and felt betrayed by my body, with its giant belly hanging low, withered and stretched beneath alien milk tits. So I bought a black skirt and blouse, as if it were a funeral, though I merely wanted to hide behind cotton shadows.

I told myself I didn't care. I told myself I was so in love I didn't need a wedding, but this was probably a lie. I knew it wasn't the "real thing." I knew if we treated it as a gesture for taxes and insurance, if I wore regular old clothes and nobody gathered in feigned joy, it would remain a flash in the grand scheme. This almost worked, but my father showed up.

•   •   •

My father was not an "absent" father. He was a physically distant father. After my parents separated when I was six, I only saw him a few weekends a year, on one or two holidays, and during one weeklong stay in the summer. For me, those visits felt strained and tricky, because he was my *father*, and I adored him, but I didn't know him well and was trying to make a good impression. This unfamiliarity alongside the paramount importance of his station in my life confused me: *I should know him and be comfortable around him—but I don't, and I'm not.*

I remembered life before my parents' divorce as an outline, a pencil scratch here and there—sleeping on the prickly floor of our boat, riding over the Golden Gate Bridge in the jump seat of my father's Porsche 930, the walls of our home and the porch jasmine—a slightly deeper mark on the day he cried and bought me a stuffed puppy from a pharmacy, and then my mother, brother, and I were gone.

How does one miss an outline?

After the divorce, my father would send me postcards of Marilyn Monroe because my favorite movie was *Some Like It Hot*. We would talk on the phone, too, but I never knew quite what to say. When we visited him, my brother, father, stepmother, and I would drive north on Highway 101 in his two-door red Mustang for what seemed like three weeks straight, taking a pee break at McDonald's in Gilroy, where life smells like garlic, and, if we were lucky, stopping completely in Santa Cruz or San Francisco, but usually driving all the way to Healdsburg, in Sonoma County wine country.

While we drove north, we listened to Bob Dylan, Neil Young, the Grateful Dead, the Rolling Stones, Dire Straits, and Pink Floyd. We listened to hippie music or Republican talk radio. On one side of the Mustang was an NRA sticker. On the other was a Grateful Dead "Steal Your Face" sticker. My father did not explain this, but he explained all sorts of other things, and I asked a lot of questions. Nobody ever seemed to exhaust my arsenal of questions. Adults looked at me as if I were annoying; my mother often suggested we "play a five-minute silent game." I unfailingly lost.

His place in Healdsburg was a fifth wheel trailer I appreciated because it was tidy, along the Russian River, and smelled of my beautiful new stepmother's hair. We would spend our days at the river or at his fancy gym down the road, where we would shower in big tile stalls with glass doors and sit in a steam room that smelled of eucalyptus. Even though there were four of us in the fifth wheel, and my brother and I had to share the "living room" at the end, it was charming in its novelty. My father made us fried chicken and we watched *National Lam-*

poon's European Vacation and *Some Like It Hot* and *Ferris Bueller's Day Off* until I had all three movies memorized. Margaret never came out in the trailer.

Somehow it became a tradition that I would cook carrots on the trailer stove, by myself, which was of great consequence at age nine and ten and eleven. I cleaned, peeled, and cut the carrots—an eternal, thankless job—then cooked them on the tiny stove, while standing on a stool that took up almost the whole motor home walkway. I had to melt the butter and then put the carrots in the pan, but I couldn't cook it too fast because the butter would burn. Then I had to add the rosemary, salt, and a little pepper. I remember feeling like I stood at the stove for hours, and that it was a mind-numbing and difficult process, but it was the only way I could get that crispy caramelized butter on the edges of the carrots. We called them "rosemary carrots" and my father asked me to make them for him every time we visited, because he said it was the most delicious thing he had ever tasted in his life.

But you can't build a life on rosemary carrots.

• • •

It wasn't these memories that made his presence at my court-house union almost unbearable. It was the way I stood on San Francisco's Pier 39 holding his hand when I was a little girl, or across the Bay at Sam's in Tiburon, or at the docks in Sausalito, when I pointed and ogled at the yachts, telling him, "Dad, I'm going to get married on *that* one." And he would laugh, and say, "Yes! You will!"

It was that he knew I held that silly dream, the one I now

denied, was too tough for, tossed aside as if I could never be bothered with such girlish nonsense.

From him, I couldn't hide in the shadows. Seeing him standing on that grass felt to me like I was crossing into womanhood, into a new family, without a proper goodbye. It simply made me sad. After the technicality, we went to dinner at a restaurant named after a duck. I drank two to seven glasses of wine.

In the photographs of the ceremony, I am holding Mac's hands and gazing into his eyes, with Ava and my mother right behind us, and a lady from the courthouse wearing wide-leg slacks, a green holiday sweater, and thick black eyeliner. She's holding a clipboard.

There are tears in my eyes. Of joy, I guess.

• • •

I soon learned as a married, stay-at-home mother that if I remained drunk about 40 percent of my waking hours, I really enjoyed it. That is not true. I did not calculate percentages. Also, I did not particularly enjoy it.

I would go to the store to "buy groceries for a nice dinner" and come back with a couple nice bottles of wine, *for our nice dinner*, which I would drink while I cooked. At our actual dinner I would have more wine and a cocktail or two. This made bedtime manageable, as well as motherhood as a whole. (They do not write this in the "new mom" brochure we get when they discharge us from the hospital, but perhaps they should.)

I drank for relief. I drank because from my first sip at sixteen, alcohol felt like peace, like coming home after a long and arduous journey. Anticipation of the day's first glass was a rush of lifted spirits within me—energy, comfort, being—and by glass number two, I began to feel the way I thought I should feel all the time.

Drugs would do the same, but they required such commitment—two a.m. runs, transactions with people I didn't know, dealers refusing to return my calls. After Ava was born, I was a drug dabbler. I was a fucking grown-up, after all, a *mother*. *Of course I don't want any blow.*

Wait. Does somebody have it, though?

More realistically, what saved me from narcotics was that I lived on a ranch ten miles outside an excessively vanilla college town where "partying" looked like nineteen-year-olds doing keg stands, not bumps of cocaine in bathroom stalls.

And I wasn't seeking drugs because I had alcohol, which was enough—mostly because it was reliable. You could get a bad baggie. You couldn't get a bad handle of Grey Goose. Plus, everyone drank. I could cling to alcohol like it was my last breath of air, but as long as I hid my desperation, the world would assume I was functioning, motherly, even sophisticated. They would believe the polish of laughter and smiles, as long as I never looked too thirsty or excited, as long as I never explained that if uninterrupted drinking was on the horizon, if I knew alcohol would soon pour into the cracks of my psyche, soul, and heart, I could handle anything—even my stale days and too-young husband who left in the mornings, and the baby sucking my life dead and dry while making it infinitely more worth living and deep and clear.

I held on that way, by drinking, and the love. Her tiny dimpled fingers.

When Ava was about six months old, I thought I had found my own groove in the endless rhythm of motherhood, possibly even beyond White Russians and steadfast denial. I started exercising and writing again. I was researching graduate schools for a master's in English, and found a friend my age with a baby.

But one morning while Ava napped, I sat alone in the ranch house, surrounded by toys and blankets and diapers, next to a baby monitor rumbling with gentle snores, and I opened an email from my brother. I clicked on a picture of him in a white doctor coat, grinning widely on his first day of medical school at one of the top universities in America. My eyes studied his proud, hopeful ones, the sprawling manicured lawns, the old red brick building of the hall of medicine. I thought of new school years, semesters in college—the pens (and how I always wanted fine-point blue), empty notebooks, literature on the shelves with its wild, disrupting ideas.

A beginning. He was at his beginning.

I was at my end.

I retraced each line of his face and smile. Each second I looked, my heart beat faster. This man, my brother, who could make decisions and stick to them, who could not get pregnant by people he barely knew, or drink too much every fucking night. *He did it.* Growing up, I thought it would be me. I thought I would send that email, yet there he was, inarguably handling the world, while I sat immobile in a room I couldn't navigate. I couldn't even find its walls. I simply saw black.

If somebody had walked into that room at that very moment, I would have run upstairs when I heard the door open so they wouldn't see me crying. If I couldn't make it out in time, I would have swept my face with my hand and laughed about having just read something sad, but I would have disliked that lie because it would have made me seem like an overly emotional female. When others cried around me, I willed them to stop immediately because I felt compelled to say something supportive, but could only think of "Pull it together, please." Or "Do you want a cocktail?" When sadness overtook me, I consciously pressed it into tightened fists, screams, and dramatic departures, but never tears.

There was nothing anybody could have said to fix it for me anyway, to give me a new way of looking at it, to patch up the hole in my brain or heart so I could pick myself up and carry on. I wouldn't have even let them try. I wouldn't have admitted how pathetic I felt sitting there, how small under the shadow of the photograph. I would have bragged. I would have said I was heading to graduate school soon. I would have squared my shoulders and acted like I had somewhere to go.

But that afternoon, in that chair, while I looked at my brother, my body shook and the tears came roaring against my will. *This? It can't be this. This can't possibly be my life. Not now, at twenty-two.* It was startling to cry like that. I could not remember having done it before. I wept in heaves until the baby cried, again, wanting to nurse, again.

I didn't go back to thinking I had found a groove.

The days began to blur.

Am I dressed? Am I ever dressed? How long until Mac comes home? How long until I can go to grad school? How long until dinner? How long until motherhood is over, or at least until wine? If I weren't here at two p.m. in my pajamas, I would be a lawyer, or writer, or something that mattered a little, at least. I would be young and hot. I would party. I would travel the world. I would do something. But I would not do this. I have to go. I have to get free.

And then, her sweaty head, puffy eyes, and rosy cheeks would send smiling warmth to my bones, and I'd think, *I'll never leave you, baby girl. Thank God for you.*

Carry on. Change the diaper. Take a shower. Make dinner. Pour another glass.

I tried to tell Mac I was barely functioning. I tried to tell him my life was in ruins, that I was no longer me, or a person at all, and sometimes I wished I had never become a mother.

In response, he went to work.

Then he came home. We did it again and again and again.

On my twenty-third birthday, he rolled in from the slaughterhouse exhausted, reeking of goat guts, and I quickly realized he hadn't planned anything as a celebration. I threw a spectacular tantrum before dragging us to dinner, where he nearly dozed off at the table, and my fit resumed. Under those conditions, though, he had no chance of performing adequately. He thought we were going to dinner. I thought we were fixing my life.

• • •

I tried to tell him I had been erased, even in body. I tried to tell him I was slipping. But he just looked at me. Always, he just looked at me. He looked at me while sitting on the floor or in a big easy chair, on the couch or in the car, on a park bench or at the pool table, or the bar. He looked at me and I couldn't understand his silence. His downcast eyes. In the hell of the morning, I loathed him, and laughed at what we called "love."

But later, as I poured an afternoon glass, I'd think, *I was over-reacting*, and when I thought of him working down at the ranch, punching the hide off a sheep, cold in the winter bite, or walking across a dusty pen in 105-degree heat, I'd realize his silence was saying, "I wish I knew how to help you."

He was twenty, and almost as empty as me. It made it worse that he was gentle and devoted to our family, that when he was home, he cradled our baby on his arm and never set her down, that he wasn't cruel or philandering. It made it worse because I knew he simply did not have what I needed. He was *there*, with all that he was, but still it was not enough.

I tried to tell him, but I didn't tell my mother. It didn't seem like the type of thing one mentions to other women. Or men, actually. So I kept it to myself. Who would I have told anyway? And what would I have said? "I chose to have a baby and now I hate being a mother even though she's perfect and the father is diligently supporting us?"

Also, nobody asked.

I thought if the doctors found out they would take my baby away, and I would be crazy and alone, and my daughter would be without a breast and the arms that craved her.

Sometimes as I walked down the stairs holding Ava, I envisioned throwing her body off the top of the balcony—not because I wanted to, but because the image slammed itself into my brain. When it hit, I would pull her hard against my chest and shake my head to get rid of the image. But I worried someday my arms would do it against my will, and as I held her against me I remembered that I could really, really never tell anyone.

So instead of telling people, I dressed her in European clothes I bought at discount stores, and took her to the park where we sat on blankets, and I was proud of us. I nursed her and fed her wholesome foods like avocado and zucchini I crushed myself, and didn't let anybody watch TV around her for fear it would sizzle her brain right then and there like an egg on a hot side-walk. There was no sugar in Ava's diet, and she slept tucked against my body because she needed me and I needed her, and I could never get enough of her milk breath.

But when nobody was looking, I scrawled in my journal, in capital letters, in thick black ink, "I CAN'T GO ON" and "I FUCKING HATE MY LIFE" and "WHEN DID IT ALL GO WRONG?" I pressed hard on the page so it would go through to the two or three pages behind it, like a little kid learning to write, but actually I was begging the page to help me.

I had been running to paper for safety since I was a little girl, since the bishop's wife handed me a journal after my Mormon baptism, saying, "You should write in this every day," and I looked at those lined pages and thought, *This is mine to fill up. This space is mine.* I wrote every day, just as she said.

But it was only after I had Ava that the page did nothing, that I felt worse after scribbling the darkest of me into sad linearity, into neat reductions of grammar and diction and punctuation. It was only then that my words made me sicker, and left me deader, as if whatever was living inside me refused to be contained, ordered, or made into meaning. Trying to stretch it into lines left me frustrated, and lonelier, because every sentence ended in conflict, in paradox, in the whimper of a baby who needed me.

There was no resolution because the revulsion was not about her. It was me. It was all that led up to her creation and birth. It was the man who didn't understand my grieving and the single bedroom we shared. It was all that and some dark thing I couldn't explain, trace, or trap at all, like a curtain over the sun blocking the light. Nobody can dodge that pain, or the exhaustion of trying to breathe beneath it.

Still, I thought if I used all my strength to scream into the page, the black would move right out of me and get taken up. I remember shuddering while I wrote and pressing as hard as I could for relief. I lifted my head and squinted my eyes and waited.

It never worked. Except alcohol, nothing worked.

· · ·

One day, while Mac was at work, Ava began fussing right after I put her down for a nap in the late morning. I stared at the monitor, then dragged myself up the stairs as her cries took over the hallway.

As I walked to her room, my thoughts were like a train crashing through my mind, accelerating with every step. *Always waking up. Jesus fucking Christ, she's always waking up. Waking up and stealing my few seconds of humanity, of freedom. Waking up and making me face her and me and all that was going to be before this hell hit like a flash flood across a broken body, and I'm crushed but somehow not dead. MY GOD, CHILD, FUCK YOU*—and when I got to her, I pinched her thigh, hard, to hurt her.

She wailed.

I cried out too, and pulled her body to mine before dropping to my knees. I gripped her against my chest, with her head in my hands and my fingers stroking her blond wisps of hair. I gasped through tears and begged her to forgive me, and in that moment I realized I did not care if they took her. I did not care if she was no longer mine, because she was better off without me. I had hurt my baby, my life, my perfect creation. I had hurt her on purpose.

I called the doctor's office immediately and explained to the first person who answered that there was something wrong with me and I could not take care of my baby. I didn't tell Mac I was going to call, because I knew he wouldn't understand my decision to give our baby away. He was not brave. He would not let her go. He would tell me to lie. He would tell me to keep hiding who I am.

That very day, I went to the doctor's office and told the nurse about pinching her, and the visualizations, and that my life was black-tar grief. I steeled myself in preparation for her words, "You know we have to take your baby, right?" I was ready to say goodbye.

Instead she put her hand on my knee and left it there as she said, "Oh, honey, you have a bit of postpartum depression. We'll have you fixed up in no time."

She shook her head and blinked like a doll. She seemed unreal sitting there, talking to me as if it was all no big deal. I got to keep the baby, because this is a thing that happens to some women after they give birth. Depression. That is its name.

Her voice was sweet and smooth and slow, but squeaky like a child's, and it startled me at first. *Why does she talk like that? With such sweetness.* It didn't matter. In that moment, I loved her.

She prescribed an antidepressant, and *just as promised* within a few months my whole life transformed from behind my own eyeballs. Doctors told me I was bordering on postpartum psychosis, that I was lucky to have come in, that pinching my baby that day could have saved my life, or hers, or both. Maybe it was the pills, surely it was the pills, but I'm not totally convinced I wasn't healed by the feeling of the nurse's hand on my knee when she said "Oh, honey," because I felt like a leper who was touched for the first time by somebody who didn't care that she was sick and deformed. I was so sure I was monstrous, some uniquely evil specimen of motherhood, that when she touched my knee and called me "honey," like I was any old mother passing through with a bit of PPD, I saw myself anew.

I was in a pit of black and couldn't see out. I felt the touch of a nurse and Zoloft and crawled to the top, looked out, and thought, "Oh shit, this ain't so bad."

And it wasn't.

4

PLAYING HOUSE IN THE SUBURBS WITH CAPTAIN MORGAN

Atop that pile of happy pills, I peered out over the edge of depression and surveyed the landscape. The first thing I saw was "I need out of this fucking house." Nothing was wrong with living in Mac's parents' house except we were living in Mac's parents' house. We were adults. We needed adult space, and in my case, employment. Stay-at-home parenthood was boldly oversold. ·

So I constructed a résumé emphasizing the honors classes I took in college while omitting the one (or two) I failed, and applied for a receptionist position at a highly respected boutique law firm about thirty minutes from the ranch, in downtown Sacramento. When they called me in for an interview, I knew I had a chance, because I did well with first impressions, particularly when sober. It was everything following the first impression that troubled me. I could give you what you wanted. I just couldn't *keep* giving it to you.

Sitting across from me in a large conference room, an extremely put-together, reserved woman with long, curly brown hair asked, "What experience do you have with administrative work?"

She wants honesty. "Well, I spent a summer as an intern at an office supplies business, but I don't have a *ton* of experience." I smiled and made a little face, as if to say, *Can I really say that?* As if I were a bit coy.

"I graduated from UC Davis about a year ago, but stayed home with my baby," I continued, "but I am a quick learner. I am very thorough." My mother had told me once while I was sweeping out our motor home that I was "very thorough." I stuck with it.

"What do you think your greatest asset is?" She offered a quick smile between jotting notes. I noticed she was left-handed and that her blouse perfectly matched her cardigan.

Humility. Tie it in with the honesty, Janelle. "I am willing to do whatever it takes to get the job done. If the firm needs me to scrub toilets, I'll do it. I'm here to work and I don't have too much ego wrapped up in that." She smiled again, and I felt bolstered. *You're doing great, Janelle.*

"We are extremely focused on collaboration. What is your greatest weakness?"

Captain Morgan.

Nope. Don't say that.

"Oh, well, I think it must be that I can be a bit of a perfectionist. I don't want to let things go if they aren't perfect, or close, you know? So sometimes I get frustrated with people who don't have the same focus as I do." I failed to mention that I thought most people around me were fucking idiots who should lose their jobs. That if I thought things, they were true, even if I had no evidence for them, and that, frankly, I was not exactly shining in my own life, and threatened to leave my husband on the daily. And, speaking of daily, I drank at that exact interval, and used to chase my brother around the house with a large kitchen knife.

I kept all that to myself and crossed my legs.

I was a master at selling my potential. My second-best talent was leaving before you figured out I couldn't deliver. Or I simply never showed up at the moment of delivery. I stopped calling friends just when they thought we were really connecting, didn't show up on the day they stopped doubting I'd show up. It was not conscious, but it was consistent. In college, a few professors wrote on the bottom of my papers, "Come see me about getting this published" or "Let's submit this to a contest I know of!" Each time, I called my mother and told her about it on the way home from class, felt proud and hopeful, told strangers about it at bars, but I never, ever showed up at their offices.

But this—this was an interview, and I believed what I was selling as genuinely as they did. As I shook the interviewer's hand and walked out the front door, I called my mother to tell her how well it went, and after the second interview, this one with a managing partner, they hired me. I landed the first "real" job I applied for, confirming my suspicion that I was *a well-equipped human ready to embark on many great successes.*

My first day of work was almost exactly two years after the February morning on the balcony. I was twenty-three and Ava was fifteen months. I woke up earlier than necessary and dressed her in Oshkosh train overalls, a white, collared long-sleeve blouse, and her favorite red leather Mary Jane shoes. I cleaned her face spotless and brushed her wavy blonde hair into pigtails. I packed a blue gingham sunhat into her diaper bag, and folded spare clothes with her name on their tags.

As I closed the babysitter's door behind me, I wondered if Ava understood why I was gone, and if I was perhaps making a mistake, and if she would be okay, and if maybe I regretted the whole job decision. I continued thinking these things until the moment I climbed into my car, put it in drive, and realized I was truly, completely, and finally alone. I glanced around the car to confirm it was real. No crying, no baby, no diapers.

Oh, thank God. Here I am again, I thought.

I stopped for a cappuccino. I tore down the freeway.

•   •   •

While I saved my receptionist money, my mother and I con-centrated with laser-like focus on the role of a house in the stabilization of marriage. She'd say, "You need a place to call your own. You need to be able to create a home for your family," and I would agree emphatically. The next day, when I would call about Mac's astonishingly disturbed relationship with a ranch—he still, after two years, couldn't take a vacation without getting ill from stress—she'd say, "It will get better as soon as you get your own place."

When I would tell her I was generally dissatisfied with life, or that I hated my body, or that the sense of monotony and seething banality of my daily existence might actually one day take me *out of the earth*, she'd say, "How long until you have your deposit?"

And I'd say, "You're right. It will be better when Mac and I move out."

We spoke as if it were a biological imperative, as if I would implode if I didn't have access to 1,200 square feet to clean, as if all that was wrong with me could be fixed with some carpets and cabinetry that were all my own. And so, when I banked enough money, I found a house in the suburbs of Sacramento, in a strip-mall paradise called Elk Grove. It's the kind of place one drives through and wonders if the civil engineers went out of their way to remove all soul from the city, or if that was simply a by-product of the ratio of big box stores to humans. I made an appointment alone, viewed it alone, and rented it on the spot.

When I got home holding a rental agreement, I figured I should tell Mac.

"Hey," I said, after a few lubricating glasses of red wine. "You know how hard things have been. We need to get our own place. That's the thing. We'll be happier."

He shifted in his seat, his beautiful eyes growing pained at the impending confrontation. But he didn't say anything. Not with his mouth, at least. So I filled the silence.

"I'm a mother, Mac, I need my own home. Mothers need it. We need a place to decorate. You don't understand. It's a big deal—like a biological thing. You know, this isn't my family." I swept my hand across his parents' living room while a familiar rage crept up my feet and all the way to my eyes as I thought about *all I had given up for him and this kid.*

He looked at me harder while his silence transformed from *space for me to talk* into a hundred-foot steel wall between us. I readied my attack. I thought it would penetrate the wall.

"Are you going to say anything?" I was done waiting.

His eyes widened but his mouth didn't move. He leaned back against the kitchen chair and picked at the label on his beer bottle. He was still wearing his work clothes, an orange and blue plaid cotton shirt, an old button-down from high school, long covered in bloodstains. His curly hair stuck out wildly above his ears from beneath his ball cap, which he had flipped up and to one side. He had dirt across the bridge of his nose, and I couldn't move close to him on account of the reek of slaughterhouse.

I took a sip of wine, wondering how he managed to stay silent for so long in moments like this, simply refusing to make a sound. Even when angry, when I swore I would punish my adversary with the severest of silent treatments, I found myself unable to quit speaking. It was remarkably disappointing. But Mac would stare at me for an entire night, look away thirty times, walk out ten times, but he would not speak unless he was so inclined. To help him along, I would chase him around the house like a puppy attacking his pant leg.

I hoped this night wouldn't be one of those nights. "Mac," I said, attempting greatest civility, "could you please tell me what you're thinking?"

Finally, after an incredible pause, he said, "We don't have the money," and watched me pour a cocktail.

"Yeah, we do. We're fine," I said, dismissing him, thinking, *God, I hate it when he has opinions.*

"How will we be fine, Janelle?"

"Because I can't stay here anymore." By then, I was yelling. I didn't want to talk about his theories of finances. I knew he was simply afraid. He was always afraid. My mother and I had already discussed the whole situation. It was handled.

He countered with more silence, and I knew it was because I yelled, because I asked him to speak and then attacked him, but what I heard in his answer was that he didn't understand. Again. He took his hat off, and a stray curl fell over his eye, and I noticed his new piercing in his ear. It was a bar that went across the top of his left ear lobe, and I flinched remembering how the piercer inserted it. He stuck a thick needle slowly through the ear and then passed the bar through. But he couldn't get it right, so he pushed the bar in and out through the cartilage, twice, while Mac sat motionless, sweating.

He was the toughest human I had ever known. But I knew it would be me who carried us someplace new.

"Whatever," I said, holding his eyes. "I already rented it." His mouth tweaked in confusion.

"You can come with me if you want," I continued. "Or you can stay here. I don't fucking care." And I walked out of the room.

• • •

He came with me. The house had two bedrooms and two bathrooms. It was one of those subdivision homes with a five-foot buffer between it and the next house, no sidewalk, one ten-foot box of perfectly manicured lawn out front, and a two-car garage. The neighborhood was neutral tones and stucco as far as the eye could see. The inside of the house felt clean and contained and new, exactly what I needed to begin my life as a fully-pilled-up, non-psychotic working mother. We moved in and bought a beagle puppy that we named Maggie May, after the Rod Stewart song.

I could not tell which house was ours from afar. Every time I drove near it, I had to check the house number in the black-and-white light-up box. The subdivision had a fake lake a few blocks down from our house, and sometimes we'd walk around the water on the clean cement walkway lined with sapling trees.

I'd look at the bigger houses around the lake with bigger back-yards and feel envy and disgust at the same time.

This couldn't be it. But damn, look how nice that pool is.

• • •

It was exactly like my mother and I imagined it, which was exactly like a 1950s sitcom, except Mac and I were the main characters.

"Hey, love, how was your day?" I'd ask when I got home from work. But instead of putting on my apron and floating around the kitchen like a house angel, I'd put my bag of groceries on the counter, kick off my scuffed fake-leather shoes, and wonder how long until I could drink rum.

"Fine, you?" he'd say. I would mention what I was making for dinner, and he would take his boots off, and we would watch Ava play in a laundry basket, and laugh. Then I would notice the laundry at the bottom of the basket, which was clean, and yet, still in the basket.

"Hey, you know I, uh, put that basket there so you'd fold it." I'd say.

"Mmm," he'd mumble.

"What?" I'd snap, leaning toward him, as if to say, "You ready for this fight?"

"Sorry. I didn't notice," he'd say in quiet apathy, an indifference that seemed to place the weight of our lives onto my shoulders. I'd watch him rub his feet and I'd notice again his flannel shirts stained with some livestock excretion. He didn't care about laun-dry or our futures. He just worked. He worked Thursday through Sunday. I worked Monday through Friday. We parented in silos. I worked five days at the office and two days alone at home, where I would do all the things that never occurred to my husband, who had moved from his mother's care to mine, his parent's house to this one, and simply steeled himself when my rage blew, hunkered down until the tornado passed, which usually looked like me getting drunk enough to no longer care.

On the days when I worked and Mac didn't, our evenings were always the same.

"What did you do today, Mac? What'd ya do today, exactly? Because the house looks the same as when I left." The anger settled across my shoulders, heavy and exhausting.

"I don't know. I drove Ava to daycare, picked her up." He'd throw me a glance and I'd notice how handsome he looked sitting on the couch with his feet up, out of his work clothes, his perfectly square shoulders and chest, and I'd marvel at how somebody who infuriated me so completely could be so fucking gorgeous at the same time.

I'd pummel him with questions about household tasks. Dog food. Dishes. Laundry. The oil change. He'd meet my inquiries with silence, and I'd wonder what beat him into silence. Shame? Resignation? Personality? How broken-down must one become to simply power off in the face of conflict? But I had no energy left to draw words from him.

"Did you watch TV this entire time?"

Silence.

"Mac have you not noticed that I work five days a week and then when I get a weekend, you go to work, so I work seven fucking days a week? Do you think I sit around watching TV for five hours? Do you think I *ever* enjoy myself? I can't do this. I want a divorce."

Silence.

I would uncork a bottle of wine, and by glass two or three, I would speak more gently, earnestly. "Mac, please. I need your help. I need *you*. Why don't you mow the lawn, take care of the car? Anything."

Silence.

By glass four or five, I would scream or cry, or drive to buy a bottle of rum, or sit on the couch and watch some British sit-coms. Or we would go into the bedroom and have sex that never left me feeling whole, but at the end, I'd think, *He's really going to change this time, on account of our highly productive talk.*

I would pass out, then wake up in a haze and sweat at two or three a.m., with a headache that threatened more sleep. I'd find the Advil and water on my bedside table, take a few, and in the morning, I'd get up and go to work. I'd feed Ava an egg or oatmeal, wash her face, and dress her warm in the winter and cool in the summer. Almost every day, I'd take a picture of her grinning and holding her little lunchbox beneath the white light-up address box, and I would send it to my mother so we could ogle at her beauty.

I decorated Ava's room with a twin bed made of pine, a white bookshelf, and a rug from the actual Pottery Barn, which felt like reaching a suburban pinnacle. We now had a real bed instead of a lumpy futon, and I hired a dog trainer for that fucking beagle. The trainer said Maggie was the worst dog he'd ever seen in his life and essentially told us the little bastard was unfixable. After Maggie ate our hose for the twelfth time, pissed on the carpet, and stole our dinner off the table, Mac and I agreed to give her away to an old man who had owned beagles his whole life and never left his house. I missed her as soon as she was gone.

• • •

Every day, I woke up and got dressed in my business casual cloth-ing, wished I exercised more, drove twenty minutes to my job in the black Infiniti four-door sedan my father had sold us. I listened to NPR on the way, specifically the old guy with the oddly soothing voice who did the news. I sucked down coffee and a cigarette. I played my music loud. It was wonderful, sort of. It was at least twenty minutes each day that felt hopeful. I was heading to a new place. A new day! Tiny potential!

At work I could drop my purse off at my desk and travel into the clean break room for a cup of coffee. While I stirred in the cream, I could stand by the counter and say hello to my work friends and feel capable and centered. In the afternoon I might get a sparkling water from the refrigerator or a caffeinated soda if I were tired. I might walk down the hall and grab a chocolate from my boss Beatrix's office.

To keep me busy between calls and visitors, Bea would give me tasks I could perform right there at the reception desk, such as calling computer companies for technological difficulties or to discuss warranties. Often I would end up shouting at the overseas customer service representative, right there in the front office. Eventually Bea banned me from making such phone calls, and I told myself she had simply realized, finally, that I was too damn smart for such menial laboring.

My receptionist skills beamed brightest when welcoming guests to our office, although my judgment was perhaps slightly off. I once asked a woman there for a job interview if anybody had ever told her she had a porn star name, because she did. She started, but grinned, and said, "I've never been in a law firm with a receptionist as inappropriate as you." That woman was hired and we ended up becoming friends, but the difficulty was I never knew how my verbal escapades would turn out, and yet, I couldn't seem to stop myself from experimenting. I'd either make a new friend or get reported to my supervisor.

I learned quickly that the superpower of low-level administrative staff is invisibility. To some, I was so unimportant I would *actually disappear*, and as a result, they would speak openly, *right in front of me*, about confidential topics. I would sit staring at my computer screen, clicking with great focus on absolutely nothing, listening to guests talk about employees of the firm as if we weren't sitting in a tiny lobby together, as if I didn't know the people I worked with, as if I were not even human. I'd think, *They don't even see me*, and I would feel powerful in their underestimation.

Fuckers. Do they even know how much potential they're looking at?

• • •

"Hey, Janelle, you can't just *say* every single thing that comes into your mind."

I sat in Bea's office crossing and uncrossing my legs, folding and refolding my hands, getting my first "talking to." I scanned the blank surface of her immaculate cherry wood desk, looking for a single stray paper clip or wadded up Post-it note. Nothing. Not even dust behind the computer monitor.

Her inbox, empty. Her candy bowl, empty. I visualized my desk with papers strewn in a thousand directions, a little bonsai tree dying from lack of water, and the pictures of Ava and Mac. I made a mental note to clean my shit up.

I had been at the firm for one year, and they had recently promoted me to administrative assistant. There's a chance they were trying to find me a less visible place than the front office. At any rate, I now had my own cubicle and a raise. I was proud. Unfortunately, the attorney I was supporting was less impressed with my performance.

Brian, the attorney in question, was a perky gentleman whose demeanor masked what seemed to me a deep-seated sense of superiority ... for approximately fifteen minutes, at which time I concluded, based on my vast professional experience, that I was dealing with a person who loved nothing more than questionable ideas and the fact that he could make me do them.

Every Monday morning, I was supposed to meet with him and listen, riveted, to his peculiar but incredibly precise requests. Then I was supposed to work hard to implement them, with glee and *to the letter*, even though I believed them to be absurd and inefficient. But every time I did a task, some horrible new detail popped into his brain, adding another act to our little roadshow.

"Janelle! How was your weekend? How's Ava?" I would begin to answer, but at mid-sentence, he'd grow bored: "Great, thanks. Would you mind researching Internet providers in my area and making a spreadsheet of what they provide and how much they cost?"

So I did it, and when I showed him my work, he'd say: "Please add a column with Internet speeds and then research what those speeds mean. Translate them for me. You know, layman's speak."

He would regularly use terms like "layman's speak," which felt as inhumane as the person in the cubicle next to me eating corn nuts. I noticed that Brian ate uniformly healthy food except on Fridays, which I imagined was a plan he had actually created for himself and stuck with. This was so profoundly reasonable and mature I contemplated poisoning his food simply to shake things up a bit. He smiled too much and never failed to say "Good morning!" as he passed each person in the hallway, making sure to use their first names. At least once a day I visualized him making spreadsheets in quicksand.

"Can you also add a column letting me know how long each company has been in business, and whether or not they outsource work in India? Also, I need this color coded, I think. Easier on the eyes."

"Color coded? Why? Brian, that doesn't make sense."

Janelle, you can't just say every single thing that comes into your mind.

"One more thing: New schedule routine. Let's try you printing out my daily schedule and highlighting each activity using different colors based on type of activity. For example, internal meetings could be blue. External meetings, green. Lunch meetings, pink! And you know, as long as they're consistent, go ahead and have fun with it."

Oh, wow, shit. For sure this sounds fun. This is exactly the kind of activity a person of my mental capacity finds pleasurable. My dream actually is to spend many years highlighting schedules for no apparent reason.

Back in my cubicle, while I worked to find the perfect shade of sea green for the AT&T column, I'd wonder if perhaps I was cut out for slightly more challenging work. I wanted to impress everyone with my administrative assistant skills, but *color coded spreadsheets?* I'd grow further confused when I'd overhear the managing partners consulting with him on major clients, as if he in fact knew how to do his job quite well and the color coding situation were a mere idiosyncrasy that could be over-looked.

"Janelle, within reason, your job is to do what he asks." After saying this, Bea held my gaze, registering my expression. She knew what I was thinking. Smiling, she added, "Your job is to be patient with people who aren't as smart as you." With this, my ears perked. *Now we're talking, boss.*

But she wasn't talking about Brian. She was talking about my impatience with all those I perceived as having subpar intelligence, which was nearly everyone.

"I try, Bea." I met her eyes while running my finger along the edge of her desk, still hoping for dust. She raised her eyebrows, knowing I was using the term "try" rather loosely. I laughed, vaguely terrified of her. She embodied all the professionalism I lacked, combined with follow-through. She was fair, consistent, and heartbreakingly organized. And yet, she had *lived*. She grew up in a goddamn desert, raised her child alone, pulled herself out of poverty. She was a single mother with an immaculate desk.

I tried to do what Brian asked, but I couldn't wipe the disdain off my face. I kept forgetting. Or it popped onto my brow before I could stop it. The fact that he was so damn friendly while he wasted my time simply confused me. Although, how very cap-italist to find yourself getting fucked and yet kind of enjoy it. I even grew to like the man. And yet he wanted me to tape his schedule in his planner in 2003. *We have computers, man.*

•   •   •

At our administrative staff meetings, I focused all my energy on making sure I didn't send my yellow legal pad hurling across the room in a fit of final unbridled rage, or fling my coffee cup at the person who brought up refrigerator soft drink organization again. The worst was when I was supposed to lead one of these discussions, telling all the women and one man how the research on a new coffeemaker was going, or where I had put the masking tape in the copy room, as if we weren't going to lie in coffins someday with maggots eating our eyeballs. By this time I had been promoted to Slightly Higher Admin Assistant, and I'd sit in the conference room listening to a person born onto earth as good as the next guy talk about parking validation methodology with the vigor of a presidential nominee, thinking, *What if I started stabbing myself in the jugular with this Uni-ball pen? Or started banging my manila folder against that lady's head, right there next to me, over and over again, without a word?*

Once again, I feared one of these days I wouldn't be able to stop my body from carrying out the vision. Meetings with the whole staff were slightly better because I got to gaze at the managing partners and imagine how big their houses must be, but still I wondered what would happen if I stood up, unbuttoned my cardigan, and smashed a scone between my tits in an act of silent resistance.

Janelle, you can't just say every single thing that comes into your mind.

This includes *shit, cunt, bastard, bitch,* and any variation of the word *fuck.* I also learned that you "can't wear black bras under white shirts" and low-cut business casual pants that show your underwear are also frowned upon. Further, copy machines have a top-loader where one can load multiple pages at once and they will run right through the copier, the whole pile, like it's nothing. This particular piece of information smashed me like a brick during the new-copier orientation meeting. I had spent an entire summer after my first year of college working as an intern at an office supply business headquartered in a desolate wasteland called Hayward in the San Francisco Bay Area. For a solid three weeks, my job was to photocopy booklets held together by removable plastic binding. All day, every day, from eight a.m. until five p.m., I stood photocopying page by page, turning the page, opening the copier, laying it on the glass, pressing the "copy" button, opening the top, taking it out, turning the page, and on and on. For three weeks.

Not a single one of those cunt bastards told me I could just take the binding out and put the pages in the top loader. Not a single human noticed that I was wasting hours and hours of my life unnecessarily. Or maybe they did notice and found it funny, thinking, "I wonder how long it will take the idiot intern to realize she can just stick them in the top loader?"

Well the answer is "never." She will never realize it. Actually, no. She'll realize it four years later. But as far as you're concerned, dick, it's never.

I never would have done that. I would have told the sad new intern how to make her life significantly easier, how to do the job better, how to make her day a little more meaningful. But then again, the people who silently watched me waste my time day after day sold Post-it notes day after day, arguing about pen quality, sitting month after month getting closer to heart disease and death, the highlight of their day being the trip to the sandwich joint around the corner, or the chocolate they'd grab from their boss's office, or the afternoon soda they'd pick up while in the break room, chatting with their friends and wondering what might happen for dinner.

5

THREE A.M. IDEAS

It was complicated to think so highly of myself and yet have a life making color coded spreadsheets while wearing size 16 Old Navy slacks and sitting in a cubicle, living in a monochromatic rental with a young husband and baby, years before any of those things are supposed to happen to anyone, let alone a person destined for greatness. I felt myself becoming like the Post-it note sellers in Hayward, but managed to smooth the dissonance of reality by clinging to the year I lived the wonder I thought would last a lifetime.

It had only been three years since I stepped off the plane in Barcelona, arriving in what I was sure must be the "prime of my life." I was twenty years old, unattached to any human, tan from my summer job lifeguarding, with newly shorn hair. Until my twentieth year, my hair fell long and straight past my waist. This had been my hairstyle since I began growing hair, but it wasn't really a hairstyle at all. It just grew that way because I didn't trim it often. But I had it all chopped off at twenty and I felt free and lighter and new. Friends told me I looked like Cameron Diaz. She must have been at the prime of her life, too.

I spent my first month in Barcelona in dorms with exchange students from all over the world, although the Americans seemed to dominate the place, as we often do. We were supposed to engage in intensive language study and find ourselves places to live, but I don't recall the language study. What I recall is the café across the street and the thick summer air—the feeling of being beautifully lost, of sitting at plastic tables in front of the dorms and feeling alien, but warmly so.

On day five, I gathered the courage to wander into the café I had been staring at every evening since my arrival. I watched the locals and tried to copy them, the way they moved and glanced at each other, but as I walked up to the counter and stared at the chalkboard on the wall, feeling the eyes of the dazzling Spaniards burning into the back of my head, I almost couldn't speak.

"Café," I said, thinking it was coffee. "Por favor." I handed her the pesetas I had counted out in advance and retreated in humiliation. Instead of coffee, I got a tiny something in white ceramic. It was pure espresso. I sat alone at a table in front of the cafe, had a smoke, and drank the espresso black, too scared to add sugar or milk. Soon I would learn that what I wanted was a "café con leche." I would have hundreds before leaving a year later, and each one would be better than the last.

While sitting in my dorm that first month, a British boy named Francis with brown eyes and wild, wavy brown hair that hung down over his forehead walked by my room, or maybe I walked by his, and we chatted for a few minutes before he said, "I'm taking the train to Madrid tomorrow. Want to come?"

Yes, absolutely, guy-I-just-met. I absolutely want to go to a place I've never been with a person I don't know. There was no voice whispering, "Hey, you don't know this fella, Janelle. You just arrived in this country, and you barely speak the language." Francis was the reason I went to Spain. I wanted adventure. I wanted to press my whole body against the boundaries of the world to see how much it could support. I wanted to be Mick Jagger and Gertrude Stein and Ernest Hemingway at the same damn time. Hemingway never would have said "no" to a friendly Brit offering a trip to Madrid. So I, too, said "yes."

I showed up the next morning at the train station wearing thin, wide-leg cotton pants and a tight spaghetti-strap tank top, without a bra. We drank beer on the train in the smoking car and as I watched the countryside speed by, I thought, *I must be in heaven now.*

In Madrid, Francis and I met his friends who were summering in Spain and somehow all looked like supermodels. We lounged by the pool and drank beer in the living room until somebody set up rows of cocaine on the glass-topped kitchen table, and I knew I was going to be just fine in this country.

"Yes, please," I said, ending a two-year streak of cocaine abstinence. I hadn't abstained for lack of interest, or because I "wanted better for myself," rather, my college-town acquaintances rarely possessed hard drugs, and I was not yet driven to find them.

But if it had appeared one night, like it did that night in Madrid, I would have said yes, because I always said yes to cocaine. I tried the drug for the first time at seventeen years old in my high school boyfriend's house. We did a couple of grams with friends, sniffing it off a mirror on the bathroom counter until it was gone, and while everybody else in the house smoked weed and drank to ease the spastic comedown and eventually sleep, I said I had to pee, went back to the bathroom, and snorted lint off the floor, thinking surely some blow had dropped to the ground and I could get one more hit.

After that night, I never found it necessary to complicate cocaine decisions, never thought twice about chasing the soaring light, the electric meaning, no matter what was happening the next day, or who I was with, or how many times I promised myself I'd never do it again. I would handle that later. In the critical moment when I needed my brain to talk some sense into me, I saw only the high at my fingertips. The Technicolor life. *Oh, the love we would feel, you and I. The truth we would speak. Let's watch the boredom burn. Let's see if we can survive. Let's do really stupid shit and get away with it.*

That night in Madrid we danced at a multilevel open-air club filled with soapsuds and bubbles, and I did bumps in the bathroom with my new friends. When we got back to the apartment, Francis and I began kissing on a bedroom floor, but I was coldly uninterested, participating solely out of a young woman's sense of obligation to deliver what she was taught men "deserve." I wished only that we had more coke. I was always the one wishing we had more coke. I was always the one spinning in circles looking for more—in the carpet, the folds of the couch, the crevices of my wallet. When the rest of the party moved on, smoked some hash, took a few shots, accepted the end of the baggie (without a fight, even), I was the one coolly dropping the idea of getting more.

"Hey, just for fun, let's call the guy to see if he's still around." I would smile, reminding myself that next time I needed to hold "the guy's" phone number.

The psychopaths around me would shoot my idea down in midair, and my heart would panic to see the amphetamine light die. My blood fumed at the impending return to regular life, and I was crushed under a wave of sadness, of fiery restlessness. So I'd make my way to alcohol, the strongest drug we had left, and I'd drink it fast and hard and smile faintly when they looked my way.

Somebody in the living room made a joke about coming down. I wanted to rip his face into shreds. Or I wanted to be exactly like him, cool and calm when the drugs ran out. I wanted to enjoy making love there in Madrid, but I was spinning in the daylight, wishing the walls of the nightclub would ever expand as they did under the moonlight, when the promise of tomorrow moved through me like God, and I danced with my face against yours, and to the stars.

• • •

After a month in Barcelona, I moved into an apartment full of Spaniards, which I insisted upon because I was strategically avoiding Americans. Most of the other American students rented apartments together, and thought I was foolish, but I couldn't understand why one would move to another country only to inundate themselves with the culture she just left.

One of my roommates, Santiago, was eighteen and from a Basque village. The second, Marcos, was from Madrid. The name of the third roommate I can't remember because he was old, perhaps twenty-six, and rarely drank with us. Our landlady, Celli, from Galicia, was also our roommate. She lived in a long, skinny, broom-closet-type room off the front hall, which she almost never left. Celli was excessively concerned with our whereabouts, which I resented, because *I did not come to Spain to acquire another well-meaning caregiver.* She smelled strongly of garlic, and I had no idea, ever, what the hell she was saying. My room was meant for two, indicated by bunk beds, but I rented it for myself because I needed space and privacy. I was very profound. Because of this, everybody in the house assumed I was wealthy. I never told them otherwise because it was amusing to be seen that way, and I had a tiny lying problem, particularly in Spain, where nobody could fact-check my stories.

When we grew tired of the garlic landlady's busybody nature, Marcos, Santiago, and I rented our own apartment down the road from Gaudi's Park Güell. My room had giant windows overlooking the city, and from my bed, which was two twin beds shoved together, I could watch the sun rise over the old red city and feel grateful.

As the days carried on and I settled deeper into the new culture, I realized I was more comfortable in Barcelona than I had ever been in America. It was an odd feeling. The siesta and drinking and late dinners and cigarettes, the bread stores and meat hanging from the ceiling of the butcher's shop. The old people playing bocce ball and men in tight jeans. Chattering teenagers on the subway. The little smoke shops with roll-up doors, the trains and taxis and "motos." The history and museums and heartbreaking cobblestone of the gothic quarter. The haunts set deep in stone, telling their stories of war and occupation and Moroccans and Rome. America felt silly and immature, like a teenager who hadn't yet realized what mattered in life. When I had a kidney infection and spent a day in a Spanish hospital, the doctors took care of me, and when I left, the receptionist handed me my paperwork and said, "We don't charge students."

Spain felt old and wise.

On Friday afternoons, when Marcos and I had money, we'd run over to the student travel agency after not going to class, and we'd see which deals they had for the weekend. They'd say, "Paris or Rome or Vienna, but you have to leave in three hours and come back on Tuesday at two a.m."

"Perfect," we'd say, and we would go.

I sat in the gardens of castles outside Vienna with nothing to do but watch the people pass, and drank beer on fountain steps in Italy. I watched opera in Paris, drank homemade wine in Sevilla, and stood at the southernmost tip of Spain, where they say you can see Morocco. Every day in Barcelona I stopped by a café to write in my journal, unable to catch all the ideas and colors and hope flooding through me. I drove a rental car up the coast of Spain with my mother when she came to visit. We had to stop to let a shepherd cross the road with his flock, and we ate shrimp in a village with buildings all in white, and we took a wrong road that ended at the ocean—simply stopped at the sand, though the map showed it continuing to the left.

I missed flights. I stayed in hostels and slept on benches in train stations. I rode mopeds in beach towns and hailed taxis in London and bumped cocaine from glittering necklaces around the necks of gay men in Madrid.

The first time tourists asked me for directions to Park Güell while I walked home, mistaking me for a Spaniard, I smiled in the knowing that I was truly, finally home. I realized I could not leave. It would be difficult to tell my parents, but I could not catch that flight back to California. My plan was to simply *stay* and explain it later.

I never made that phone call, though, because a week before

my scheduled flight home, I found myself reading a letter from our landlord saying we hadn't paid the rent in three months and the police were coming for us. My student loan was gone. I had spent every penny on "partying" and had no reserves. My family had given me plenty. There was no way to ask for more. I packed up what meant anything to me, rented a motel room with Marcos, who was my only friend left, and waited for the days to click by. I had a plane ticket. I had enough money to buy cigarettes and beer for the next few days.

I had banished myself out of the country I was meant to live in.

Still, I swore I would return. I knew it in my bones. Like the haunts in the gothic quarter.

Eight months after returning to America, I was pregnant.

•   •   •

"We have reorganized the copy room and the masking tape is now beneath the binder clips."

Joyce, a more senior administrative assistant at the office, was very serious in her coral cardigan and khakis. When another secretary raised her voice to argue with her about the suggested tape placement, I slowly lifted my eyes toward them and let my head fall to one side, refusing to hide how much I hated this moment. They finished in time for someone to bring up parking validation.

The waist of my black slacks cut into my belly. As I looked down to adjust them, I noticed my shoes were navy blue. I thought, *Wow, I can't match shoes with pants. Guess we're there now, huh?* My shirt was faded purple and probably a polyester blend. I looked ridiculous. A fat roll spilled over the top of my pants, and I considered pulling the waist down beneath the roll, so the fat bubbled out in one billowing mess. It was more comfortable that way, but felt like giving up. I sat up straighter and pulled my shirt away from my stomach, trying to hide my bulges in that classic self-conscious fat person gesture.

Perhaps there was going to be more.

Between emails at my cubicle and commutes home, I dreamed of nights in Barcelona. No, I dreamed of some. Because there were failed classes, lost friends, mornings of regret and shaking desolation. Twice I escaped being raped. Once, barely. I was pinned against a wall in a bar's cellar while a man lifted my skirt and pressed his body against me when my friend "had a bad feeling," came downstairs after me, and began shouting and pounding on the door next to my head. It startled the man long enough that I could shove him off, unbolt the door, and run out. As my friend walked me out of the bar, she said, "I'm tired of taking care of you. I'm tired of wondering if you made it home okay." She got in a cab and didn't call me again.

Once, I couldn't speak on our couch. I must have done too many or the wrong drugs. I tried, but couldn't make my mouth move. My roommates stuck me in a freezing shower and slapped my face while they looked at me, bored.

There was all that, plus nights of empty insomnia, which I spent scratching in my journal and at scabs on my legs, but what you remember when living in a house that can't be told apart from the others is walking the brilliant streets of a European city on a bright morning on your way to the subway, realizing that nobody is treating you differently than all the Spaniards around you. If you want, you can walk into any café, order a "café con leche," and smoke a cigarette—and you'll know it will be right, and you will fit, and life will move in luminous color. What you remember is the feeling that life was going to happen, or that it is happening now, and that it would always move in meaningful directions. But I couldn't stay.

Mac, are you going to go to college? You don't earn enough. We have no benefits.

What are we going to do, Mac?

Why are you just staring at me? Why don't you care?

We need to extend the warranty on these five computers.

Yes, I'll hold.

Okay, here are the serial numbers.

I lay on my back while we fucked and stared at the ceiling because I was not drunk enough to make it interesting, or sober enough to make it satisfying, or wasted enough to deny that it had been so long I couldn't run anymore.

The pills gave me just enough to get my body into the car to drive twenty miles and listen to the guy from NPR, and on the way home, just enough to stop at the grocery store to buy one, maybe two bottles of wine. Walking down the liquor aisle, I'd tell myself, *Janelle, you just can't drink so much again tonight, and dammit, you can't wake up with that hangover like you did today, or put your kid to bed half passed out. One glass, maybe two.*

The pills carried me to the moment I drank my first glass and it all started feeling manageable again, the stucco and lake and office chair and gorgeous blonde-headed child. *Another must be okay* (of wine, that is). With the second, it was so much better still. Mac would seem witty again, and television would make me smile, and reading Ava a story would entertain me. *Who needs Spain? Who needs love? Who needs what I thought I needed?*

If I go to the store and buy a bottle of rum, I'd think, *I could drink it fast, and things would be that much better still.*

Even still!

Until the morning, when I would wake up and swear I wouldn't do it again, not this time, because *I can't keep living like this.* Again. Again. I'd take some ibuprofen, make some coffee, and shuffle into the car from behind sunglasses, where I drove and smoked and listened to music, loud, almost like the girl flying down the rails listening to the Grateful Dead, wondering where the end of Spain is, and how long it would take to get there.

· · ·

Once a week, I would call my mother to inform her I was leaving my marriage. She would listen, genuinely fascinated, and then suggest I talk to him, really explain how I was feeling, and I'd recall the seven hundred and fifty thousand conversations he and I had endured to the bitter end, and she and I, too, to fix her marriage or mine. They never worked, but what the hell else does one do with a failing marriage other than *talk about it incessantly*?

Well, Mac and I would go out together. Grandparents would watch Ava while we concentrated on our sole purpose, which was to get hammered at a bar with no windows. Unfortunately, since he worked weekends and I worked weekdays, one of us was always going to work hungover, but that was a risk we were willing to take. We did it for marriage. It was like a commitment to therapy, but for alcoholics. I'd wedge myself into jeans and drink wine while he got dressed. I'd paint on makeup and style my hair, and we'd smoke cigarettes on the way to the bar, with our best songs playing and each other.

Occasionally we would visit my mother in Mendocino for the weekend, and she would babysit while we went to the Caspar Inn, which is a bar in the middle of the five-building town of Caspar, across the street from a nineteenth-century church. It was packed on Friday and Saturday nights, smelling of whiskey, convenience store perfume, and alcoholism. One night we went to hear Tommy Castro, a local blues-rock band, and out on the deck in the fog we met a man named MYQ, but not pronounced "Mike." His name was pronounced "M-Y-Q," as in the letters themselves. He was making a coffee table book of his facial hair configurations. At the time, he had a spade shaved onto his chin.

A few minutes later, down at the end of the bar, MYQ, Mac, and I met a seemingly homeless man with a kitten in his jacket. Impressed, we bought the man a drink and became fast friends, though I can't remember his name. The kitten's name was Rufus. After talking for a while, we bought him a couple more rounds, smoked a few cigarettes on the misty porch, and shut the bar down. Rufus's owner needed a ride home, and we figured giving him a ride sounded as good as any plan ever sounded, so we hopped in my car and drove north on Highway 1 along the ocean, eventually turning east, into the mountains, then right down a little dirt road. He said he had some beer in the "main house," so I killed the engine.

"Come on in," he said. "But these people are a little weird." Considering he went to bars with a cat in his jacket, I was intrigued to meet somebody he thought was weird.

When he opened the front door to the house, I faced a wall of indiscernible material to the ceiling and a smell I can only describe as "absolutely not." There was a single trail through the house, forming a reeking canyon of trash.

I forced a laugh and said, "No thanks," turned around, and walked out. They must have been hoarders. A few minutes later, Mac and Rufus's dad brought out some beer. *Did we just steal beer from hoarders?* I thought, grabbing one.

Our new friend walked us over to his home, which was a converted school bus on the other side of the property. The inside was covered in quilts and packed with wood carvings and stained glass and paintings, trinkets from every town in northern California. While we sat with him, he filled a little bowl with tofu and pulled a plastic sack out of his pocket. I thought it was bee pollen. Sprinkling it on the food, he said, "Rufus eats tofu with brewer's yeast on it. It's the only food he likes."

"Oh." I nodded, seeing the dirt under the man's nails and his thick, filthy fingers sprinkling the yeast in a little mound right in the center of the bowl.

"It's hard for me to get to Fort Bragg to buy it, but it's so expensive in Mendocino." I almost offered to drive him there right then, but I knew it was a three a.m. idea, and three a.m. ideas are almost uniformly bad. Rufus devoured his dinner.

"I'm a stained glass artist from Humboldt. I used to travel around to shows with my old lady, but she's gone, and there isn't work anymore. I have this beautiful place though." I watched him and tried not to look around, tried not to be the one to break it to him that his bus was not beautiful.

When we went outside, I realized he was not talking about the bus. He didn't care about the bus. He was talking about the little river below, so close you could hear it from inside, and the ferns and redwoods, the thick fallen trunks and moss, the scent of ocean in the distance. The silence.

Mac and our friend and Rufus went back inside, but I stayed

alone and looked out at the little river and the stars and trees, which were mostly sound and shadows in the dark, and I thought about his kitten, and that I had little idea where I was, and I wondered if this was how people got cut up and eaten by axe-murdering psychos. But he was not an axe-murdering psycho. He was a misunderstood stained glass artist who fed his cat brewer's yeast.

I loved Mac on those nights. I loved our adventures, our chemistry, the way we seemed to attract endless weirdos. Everywhere we went, the misfits came running. Reno. Davis. Tahoe. San Francisco. Santa Rosa. Caspar and Mendocino. How many nights had we spent with the outliers of those towns, the loner eccentrics?

Mac and I were friends. We were young, lightly renegade partiers, but we had our baby, and we loved her, and when the mavericks at bars would ask about our lives, we told them about her. We told them how smart and beautiful she was, and we seemed to have a better life than them because she existed, and we had each other. That dive-bar life was a tiny piece of a brilliant whole. We had a real life out there in the world with stucco houses and cubicles and cement lakes and neat lawns, where the sane people live, as opposed to the ones making coffee table books out of facial hair photography and stealing beer from hoarders.

And yet, I needed the misfits to exist. I needed to party with them and drink with them and inhale deeply with them. I needed to shut down bars with the local drunks, because next to them, we were a millionaire family. Next to them, we really had our acts together.

We navigated the crazies just fine. It was only at home we

lost our way. We tried, though. We talked. Sometimes I'd get my hands on some cocaine and we would really talk then. High as kites, I'd encourage Mac to wake up, liven up, go to school, do something! Grow up, son!

He'd get excited too, and after a few lines, he'd come up with a plan. "Tomorrow," he'd say, "I'm going to join the rodeo circuit."

"Yes! You should do that, Mac. You can do it!"

It was a three a.m. idea, but it was all we had.

6

ROCKETSHIP ROCK-ON

After two years at the firm, I got a promotion and raise that made me question the institution of marriage as a whole. *Janelle, I thought, this is the moment you've been waiting for. Your big fucking break. Time to get out on your own and soar.*

I found a little house in a 1940s neighborhood of Sacramento and rented it alone, again, announcing my departure one evening while Mac finished his spaghetti. But this time, I explained, he could not come with me because our marriage wasn't working.

"What do you mean?" he asked, and then it was my turn to stare silently into the void.

I was horribly confused by his confusion since we had discussed that exact topic every week for two solid years. And we had only been married three.

"Mac, you're not going to change and I need a future, a life." I was pontificating loudly, but lost some gusto when I added, "I'm not sure I love you anymore."

"I still love you, Janelle," he said in a sort of whispered resignation.

I scowled, thinking, *Who would say such a thing at a time like this?* His eyes were wet and the same as the night we met, and I wanted to love him but could not. I was looking for something lost. I was looking for Barcelona.

"Mac, look at the way I drink every day. I am miserable. I'm dying like this."

"I don't think you should go," he said, holding my eyes. I felt like I was smacking him with the back of my hand while he crouched behind a table, and I think somewhere I knew he could not defend himself or understand or even beg. Life washed over him. He seemed like a boat without a rudder, and I was simply a current that came along once.

One week later, I was gone. I took the furniture and left him to pack up the house I had rented without him, returning a week later to get the last of my belongings. I found him sitting on the floor in the empty living room, leaning against a wall with his knees up in front of him, watching a movie on a laptop. From the loneliness of that view I had to turn away quickly, but glanced back when I opened the door to leave. He was looking across the room at me with hungry eyes, but I felt only rage.

I couldn't hear his voice again. His broken, thin words. His even-toned flatness. His control. His agreement. He would tell me a hundred times that it would be different. He would do something new. He would go to college. Get a different job.

We would grow close again. We would not sleep together in machine-like coldness. We would rediscover love.

Ah, fuck your tears. Fuck our voices.

I gotta go.

I am a master of beginnings, and this—this is a goddamn grave.

• • •

My new home had old wood floors and a front porch behind a sprawling oak tree. The only time I had to look at the address box was the first time I pulled up and thought, *Well, this place is damn adorable.* It was white with blue-gray trim and had a big lawn out front and a huge backyard with a fountain and lavender plants where bees buzzed. Inside there were two bedrooms to the left of the living room, one in the front and one in the back of the house, with a bathroom in between with tile floors and a pedestal sink. It had a big brick fireplace, and a kitchen with barely any storage or counters. It was perfection.

Mac returned to live with his parents at the ranch.

We split the week with Ava so each of us only had to endure a few days without her. When she was with me, I dressed her in colorful tiered skirts and leather shoes, took her to the bakery down the road for a croissant, and to the park, where I would lie to the other mothers about my marriage. We'd go home and eat lunch, and then I would snuggle into my bed with her, her head on my arm. I'd kiss her over and over again. She'd drift off for a nap, and I would too.

Sleep was harder at night, though, because I had never lived alone. The neighborhood was largely retired folks who enjoyed trimming roses and talking to each other, but my house had windows and doors right near the ground, where people could walk up and *climb in* if they felt so inclined. And I was sure they were so inclined.

So, before bed, particularly if it was just those wood floors and television and me, I protected myself using a complex inspection routine. First, I of course checked every door and window lock. Then I had to look under my bed and Ava's twin bed, but because I couldn't see to the back of my queen bed I would sometimes do a quick sweep with a broom to make sure nobody was curled up in the corner, where no human could ever fit. I also sometimes had to do that under Ava's twin bed. I then looked in the closets, in the corners, behind the coats I hadn't worn in five years. I could have just looked for feet on the ground, beneath the coats, but that didn't occur to me. I looked behind bedroom, closet, and bathroom doors. I looked in the shower. For people. Intruders. Lurkers. Rapists.

I was not on meth. I was not suffering from schizophrenia. I was scared, and I thought if I knew every corner of the house was clear, I would lie down in my bed and turn off the light and feel safe. I thought I would feel comfortable knowing I had secured the perimeter.

But it never worked. It didn't matter how thoroughly or often I checked, or how many days passed without incident. I could examine every millimeter of that house, but somehow at the end of the process, I was just as terrified as before I started. I left a light on in the living room and glanced out my bedroom door too many times as I fell asleep in twitchy half-sleep inspection.

I knew it was crazy. I would tell myself when I looked behind a door, "Janelle, nobody can fit there," but I was compelled to look anyway. I had to *do something* to become unafraid.

It wasn't my mother on the chopping block as I had imagined when I was younger. It was me. Something was coming for me. Somebody in the closet. Somebody under the bed. Maybe the same man who threatened to chop my hair off when I was a little girl also lurked in the closet of that 1940s house, a monster I never quite saw, for whose existence I had no evidence, but whose power over me was undying and uniform.

• • •

On the evenings when Ava was gone, I would lie on the couch and watch *Sex and the City* reruns and sip white wine until I was good and loaded. Then I would make phone calls.

"Hey, you want to go to SoCal's?" I'd usually call my friend who'd walked into the law firm with a porn star name.

"Janelle, it's nine p.m. on a Tuesday." she'd say, fake exasperated.

"So? I know. Come on. I'm bored. One game of pool and a shot." I'd soften the urgency in my voice. I'd play it cool.

"Well, okay."

Oh, thank you, sweet baby Jesus.

I'd be at the bar within fifteen minutes, and I would have a grand time right up until the moment my friend would realize it was eleven p.m. and she needed to get to bed for work the next day. Then I would find myself alone, again, as the world moved on and I looked for more. More.

Hours later I would wake up in my nice bright house and whack my alarm, squint beneath the throbbing in my head, the chilly sweat, the strange panic. Advil. Water. Shuffling to the shower. Coffee. Cigarette. There I was, with my promotion and house full of character and freedom, and not a goddamn thing was different.

Drink more water. Take another pill.

But there was no pill to fix the regret, the abhorrence of myself each morning. I never woke up hungover thinking, *You know, Janelle, you're really winning at life.* I never thought about the "fun" I had, or decided the hangover was "worth it." I never looked back with a flippancy like other people might, the way they do in the movies: "Wow, we really went on one last night, huh?"

I woke up with mind-bending shame and deep confusion. *Why can't I stop drinking? Why can't I drink like my friend?*

What got me through those mornings was that I knew with every drop of blood in my body that I would not drink that day. I would dunk my head in a sink of ice water and hold it there for as long as I could stand it, in a miracle hangover cure my father had inadvertently taught me. He always laughed and told me it was for his complexion, but as I grew older, I realized it was for the headache. After "icehead," our loving name for our loving cure, I would focus only on getting through the morning, one second at a time: eat food, drink coffee, get to cubicle. Let some hours pass.

But when I started to feel human again, when my thoughts became crisp, the furious remorse would fade to a whisper in the back of my mind, and every day, as soon as I was well again, I would suspect I was overreacting about the whole "not going to drink today" verdict.

That seems a little extreme, I'd think. *Maybe tonight I'll just stop by the store to buy one quality bottle of white wine because I need to relax. Make myself a nice dinner.*

Life was officially not getting better without Mac. The only new feature of single life was worrying about Mac falling in love with some broad who would tell Ava what a loser her mother

was. Well, that and I didn't have magical nights in buses anymore, or my best person to call to hit the dives and play pool.

But mostly, when my drinking didn't improve without Mac,
I invited him to live with me again because if I was going to be
a fucking drunk, I thought I might as well do it with my best
friend, and at least some ability to pretend my life was working.

•   •   •

I made it six months without him, and we made it one week
without drunken domestic violence. One night in the parking
lot of a Thai restaurant, I sat in Mac's truck and scanned his text
messages, engaging in a process of snooping I had only seen in
sitcoms. Before I left to pick up our takeout he was quite obviously trying to shield me from his phone, which he had left on
the seat of his truck. *What a fucking horrid liar he is*, I thought. I
found messages from a woman who "really missed him." They
were sent at eight a.m. on a Saturday. She appeared to have seen
him the evening before. He assured me it was "nothing." I assured him I knew all the various ways he'd slept with her.

I was the abuser. He could have killed me if he wanted to,
flattened me with one hit, but he didn't touch me. I shoved him
while he stood in the entryway. He stumbled backward to the
ground against the front door, and I remember him looking up
at me in shock and wild confusion. He got up, grabbed his car
keys, and tried to leave, but I snatched them away and continued
screaming while our daughter slept in her bedroom.

At this, he walked to our bedroom and I threw his keys at
him, but missed. The sight of his back, of his silent retreat, reminded me that I was nothing more than a current that came

Mac's way—something that pushed him along through a few years, and when I was gone, there would be another.

He was not loyal. He was just another man. He could leave me. Those daggers sat in me like metal in a fire—poised and red hot.

•   •   •

Mac never joined the rodeo. Instead, he signed up for calculus and geology courses at the community college down the road.

A few months after I learned of his non-girlfriend girlfriend, he was supposed to go on a weekend field trip with his geology class to Lake Tahoe. On the evening before he left, he scanned the checklist of items he needed, packing and repacking his backpack. He was eager and anxious like a kid before the first day of school. When he was all ready, I wanted to go to a bar, so I commenced begging.

"Let's go out for a couple games of pool!"

"What? No. I have to leave at six a.m." He shook his head and looked at me from beneath his hat like I was insane. I was standing above him, hopping around like a puppy.

"We won't stay out late. Come on!" I smiled and yanked his hand.

"We always stay out late, Janelle."

"We won't this time. I promise, I swear, I promise! Please, baby. Just a couple of games. Come on. We never get to hang out, and Ava's with my mom." I pulled his arm and flirted with him until he agreed.

We played our games of pool, but in the back of the bar I ran into some men with cocaine and did a few lines on the back of a toilet seat, without telling Mac. Then I bought a baggie from them in the dark parking lot, alone, and by the time I got back to Mac it was too late. He was now the husband of a wife on coke, and if he didn't join me, he would be the man who "didn't party." It was already done. Already purchased. To me, his words of "no thanks" were a mere inconvenience, an obstacle to be overcome. I was a boulder smashing down a mountain.

"Have another drink," I said, knowing if I got him drunk enough he would get high with me. Sure enough, we went back to somebody's place and did more, and more, and more—until five-thirty a.m. arrived and I drove a sleepless, trembling Mac to meet his class at the school. He pulled his carefully packed backpack along on his drooping shoulder, red-faced and wild-eyed and never supposed to be like this. I watched him get on the bus alongside a bunch of bright-eyed students cradling cups of coffee and smiles, and I thought I had never seen a man look sadder in all my life.

Through the window of the bus, he mustered a little smile. It broke me.

Through all that, he smiled at me still. He forgave me already. He already loved me again. I drove out of the parking lot seeing his face and the way he looked at me, and I thought about how he must feel coming down off alcohol and blow among strangers, already shy and reserved, miserable and frantic with nothing but static in the brain, without sleep or a place to rest and get well. But more than that it was the way he refused to not go. He wanted to be better. He wanted to try. He wanted to be with the regular humans, and I ruined it. He wanted to sleep, and wake rested, and join the students on the bus to learn and be good and right and clean.

I sent him off sick and twisted and lonely.

He could have not gone with me. He could have left his wife with a bunch of men doing cocaine—because he knew I wouldn't leave. I would stay where the drugs were. But he wasn't that kind of man. Or maybe, he wasn't healthy enough to let me go.

As I turned the corner onto our street to get home and sleep off the disaster, I realized I was wrong about all that "potential." I was not capable. I was not destined for anything. *How do you keep making these decisions, Janelle? How do you keep knowing what's decent and true and then doing the opposite? How do you do it over and over again?*

My next thought was, *I must have been born without a moral compass.* This wasn't pity. It wasn't groveling, or vapid self-deprecation. It was an observation of the facts, and I accepted them as such. *I was born without morality. I must not care. I am not capable of caring.* I thought about the way I used to chase my brother with the knife, the way I raged at my mother. It had been a long haul of depravity.

I could see my home crumbling. I could see any hope we once had for a decent family fading into an old memory. I could see myself turning into a person not even I recognized.

I begged him to forgive me when he got home, but he already had.

"We need a new life," I said, clinging to him. "We need a new start." And I had been thinking, *Nothing says "new start" like a new baby.*

In my mind, if I had two children, *I would join the fucking PTA.* I would carve carrots into little owls and place them lovingly into bento boxes with sober, manicured hands. I would wear yoga pants and actually do yoga. I would decorate cupcakes. I would have a special birthday breakfast plate and a Waldorf candle ring. I would clean up my act and get right with heaven and hell, but mostly, I would stop drinking, and if I stopped drinking I would also stop snorting cocaine, and Mac and I would be in love again. I wouldn't leave him shivering in the cold on a curb, in line to board a bus, waiting to inspect shimmering pines with pupils aching for darkness.

. . .

The two lines popped up again without hesitation, no longer a "fuck you" pink. Mac and I hugged and hugged.

"Mom, I'm having another baby!" I told her ten minutes after I took the test.

"You are? Oh my goodness! I'm moving there."

Of course you are, I thought, *because this is our refreshing new life.*

My mother, Mac, Ava, and I moved into a giant house we rented on a big fake lake in Natomas, a slightly fancier suburb than Elk Grove, but still soulless. I was now living in the house I used to admire from afar. I knew which one was ours without looking at the number because the houses were at least large enough to *appear* different from the others. It had five bedrooms and three bathrooms, an office and a laundry room, and a backyard that opened onto the cement lake. We put a pool table in the formal living room.

At the four-month ultrasound, the doctor jellied up my belly while Mac and I held hands in the dimly lit room. Ava sat near us on a stool, her blonde ringlets frizzy and wild around big blue eyes. "You're having a boy," the doctor said. He pointed to something on the ultrasound screen that was supposed to indicate this, but all I saw were squirming yellow lines. Still, I gasped and cried, and Mac's eyes filled with tears as Ava hopped off the stool and marched up to the doctor with her hands on her hips, announcing, "No! We are having a girl! I am having a sister!"

The doctor laughed and confirmed that indeed she was having a brother, and then Ava's sobbing ensued.

To cheer her up, we sat in the parking lot for a moment with Ava in her car seat and asked, "What should we name him, Ava? Can you help us?"

Within seconds, as if it were obvious, as if it were the only name possible in such a situation, she proclaimed: "Rocketship Rock-On. We need to name him Rocketship Rock-On!"

We roared and said that was an excellent name. I looked at Mac and said, "And because we are Frank Zappa, that name is perfect!"

He laughed. She beamed.

She told everyone we knew, "I'm having a little brother, and I named him Rocketship." She was so proud nobody had the heart to tell her we weren't Frank Zappa.

With Rocketship, I had a whole room to decorate. I bought an oak crib and changing table. We installed a chair rail and painted it white. We painted the bottom of the room a pastel green and the top blue. Because I wanted him to use it for years, like an heirloom, we spent real money on a matching honey-colored oak dresser from the fancy baby store.

A boy. A son. *My son!*

My job was rising. Our home was huge. I was sober as hell and decorating a nursery. I bought playful maternity skirts and ruched blouses and strappy sandals. He was due in September, the most beautiful month, and every appointment was happy news. I sat in the rocking chair of his color-coordinated nurs-ery, a room straight out of a catalogue. I hung his tiny clothes on fuzzy little hangers, organized by size. I washed it all in baby-friendly detergent and folded the washcloths into tiny squares. All the cloth diapers were ready, folded, cleaned, and placed in gingham-lined baskets. There was even a patchwork quilt draped over the back of the rocking chair.

Labor began two days before his due date, four days into my maternity leave—because he was a gentleman who would never imagine arriving late. His birth was the kind they show in hippie movies trying to convince women birth is like dancing among lilies in morning dew. It lasted seven hours, beginning at home. When a contraction came, I leaned against the wall and swayed, moaning, resting on my bed in between. I took showers. I swayed some more. Around seven p.m., Mac told me we had to leave for the hospital. I told him I was okay where I was. I had never been so okay.

While in the shower, I felt the familiar agony and delirious pain of hard contractions, and I thought, *No! I cannot do this again.* I began panicking, resisting the pain, but I had read some-where in those hippie books that you should think of all the women who were birthing with you in that exact moment, and that you had to let go and ride the pain through, because fight-ing made it unbearable.

So I surrendered, consciously. I let go. I visualized myself among a few thousand women all over the world—in rivers and huts and hospitals. By the time Mac told me again we had to leave I was in another world with those women, peacefully birthing my baby like those bitches in the movies nobody be-lieves are real.

In the car that September day, the sun pounded through the glass and it was, of course, Friday evening, when the traffic is terrible. I even screamed at Mac about how much I hated him. I tell you it was a perfect birth. When I got to the hospital, the nurses didn't believe I was in active labor because I was "so quiet and calm," but they booked me into a room and demanded I get on the bed for twenty minutes of continuous fetal monitoring. I told them to go to hell. I was standing and swaying. That's how I was riding the pain. I ultimately agreed to stand against the machine so they could do their monitoring, and then they left. I was delighted to see them go. I wanted to be alone, alone with this boy, alone to have my baby.

I almost immediately felt an urge to push. My mother yelled down the hall, "Somebody better get down here! She wants to push!"

I wanted to deliver in the water, so the midwife helped me into the birthing tub. I had three more contractions and pushed twice, and then turned over onto all fours. In one contraction he was born. I heard the midwife say, "Turn around and pick up your son."

I flipped my leg up and over the umbilical cord and looked into the water and saw him there, pushing the water, eyes wide open, with his palms out and his arms and legs reaching. I brought him to the surface and pressed my face against his as close as I could without crushing him. I felt his velvet cheeks and inhaled the sweet newness at his neck. I cradled him against me on my arm, and I watched him pull his first breath of the air we shared, and his body flood pink with my blood. He looked me right in the eyes and sputtered. They rubbed his palm to make him cry, though I thought that was unnecessary. I didn't understand why they needed to hurt him, even a little. Mac was pressed against me, his head on my shoulder, and my mother and Mac and the midwives were hushed and whispering in the gray room. When they asked how I felt, I said, "Elated."

He came two days before his due date in a birth that felt like the sunrise. When I walked in the door of our home I knew life was going to be different. This son. This perfect son. Nobody could ruin this life, not even me.

PART TWO

7

FAILURE THAT ISN'T FUNNY

I woke from a few moments of sleep, or maybe just shut eyes, shaking. Not the shaking of a chill, but a quiver I couldn't quite feel. It drove me up and out and around the house in circles, though my body perhaps stayed on the couch, drinking leftover alcohol out of a coffee cup and rocking back and forth, like the baby on my left who wanted breakfast. It was as if the blood in my veins wouldn't settle down, as if it were pulsing out of me rather than through me, scratching the walls for escape, tossing me around the room and into every insane thought, regret, and memory of the past twenty-four or forty-eight hours, or maybe my entire life.

It drove me outside for yet another cigarette, the twentieth or fiftieth in the past two days, but it was worse in the sun, in the flickering leaves and slamming roar of passing cars. I squinted and hid from my neighbors behind our house, pulling that cigarette with all my strength, but it didn't have what I needed.

I fed my baby, Rocket. This was the only variation of "Rocketship" Ava would allow. For an entire year, none of us had the heart to tell her we weren't rock stars. The name grew on us while we waited for her to change her mind.

When Ava shuffled into the living room in her flannel pajamas, I turned the channel to PBS because it was a decent learning channel with soft colors and slow images. I hated the cartoons that screamed and slammed her little mind with fluorescent images and rapid-fire, vapid dialogue. She was five. I wanted her to see wholesome things.

Mac and I had been on cocaine for two and a half days. We went out on Thursday to have a few drinks. Then it was Sunday at eight a.m., and we had been awake the entire time.

But this Sunday was Rocket's first birthday, and I had an enormous party planned. I had bought an outfit for him weeks before—a deep blue button-down shirt, black pinstriped pants, black leather shoes, and black socks to match.

Seven hours until the party, I thought.

Maybe I can feel better by then. Maybe I can sleep.

But the quiver would never let me rest, and I knew it. I considered drinking enough to pass out for an hour or two before the party, but then I would be drunk at the party, though I probably wouldn't wake up anyway. After spun-out days, sleep, when it finally comes, is cavernous.

I had decorations, streamers, and presents. I had Brie and blue cheese and baguettes and figs. *I have it all ready, son. I prepared it all, thinking of you, my boy, and loving you, with your endless blue eyes and curls of strawberry red hair that stick to your forehead when you sweat. (I always say you got the red from Daddy's beard.)*

I can't do it. I can't show up like this.

I resolved to cancel, then immediately remembered how

grandparents and great-grandparents were coming from other towns, and twenty friends. It was too late.

Here I am again.

Six months before, when I felt myself slipping back into drinking after Rocket's birth, I enrolled in a master's program in English to "challenge my brain," thinking, *Surely, I must be bored. Surely, my vanilla admin job is driving me to drink.*

When the red wine continued to pour despite rampant critical theory courses and Marxist analyses of lost generation texts, when I looked down and noticed my very own hand pouring that wine, night after night, despite continued daily declarations of *not tonight, not tonight, not tonight,* the thought came to me: *Janelle, maybe you are an alcoholic.*

I thought of my father, newly in recovery. I thought of when we were sure he was going to die from alcoholism. I thought of his brother, my uncle, who did die from it. I thought about how those D.A.R.E. cops always told us alcoholism is genetic.

And then I thought, *If I am, so be it.*

Because by then, the consequences of not drinking were far greater than anything that could have happened from drinking. Internally, that is, because I drank to repair my inner self. The external penalties for my habit were damn near imperceptible in the shadow of the colossal misery that was sobriety. I drank because sobriety was intolerable, and that intolerability arose from within me, slowly from my guts, increasing with every passing sober hour, until I found myself drinking again, only to soothe the wild discomfort. If not the bottle, it seemed a bullet to the brain would be the only viable alternative.

Alcohol was my most reliable friend, offering me with every

warm hot kiss that which the rest of the world promised but never delivered: peace and meaning.

I knew this somewhere. I knew I drank to fix the unfixable, and I knew it when my outer life was "perfect" and nothing had changed. *Here I am with a good job, a good house, two perfectly good children, physical health, a scintillating life in graduate school, and I still cannot stop drinking.*

I imagined my childhood must have really fucked me up. Psychiatry was the obvious answer. I began seeking help to fix my insides, thinking, *If I just get happy, I won't need alcohol anymore.* But on the night I met Ben, the cocaine dealer who delivered straight to our front door, I wasn't wondering what was wrong with me anymore. I was simply buying more.

• • •

My crying on the morning of Rocket's first birthday was unhinged.

"What's wrong, Mama?" Ava asked. She had changed from pajamas into a green Tinkerbell costume with a tulle skirt and jeans underneath. Her eyes were wide with concern beneath unbrushed waves of blonde.

"Oh, nothing, sweetie," I said, but I didn't mask the lie. I was still in jeans. My eyes were set in deep black circles. I said it through gasps and tears.

Mac was at work. I tried to imagine him there, wet and muddy, punching the hide off a lamb, handling knives with vibrating hands. It felt like the morning I left him at the college field trip when he tried to smile.

What kind of fucking people have we become?

I feared he would die. I feared he would cut himself, or fall asleep in front of the meat saw, or flinch while killing a cow with a shotgun.

I called him, and said words I knew wouldn't do a damn thing. "Mac, this is insanity. You can't stay. I know you feel like I do. Please come home."

"Alright. I just have to finish cutting this meat." I was correct. He was standing next to a meat saw coming down off a three-night cocaine binge, and I realized it had gotten so bad he agreed to come home.

• • •

I wanted it to be just right and nice for you, son, the cake I ordered from the fancy bakery, food from the nicest store in town, the recipes I chose a week ago. I wanted it all to come together in this exact moment, and for me to be there, and for all the guests to celebrate you, but instead I am sitting on a couch, shaking but not shaking, reeking of dirt of the internal kind, and wondering if anybody would notice if I just drove away. Maybe into that fucking cement lake in front of me.

I stared at the shifting water, smoked another cigarette, and wondered how much money we had stolen to make the last three nights happen, how many checks I had written to myself with money I couldn't cover to put in the ATM machine at three a.m. to get cash out, knowing they would only bounce and be deducted from the same account from which I was trying to pull the cash. *One more bag, just one more bag.*

With renewed strength rising from self-disgust, from a will to never repeat the hell I was then living, I decided not to cancel the party. *I will get through today to make this pain mean something.*

Right now it all changes. This failure, this coke-addicted drunk fuck of a mother in a suburban home on her son's first birthday. It will not happen in vain.

This is it. This is the day I learn.

It's okay, now. It's okay, son.

I meant it. I had the party because I knew it was the end, and I succeeded. Nobody knew, because I smiled and laughed and only collapsed after the last guest had driven away.

• • •

Three weeks later, nine a.m. rolled around on the day Ava was supposed to attend the birthday party of a little girl at her school. I didn't wake up like the day of Rocket's first birthday, because I was already awake. Still awake, still high. The quiver remained.

It occurred to me we had no gift. I considered telling Ava she couldn't go, but it was the first birthday party she'd ever been invited to, and I couldn't disappoint her. Not again, not now.

"Hey Ava, let's pick something out of your closet to give to your friend, and I will buy you another one tomorrow. I promise. We will go *tomorrow*. Is that okay? Can we do that?" My words rushed together in idiotic cocaine excitement.

"Sure," she said. "That's fine, Mama." And she ran up the stairs with her blonde hair bouncing around her, and me, behind, nearly dead weight.

"You're so awesome! Thank you for being so patient and giving, Ava!" In her closet, I found a silk rainbow streamer. I grabbed it and thought the girl would like it because they went to a Montessori school and that was a good hippie gift.

"How about this?" I asked. "Can we give her this?" I held it up and tried to smile.

"Okay, Mama." Ava said. She didn't even look disappointed. She didn't even look at me like I was shoving all my words together or stinking of cigarette smoke or scratching scabs on my shins because I couldn't stop picking.

•   •   •

Ava put on a pink dress with tiny white smocked flowers around the chest while I wrapped the gift and snorted a line in my bedroom before getting Ava into the car and driving to Woodland, a town twenty minutes away. Mac stayed home with Rocket. He was missing work. He did that more often now.

He had offered to drive, but I didn't trust him. I was as loaded as he was, but I never trusted anybody to drive as carefully as I did when intoxicated. People were idiots. They got swept up in the euphoria. They got carried away in the feeling. They forgot it wasn't real. They forgot that you have to focus on signs, on sober reality—signals of truth—to differentiate between what you see and what's actually happening. Whenever a friend in high school was tripping too far from us on some psychedelic, I'd say, "Look at the clock. The clock is always sober." It was a grounding device. And I thought I was a master at that game.

So I looked at the clock, double-checked my seatbelt, lights, and mirrors, made sure I had my purse and license, moved my baggie from my wallet to a CD case on the floor. I had to take it with me, because I knew I'd need it before I returned home. I drove deliberately, exactly at the speed limit, focusing three times harder than I normally did, watching the lines and speedometer, studying the cars around me in a routine I knew like air. I hated driving drunk and on drugs, and every subsequent morning I would shudder in shame and horror at what I had done, but I knew in the moment I must minimize risk of swerving or speeding or missing somebody's sudden turn or braking. I refused to turn on the radio. It would interrupt my attention. Ava tried to talk to me, excited about the party, but her voice was like the chattering of a squirrel. In my mind, it was a stream of impossible sound.

"Honey, please let me focus on driving." She quieted down for a moment, then started back up again. I tuned her out the best I could and kept my eyes on the road and clock.

I parked unreasonably far away from the house, put on sunglasses, and walked my daughter to her first birthday party. I was high, half-drunk, reeking of cigarettes, with a stolen gift and a little girl holding my hand, elated, wearing a pink dress and pink Western cowboy boots. I reminded her I would buy another streamer.

"I know you will, Mama." She smiled at me, and for a moment I felt better. She believed I would do it, so I could believe that too.

The girl's mother invited me in when we arrived at the doorstep, but I mumbled something about an appointment. I told her how sorry I was to miss the party. Then I walked alone back to the car in the relentless sunlight to do another line on the back of the CD case while parked right there on the street. I needed it to get back home. I wondered how I was going to pick up Ava in three hours, but set that aside as a concern of the future.

As I put the CD case away, I thought of her laughing and playing at the party without her mom, while all the other mothers stood around smiling at their kids' antics and games, and I felt so blackened with my own sin I slammed my fist into the steering wheel and dash until I couldn't anymore. I lit a cigarette and drove, telling myself this had to be the end.

Please, God, let it be the end.

• • •

"I was not fired. I was placed on a mental health leave." That is what I told my friends when they asked why I wasn't working anymore.

"Oh, I needed to take a semester off to focus on my mental health." That is what I told my family when they asked why I wasn't in graduate school anymore.

My mother moved out of our big house on the lake, and Mac and I were supposed to move out too, but we decided to leave a couple of months after my mother. None of us could afford the big house anymore. It was 2007 and everything was tanking.

Two weeks after she moved out, my mother knocked on our front door one Saturday morning and told me she was going to take the kids to the park. I knew this was not true because it was seven a.m., raining, and January, but I told her okay because I wanted to go back to bed. And I knew somewhere they were better off without me.

Back in bed, I told myself it would only be a couple of days.

• • •

Two days later, I reminded myself they would be back soon, but I told my mother, "I'm just too sick to have the kids, Mom."

"I agree, Janelle." She said softly.

"I just need some time to get better, Mom."

"You know I'll do anything for you." The sweetness in her voice was relieving this time. Her unquestioning devotion. Her acceptance. I knew I would get what I wanted that day—wide open space for addiction.

By "sick" I meant "what my shrinks told me," and I had seen many as I sought answers for my inability to quit drinking, as I sought answers for where exactly all my "potential" went. *How does a smart, middle-class honors student with a "good head on her shoulders" end up unable to quit drinking and pumping herself full of powdered stimulants?*

That was my question for the professionals, and in response, they told me I had borderline personality disorder (which seemed accurate but is basically incurable, unfortunately for me), bipolar II (when they asked me about mood swings I said, "Um, yeah. I'm a coke addict," but they gave me the diagnosis and anti-psychotics anyway), chronic depression (obviously), and PTSD (*Oh, come the fuck on, that's just ridiculous*).

The psychiatrist prescribed seven psychotropic medications but never explained the source of trauma that ruined me. Walking out of his office, I felt myself fully armed with the reason for my drinking, drugs, and failure.

I'm broken, I thought. *I'm a broken insane person. It's not my fault. I'm self-medicating.*

Nobody mentioned I might just be an alcoholic.

Lamictal. Klonopin. Seroquel. Neurontin. Effexor. Zoloft. Ambien. I took them all, mostly. I took them all, usually. I often took the Ambien and always the Klonopin. (*It's not my fault. I have mental illnesses.*)

The therapists fixated on events of my childhood, particularly those of a sexual nature. Another one spoke of my father's absence. During our next session, we discussed how my mother and I had an "unstable" relationship that left my personhood ill-defined. I never knew I was so damaged by those things. *But now that you mention it, doc, I do feel damaged.* I especially felt damaged when people came at me with criticisms of the way I was living.

If what happened to me had happened to you, you'd be living this way, too, I'd think.

Just try to tell me to clean up my act again. Just try *to fucking tell me.*

• • •

Mac and I began frequenting a tiny, dark, terrifying hovel belonging to a man I called Charlie, although that was not his name. When we arrived, he had recently spray-painted the walls of his kitchen with unrelated German words. His girlfriend was unimpressed. There was always a large selection of people there, none of whom we knew. I wasn't even entirely sure why *we* were there, but we always stayed awhile, often talking to half-naked people on a bed.

The children were still with my mother. I reiterated to Charlie and the half-naked people how very sick I was, and how beautiful and smart my children were. They listened, spellbound, warm in cocaine compassion.

One night after returning from Charlie's, in the kitchen of our home, I couldn't stop shaking my head and saying strange things. I gently tapped my head against the wall. By hour one, Mac was weeping, but I couldn't stop the tapping.

"Janelle, please don't stay like this. Please come back. Please be okay," I heard him talking. His voice was slowed down and I thought I could see the sound waves. His mouth and the sound were not lining up, so I merely observed him.

I stood by the dining table in the corner of the kitchen in the early morning light, and I saw him looking into my face. I knew he was seeing me insane, and I wanted to be better for him, but I could not.

"Janelle," he said with his hands on my face. "You're talking nonsense."

I was speaking in tongues, my mouth moving against my will. As he paced and begged, I faced the corner of the wall and began hitting my head harder and talking, and then I was sitting in a kitchen chair I had towed to the middle of the garage, smoking. He sat behind me with tears and concern, trying to give me space. Our border collie whined from the crate. Mac let the dog out, fed him his breakfast, and, I imagine, patted him on the head. He returned, handed me another smoke, and crouched down to watch me. Right in front of me. I saw terror. In his big brown eyes I saw terror. He watched me silently and waited.

Over time, I moved a little closer to him, to the ground, spoke in a language the people understand.

•   •   •

I was not fired. I was placed on mental health leave.

From our motel in Sacramento, Mac suggested we go home. "It's a half-mile away, Janelle. We can't afford to stay here." He was puffy-faced and had put on a few pounds. He wore a huge camo jacket with pockets everywhere. We had bought it two years before at an army surplus store. He hid liquor bottles in it when he returned to our motel room from the grocery store. He believed they should be hidden, even from strangers, and even though they were legal.

"No, we can't go home. Somebody will find us."

"Who, Janelle? Who will find us?"

We just need to stay here in this motel room with towels shoved under the door because I think I see feet. I'm 90 percent sure I see feet. Those are definitely feet. How do you not see them?

"Fine, we can run home for clothes," I said. "I can do it. I'll do it. I'll run home for clothes. I can do it. Don't come with me. I want to go alone." I saw him as a liability. If we had to do something as dangerous as drive across town and enter our home, I needed to do it myself. I was the only one I trusted.

Back in our house, the big one on the lake where we had brought Rocketship Rock-On home in his blue pastel smocked bubble, I decided we could stay for a few days, so I called Ben, the cocaine-delivery guy, and told him we had relocated. He brought me more.

But there was too much blood in my nose to do another line and my heart was doing something strange and I wasn't entirely sure I could feel my feet, so I asked Mac to Google "heart attack from cocaine." He yelled from the other room, "Does your chest hurt?"

I could tell by his voice he was scared, and if he was scared, he might block me from doing more drugs, so I yelled, "No," and then he yelled, "Are your fingers tingling?"

And I didn't think so, so I yelled back, "No, baby!" And at first I enjoyed the "possibly overdosing" attention, but then it turned on me. I just wanted to do more, so I told him "never mind" and asked him to come back and told him all the racing heartbeats were gone.

I'm okay. Bring me a straw and the baggie after I rinse my nose to wash out the blood. Bring it to me on the couch because I cannot stand. Bring me a cocktail to slow my heart. Tilt the straw because I cannot lift my head. Bring me my pills because I'm getting dizzy. If I don't take the Effexor I get very dizzy. Has it been two days already?

I staggered up the stairs after the Effexor kicked in and I could walk again to do a line off our wall mirror, which was lying flat on my bed now. When I got to the top stair and turned toward my bedroom, I heard it: "You are going to die if you do another line." I thought it was God. No, I knew it was God, and I knew it was true. It was a voice that rose clear and clean from the thick mud in my mind. It boomed.

It roared, and when it came, I knew it was not from me, and I didn't want to die.

8

NOTHING LEFT TO HIDE NOW

That morning, instead of walking into the bedroom, I turned around and went back downstairs, leaving half of our last baggie of cocaine untouched. This was an act I had never accomplished before that very moment. I had voluntarily faced the beginnings of detox. I knew then it must have been God.

"I'm done, Mac. I'm going to die if I do more," I said. I paced the kitchen and then filled a beer stein with Captain Morgan, capping it off with flat Coke, readying myself for the feverish craving already crawling up the floor into my feet. It would get worse before it got better, but I had endured the withdrawal before. I had done it countless times before.

But this time, I had no desire to continue. *I could not continue.* I recoiled from the drug as if it were a food that had just poisoned me. My body rejected it on a visceral level.

Mac was still wearing his camouflage jacket, after all these days, and in our warm house. His black curls were wild, flat on one side, and his eyes were deep in amused skepticism.

"You don't have to stop, Mac. I don't care. Finish the bag. It's right upstairs."

"No, it's cool. I don't need more."

Weirdo, I thought.

He approached me in a motion I feared preceded a hug, a touch I knew would set my skin burning hotter than it already burned. He often wanted to touch me when all I wanted was to disappear into the black alone—the black of cocaine, of alcohol, of sleep. It didn't matter what it was, I simply did not want him close. I wanted him to get the hell away from me until I felt some control again.

"I have to call my mom," I said, sidestepping him and grabbing cigarettes and the house phone on my way to the backyard. I looked out over the fake lake and then squinted at the pulsating numbers on the phone, knowing my eyes were amphetamine eyes. I pressed each number with stupidly measured focus. She answered immediately.

"Hey, Mom," I said, cracked.

"Hi, Janelle." Her voice was thick with worry, a tone I would have called "overly dramatic."

"I need help. You have got to help me. I'm addicted to cocaine."

I thought she would cry or yell or pass out in shattering surprise, but she said, "I've been waiting for this call."

Strange, I thought, *since I had been so sly.*

"I'll be right there," she said. "Do not move." She arrived thirty minutes later with a furrowed brow and stood in the kitchen looking at Mac and me, in the awkward awareness of a lie just brought to the surface. *Nothing left to hide now,* so I took huge early-morning swigs from my stein and smoked the cigarettes I used to hide from her.

I fell finally into a deep sleep, and that evening, when I could sit still again, I sat on the couch with my laptop and began searching for the rehab that would cure me. Mac and my mother looked at me with irritating severity from across the living room.

"God, why are you two so serious? None of this is that big of a deal." I wished they'd both settle down.

"Not a big deal?" My mother appeared incredulous. "You just told us you were about to die from cocaine."

"I know, but—whatever. You guys are making me nervous. I don't know why everybody's gotta be so fucking dramatic."

"Why don't you just find a rehab you like?" My mother looked at Mac for support, but he looked at me, and I typed "Northern California rehabs" into Google.

I had two stipulations for a treatment center: First, it couldn't be part of that coffee-drinking cult. Second, it couldn't be one of those God places. It was quite thoughtful of God to speak to me in a mental lightning bolt, but I had no need for a relationship with the man. *Besides, I had one with Him once, and look where that got me.*

I found a rehab near the ocean in Northern California among the redwoods and hippies. It boasted science-based therapy, and on our way there the very next evening (the intake specialist told my mother, "Come now before she changes her mind"), Mac and I stopped at Nordstrom and one of those import stores where white people buy drapes, couches, Italian sodas, and small statues of Ganesh.

At Nordstrom, I bought a pair of leather tennis shoes, perhaps as some sort of consolation prize, or because I had no closed-toed shoes even though it was March and had been raining for weeks. Every day, I wore a long skirt and flip-flops, possibly with a sweatshirt, mostly due to all the weight I gained after starting the medications that were supposed to heal me but only made me fat.

At the import store, we bought a silk and cotton blanket with elephants embroidered along the edges to decorate the potentially drab rehab bed (*nobody wants that!*) and a tiny Buddha statue, to represent my new life of spiritual greatness. I packed a journal to record my transformation, pictures of Ava, Rocket, and Mac, a copy of Emily Dickinson's collected poetry, pajamas, and my flowing, ripped skirts.

Sure, I had lost my job, children, dignity, health, mind, and respect as an unfit drug-addicted mother, and was on my way to an institution hoping to save me from myself, but what occurred to me was that I needed $80 Nikes and a throw blanket.

Mac and I drove quietly through the rain. We were headed for the coast again, but for different reasons. This time we sat in a bath of misery and hope rather than excitement, a sort of determined agony that comes when you've reached the end of a long catastrophe, or think you have—and it all feels urgent and heavy and new. We listened to live Grateful Dead, the same songs my father sent me on cassette when I was a little girl, which I replayed for hours on my boom box. I wondered if they allowed music in rehab. *I should have brought some,* I thought. If I were to bring music, I would have brought the bands I grew up on: the Rolling Stones, the Dead, Bob Dylan, and Neil Young. Some Janis Joplin, perhaps.

When "Ripple" came on, I glanced at Mac and thought about him—my old friend sitting there, driving me through the rain—and how it had been a long time since I watched him chase unruly chickens, since we shot pool in dive bars, since

M-Y-Q and the almost homeless man with the kitten who ate brewer's yeast.

When Jerry sang, "If your cup is full, may it be again...," I thought, *Alright, is this going to be when my cup gets full again?* It was almost too sad to think about, his tunes, his black-tar humanity. I wished we had gone in the daylight. My mind drifted to the goodbye I would soon face, and the time I said goodbye to Mac that Saturday morning while he stumbled onto that goddamn bus with all those goddamn bright-eyed students, and how we were so much sicker now. I had thought we couldn't possibly get worse than that day, and yet, *here we are.*

Well, here I am. I suspected it was mostly me.

"I can't believe the shit we've done, Mac," I said. "What happened to us?"

"I don't know," he shrugged. I wished he'd say more, but he never said more. If I had looked harder at his eyes I probably would have seen they were damp with tears.

"I don't want to live that way again," I said.

"Me either." He smiled at me while I kicked off my shoes and reclined the seat, put my feet on the dash, and lit a cigarette. We had traveled the road to hell, but we had done it together.

I heard Jerry sing "If I knew the way, I would take you home," and I had to hear it again, because I've always thought it was the most beautiful lyric ever written. How simple the thought, how true, to want to lead with love, back home, into safety, but having no idea where to even begin.

I reached down and skipped the song back.

Mac was the only one who knew the whole truth, of me, of my life. Insane nights in motel rooms. Beating heads. Speaking in tongues. Broken tears and the homeless guy who asked us if we would please take him back to his spot under the overpass. "You frighten me," he had said. That one night when Mac knelt for hours naked in the bedroom doorway, to "guard" us from intruders (in our minds). He explained, "Well, if someone opens the door, they'll see me here and turn around." I laughed, telling him it was a really shit plan.

Since the day we met seven years before, we had never spent more than a few days apart. Even when I lived alone in that 1940s house, we always somehow ended up back in each other's arms. We were friends, I guess. We were always good friends.

Beginning that night, I would live thirty days without my friend, and my beautiful Ava, and my baby Rocket.

My boy. My sweet boy who was going to fix me up. The pregnancy that was going to straighten me out for good. I thought about the day I found out I was pregnant, the day I found out he was a boy, the day I brought him home. I thought of the ringlets that bounced under his chin, the way his knuck-les dimpled and his tiny perfect hands held dolls and hammers in that endless toddler fascination, and I thought about his silence. He barely said a word, except "no" and "mama." He was so quiet, a hushed angel with giant blue eyes who toddled around, smiled, climbed things, cuddled, and laughed, until he was gone. I thought of the morning my mother took them and the way I let them go.

I am here now. It won't be in vain.

I couldn't stop looking at Mac while we drove, as if I wanted to burn his image into my mind. I wondered if I should say something, but I couldn't think of anything, so I kept staring until he smiled again, his face small and childlike with the same heavy yearning eyes, offering still a thousand years of love and adoration. I looked away, partly in disgust, in that old familiar repulsion, because he loved me unquestioningly. I threw my weight against him because I had nowhere to lean, because he was there and I loved him, but why did he stay with me? I thought it was all he could do, all he knew how to do, some weakness, some sad routine he developed over the years because he couldn't find a better one.

I didn't think it was a choice he'd made, or some gift, some beautiful generosity of spirit he was born with. It seemed more like blind devotion—weak and frail—to love a woman like me.

Yet I hated myself for abusing his love. I wanted him to stand up to me. I wanted him to fight me. I wanted him to shove me back or scream in my face or walk out or fuck somebody else. Anything. But the second I thought he was pushing back, or walking away, I panicked and begged him not to leave. In therapy, they told me this was "borderline."

But he never did any of that. He simply stuck around and asked me to stay too. He stuck around and drank and took drugs with me even though he almost always responded to my first request with: "No, this is a bad idea," and "Janelle, let's just go home." He stuck around while I begged and pleaded for one more baggie even though the night had already gone horribly sour, and we were stuck in a stranger's house downtown with blabbering idiots on a four-day drug run. He stuck around the next day while I paced the house, barefoot in a ripped skirt over bleeding scabs, and he stuck around when I told him I hated him and that he had ruined my life. He stuck around even when our children were gone. He stuck around waiting. For me to get healed.

"I'm going to miss you, Mac." I closed my eyes when I said it and looked away.

"Don't cheat on me in rehab," he said, smirking.

"Who the fuck would I cheat on you with?"

"I don't know. Some dude." His jealousy made me smile.

"I love you," I said. "Everything is going to change, Mac. It has to."

"I know, Janelle. Okay," he said, but I wondered if he believed me.

"If knew the way, I would take you home," Mac sang along this time, not mentioning that I had started the song over, to hear that line again.

I wanted to hear Jerry sing it. And I wanted to believe him.

• • •

In the rehab parking lot under the drizzly rain, I refused to cry. Instead, I held on to Mac too long. He felt giant in my arms, like pure rock warmth, and I couldn't believe I was leaving him. I wondered if I had even noticed that warmth before.

I regretted coming to this place immediately. I wanted to get back in the car and head out with Mac, anywhere. Like we used to.

Almost as if he knew I was about to bolt, a lively redheaded man in his early twenties came bouncing out the front door to retrieve me. He shook our hands with the enthusiasm of zealots trying to sell religion on a doorstep, then merrily picked up my bags. Mac stood shifting back and forth, looking at me from under his downturned face, watching, waiting for a cue how to behave.

I mumbled an encouraging platitude and realized it was time, so Mac and I hugged again and kissed. I watched him back out of the parking spot, waving to me out the window. My guts turned into lonely disgust, as if the reality of my life were unfolding in that moment, when the last of my family drove down a hill without me.

The bouncing man reappeared, and I observed that he was wearing cargo shorts and flip-flops. He appeared too young to be escorting people into their new lives. I seriously doubted his qualifications and wished he'd talk less—or better yet, stop talking entirely. Nothing is more nauseating to a drug addict facing clean living than a joyful person already there.

To make matters worse, his name was Brent. *Of course it fucking is*, I thought. *I bet you also drink soy lattes and wear those shoes that look like feet*. I wondered if I was going to have to see him every day, and, if so, whether or not anybody would notice if I killed him.

Once inside, he led me to a small room for the beginning of the "intake process," which involved him and some equally elated young woman relieving me of my cell phone and face toner (it had alcohol in it and could be consumed) and requesting that I get naked to make sure I didn't have any drugs duct-taped to my body. Luckily, only the woman was there for the strip-down part. I wondered if she was also going to make me bend over and cough to check my asshole for heroin. I had seen that in the movies.

Jesus, these people are serious. Who the fuck would drink face toner? I wondered if perhaps I wasn't as sick as I formerly imagined.

After the body search, which did not involve my anal cavity, they led me to the office of a somber man with white hair who appeared to be in his fifties. He wore a striped, collared short-sleeved shirt and khakis. His desk and office seemed very official, with diplomas hanging on the wall in frames and tasteful plants by the window. When he said hello and began perusing a file, he struck me as a middle-management type, the kind of person who was always trying to prove his worth. He asked about when I had last used drugs, which medications I was on, and whether or not I was having suicidal thoughts.

Though he smiled incessantly, the way he spoke to me—slowly, skeptically, with a touch of condescension—reminded me of being a receptionist, of being considered so irrelevant you disappear.

"Sign here," he said. "And give Brent your purse so he can look through it." I handed it over.

"Good, now Linda will show you to the house."

"Oh, we don't sleep somewhere here?" I asked, looking around. I thought the place looked pretty homey.

"No, this is where you'll come each day for group."

I had no idea what "group" was, but it sounded awful. Like the kind of place where one is expected to "process feelings."

"Sounds good," I said, and smiled, wondering if it was possible to get released on good behavior.

Linda was a woman in her forties with brown wavy hair and several pieces of turquoise and silver jewelry scattered across her ears, neck, and arms. By the time she arrived, I was already bored and impatient to get to the self-improvement portion of the adventure—the part where they fixed me. The part where they showed me how to quit abusing drugs and alcohol so I could get my life back. The part where I no longer *wanted* the drugs and alcohol because I was healed. The part where I got happy. Or, if they couldn't teach me all that, perhaps they could at least tell me how to stop buying eight-balls of cocaine on a Tuesday.

Or any time, really. I guess no cocaine at all is the thing we're shooting for now.

●　　●　　●

Linda drove me down the road a half mile or so, and slowed down in front of a house right in the middle of a remarkably standard neighborhood, among the homes of the regular people. We pulled into the garage and walked into a kitchen smelling of bleach. It had brown tile floors and immaculate counters, and I noticed on the wall by the pantry a large bulletin board with laminated rules, schedules, names, and numbers. I stopped to read them, but Linda said, "Oh, you have all that information in your packet," and I remembered I had a folder in my hand.

My room was toward the back of the house, down a long hallway with gray carpet, and as I walked by other bedrooms, I peeked inside hoping to catch a glimpse of some shivering junkie, but they were all empty.

"Everyone is at the bonfire tonight!" she announced.

"Bonfire? That sounds fun," I lied.

"It is. It's really fun. There are a lot of fun things you can do in sobriety," which was the exact moment I decided never to listen to anything she said again. But I smiled anyway and said, "Yes! Looking forward to that."

My room was plain and comfortable, with two twin beds against one wall, a nightstand for each, and a dresser at the foot of each bed. The comforters were thin like motel bedspreads, but the pillows were big and fluffy. Mall art hung on the walls—watercolor posters with egrets and oceans and rivers, framed in blue pressboard.

The second bed was empty, but Linda let me know it would be filled soon. I said a quick prayer that she was mistaken.

Looking around the room, I missed Mac. I missed my babies. It was strange to be so fully alone, in a new place around new people who knew nothing of me, people who would judge me only for the way I presented myself. I grew exhausted just thinking about it.

I folded my red silk blanket on the foot of my bed and missed Mac even more, remembering how Brent had confiscated my phone when he inspected my purse.

"You can use the pay phone in the kitchen!" Brent had said, as if he were announcing the most thrilling of news.

"That sounds fun," I said, thinking how I could never understand perkiness as a personality trait. It just seemed so damn unnecessary.

So I couldn't hear Mac's voice. I set Emily Dickinson on the nightstand and Buddha on the dresser next to my journal and pictures. I unloaded my clothes into the drawers, noticing that some of the shirts and skirts weren't even clean. I had packed in a hurry and left in such a rush, I never said goodbye to the kids.

I hadn't seen them for a week, since before the final coke run, and I knew they were safe with my mother, but I couldn't shake the feeling that I shouldn't be in this place. I didn't belong here.

How do I explain to these people that I am a mother, not a drug addict? I picked up a picture of Ava and Rocket on Mother's Day the year before. Ava was sitting on a couch looking up at the camera, wearing a navy and white linen dress. She had pigtails in her hair and they were perfect, no lumps. Rocket sat on her lap, a baby of eight months—my favorite age, when they are fat and giggly but still can't walk. He grinned widely in a green jumper with smocking and embroidered rabbits across the chest, his hair an ineffable strawberry blond. I felt sick to my stomach.

Rocket was now seventeen months old and still not fully weaned. Although he had been away from me for two months, and my milk was gone, every time I visited him he wanted to nurse. But he was used to rejection, used to replacements, used to his mother's body as a site of toxicity. On many nights in our big house, I had to hide. I had to not comfort him when he woke up crying. I had to rely on Mac and my mother. A few times I went upstairs anyway, and, when I sobered up, wanted to die. Every time I sobered up, I wanted to die. Because *what kind of trash . . .*

And yet, I never wanted to give up on us entirely. On me, I suppose. On my ability to be a good, nursing mother. *Good mothers breastfeed. Tomorrow I will be different.*

And now, now I would be gone thirty more days.

He doesn't even know where I went.

I knew he would stop trying to nurse by the time I returned. *It's okay. I had no business doing that anyway. Poisoned. The most beautiful act, I poisoned.*

I threw the pictures in the drawer and walked out of the room to have a smoke in the backyard.

On my way back, I reviewed the house rules in the kitchen: when they would give us meds, what we could eat, where we could go, what would happen if we shot up. I wished the other addicts were there so I could have a distraction from the swirling anxiety in my brain.

From my bed that night, I heard the housemates roll in, their laughing and cheerful talking and shouts of "good night," and when it all quieted down, I got up and locked my door.

9

WHO'S THE SICKEST IN THE ROOM?

On my first morning in treatment, I woke early, got dressed, and put on makeup, which I hadn't done in weeks. I was the last person to climb into the van, nodding and mumbling quick hellos to the other clients. The man next to me looked about twenty, and I could hear his music rattling out of his headphones. I liked him already. He didn't want to talk either. Back at the main building, we filed into a large conference room and found seats around a huge oak table. We sipped coffee and stacked our journals, pens, and cigarettes alongside us.

Ned, a therapist and substance abuse counselor, rose in front of the room and handed out worksheets. He was about fifty years old, short, with a square jaw and gray hair. He obviously exercised on a regular basis—and probably outdoors too, for the added mental benefit of sunshine. To me, he looked like some sort of Herculean god of health. His body was firm, muscular, and rationally tanned. I hadn't seen a human like him in a long time. His clothes fit perfectly, and he even wore a belt that matched his shoes. His eyes were bright and clear, his hair strategically disheveled, just enough to make him accessible—an everyday, chilled-out California bicyclist guy.

While I constructed a yuppie past for him, he told us how he had spent ten years on the streets of Los Angeles shooting cocaine and drinking. My head cocked to one side while I contemplated whether or not to believe him. His details seemed accurate. *Alright*, I thought, *he appears to know things.* He explained how he was twenty years sober and a cognitive behavioral therapist. He didn't believe in God and wasn't sober through anonymous meetings. I liked him more than before.

Ned stood in stark contrast to the mostly white, twenty-something misfits in front of him, fumbling, fidgeting, and analyzing each another. The new arrivals were red-faced and pale, with big black circles under their eyes. The addicts completing their thirty days were bright-eyed, high-fiving the staff, bouncing like the teenagers I knew in high school whose confidence I wished I could steal and make my own.

Looking around the table, I noticed we were all either fat or emaciated. Drowning in clothes or barely wearing them. We had our hoods up and chins down or our chests puffed out. Our eyes darted around the room or stared unflinchingly at a scratch on the table, a spot chosen as to avoid eye contact. *We are the human embodiments of excess,* I thought.

I watched a quick-talking, black-haired man with a nose ring and tattoos covering his arms and neck flirt with the girl next to him. He had been in the rehab twenty-five days and clearly believed himself healed. She had arrived that morning. I watched in disgust at his opportunism—*quick, get the sad new addict before she cleans up enough to realize you are dull and slimy.* Ten seconds later, I felt a touch of jealousy that nobody was flirting with me. I recalled Mac's words, "Don't cheat on me in rehab."

None of these assholes are going to stay sober, I thought. But I would. I wanted it more than them.

"This chart outlines the Stages of Relapse," Ned said. "It shows what happens when an addict starts using again after a period of abstinence." He looked down at the paper, his page highlighted with notes everywhere, and I followed his lead, scanning the page, picking up my pen and underlining words like "drug glorification," "negative emotions," "coping skills," "loss of daily structure," "social isolation," "triggers," and "problematic thinking."

Oh, I thought. *I don't have that. My thinking is just fine.*

I took notes, underlined important concepts. *So, rehab is like school,* I thought. *Perfect.*

After defining each term, Ned asked us to go around the room and explain our most recent relapse. A tiny dark-haired woman named Danny with librarian glasses and Sailor Jerry tattoos on her forearms spoke first: "I moved back to Portland, got a job, but one day after work, I went to a bar for happy hour. I just went for a beer. But there were old friends there, and they offered me a hit, so I took it, and nearly overdosed. I was high for two more years."

Ned paused, smiling, and asked, "Why did you go to the bar? Why did you go back to the place you knew would trigger you?"

"I don't know. I wanted a beer," she said.

"But you ended up shooting heroin," he said, framing the question as a statement.

"Yes. In the bathroom."

"You weren't there for a beer," responded Ned. "You were there for something else."

"Okay." The woman narrowed her brow. She had no idea what the hell he was talking about and neither did I. *I would go for a beer too, Ned. You go for a beer and shit happens, Ned.* I wondered if Ned was lying about the whole ex-addict thing.

What kind of addict doesn't understand stopping by for a quick drink only to find yourself two hours later doing hard drugs in a bathroom stall?

Sitting next to the junkie was Shelly. Shelly had bleached, frizzy blonde hair with black roots that fell into a deep V down her back. She was impossibly thin and wearing huge gold earrings and tight jeans. She had no visible muscle. Her bones held pockets of waggling skin, like silk draped over a stick. I noticed her forearms were dotted with scars and scratches. She began explaining: "I was doing so great. I was working and back with my family and everything was going so great, but then my mom died, and I found out my husband was fucking around with his ex—the mother of his kids, who I've raised since day one—because that woman is a useless bitch, never given us a damn penny, and her kids? You know what? They call me Mama. They've always called me Mama. Do they call her Mama? No, cause she's not there. Who went to their kindergarten graduation? Me. They aren't even my kids. And when the oldest had pneumonia, who took him to the doctor? Me..."

It was then I realized we had a tweaker on our hands, and I glanced at Ned to see if he was going to shut the chattering woman up anytime soon. He merely gazed at her compassionately, which felt to me like an underhanded insult, as if he were trying to say I was an asshole.

She continued, "So I find out my old man is fucking around with her and you know how I found out? She told me. She just showed up at my work one day and told me she and him had been screwing around for months. And she's pregnant again, but I don't believe it's his baby. And then I find out I'm pregnant too. But I know it's his baby. So here I am, pregnant, and I was so sad and angry, so one night I scored some dope—"

At the word "dope," I hit my breaking point and rolled my eyes, because she wasn't a junkie, and "dope" is heroin. She was trying to sound as hard as the junkie, and it infuriated me. *Everyone knows you're smoking rocks in a barn, lady.* She probably didn't even shoot up.

She wrapped up her inane diatribe with the words "and then I was off and running," which hit my ears like somebody eating potato chips with her mouth open. *Why the hell say things like "off and running"?* I wondered how she could afford this place, and if, perhaps, they offer government subsidies for rehab. I made a mental note to avoid Shelly for the next thirty days and the rest of my life.

The next speaker looked vaguely promising. She was clean and less jumpy. Her name was Shannon, and she reminded me of the mothers in my suburban neighborhood. She wore jeans and a sweatshirt with the words "Lake Tahoe" on the front.

Her face contorted into a pained expression while she said, "When my two-year-old pretended there was wine in his sippy cup, I knew I couldn't drink any more. I saw right then what my life had become." She looked at her feet, as if that were the saddest image she'd ever conjured.

I suppressed another eye roll, thinking, *Oh, did you lose your Mercedes-Benz too?* I wished I could say it out loud, but I couldn't (not yet at least), so I tried killing her with my eyes. *Your kid pretended to drink wine out of a sippy cup and you check yourself into rehab? My God, did you even get a hangover once?*

It occurred to me that I was going to spend every day for the next thirty days with this horrific conglomerate of humans, and I had no idea how I would survive it. I hated everyone in the room except the dude with the scruffy half-beard who refused to remove his headphones.

Shannon was obviously the healthiest person in the room— with her bobbed hair and polished nails and rampant sanity. *What a loser.* I considered letting Ned know he should probably send her home. But he nodded encouragingly at her while she explained how her husband had been sleeping in the guest room for six months, and I returned to wondering if Ned was ever a drug addict at all.

Harvey, a red-faced man in his sixties wearing a button-down plaid shirt and blue jeans, began: "I have never been able to quit drinking for long. I made it six months after my baby son died from crib death and I was out drinking when it happened, but I don't know. I always start again. I've never done a drug and I still own a little company, but I can barely show up to work any-more, and my wife and kids are gone, but I think this time it's going to be different. I think for sure—I mean this is my fourth time in rehab." He forced a small, sad smile.

I was bored just thinking about him, and decided he must have some intellectual deficiency. He went to rehab four times just on booze? *How do you get taken down by alcohol alone, man?*

He kept speaking as Ned asked him questions, but I had ceased listening because I knew I was next and needed to figure out what sort of first impression I was going to make to the group. *Do I go quiet and reserved? Do I go loud and funny? Do I hold my shocking story close or lay it on them right now?*

"Why did you relapse?" Ned asked me with a smile.

"This is my first time in rehab, so I don't think I've done that," I said, feeling immediately embarrassed.

Ned sat down, as if settling in for the long haul. "A relapse doesn't just follow treatment. It's any time you start drinking again after a period of sobriety, after really trying to stay sober."

"Well, I do that with alcohol every day." I laughed.

"Right," Ned said. "But have you ever been sober for a long period, then started using again?"

I thought about the way I *knew* Rocket was going to turn me into a PTA mother but instead I ended up doing blow in the bathroom. "Yeah, I guess I did that with cocaine after my son's birth. I was sure I'd never use it again, and then I did after a long time."

Ned looked at me, waiting for me to continue, but I had nothing to add, so I resorted to honesty, saying, "But I don't know why I did it." I looked away from his face.

"Do you mind sharing the circumstances?" I flinched, because I hated when people said heartfelt words like "sharing." It made me uneasy.

"I was nursing my newborn son and wanted a beer, so I had one—a really yeasty one—because it helps with milk production. That was what I told myself: 'It helps with milk.' And everything was fine for a few months. I even started grad school. I only drank beer and wine, but as my son got older, and I could leave him with my mom, my husband and I started going to bars again, and one night I met a guy who would bring blow to our house, so I bought an eight-ball from him, and then every time I drank I wanted cocaine."

"So your relapse started with a beer?"

"I guess, but beer wasn't my problem. Cocaine is what always takes me down."

"Sounds to me like it was that first beer that took you down." Ned didn't smile this time, but instead leaned toward me and looked right in my eyes, and I decided for sure he was not a nice man. Once again, I had no idea what he was talking about.

• • •

After lunch, we gathered in a large room for our first "group therapy" session, or "group" for short, where we all sat in a circle and took turns speaking of "how we're doing," with or without a Native American talking stick. In addition to "processing" and creating "relapse prevention plans," I learned we were defining and cementing our own special disaster hierarchy.

Nobody was in that place because life was spinning out of control in success. No, we were there because we were failing, for whatever reason, and probably miserably. And yet, every one of our egos remained miraculously intact. But since we couldn't battle each other for top position of highest achiever or smartest—clearly, that ship had sailed—we focused instead on a one-upping contest I liked to call "Who's the sickest in the room?"

In rehab, we fought for the bottom. We shuffled and scooted for the lowest rung. Everybody in that place believed he or she was the most desperate case: the most addicted, the most fucked-up, the most shocking. We wore our catastrophe like shimmering medals.

The heroin addicts were royalty—not only because sticking

a needle in your vein is terrifying, but also because shooting heroin has that screw-it-all suicide vibe that most of us found "just too far." I would watch Danny like a character out of *Trainspotting.* She and the other junkies had a sort of stoic, matter-of-fact approach to addiction that awed the rest of us. When Danny spoke, we stopped muttering to neighbors and listened, in deep regard. I thought I was hard, very tough, but soon realized I hadn't done "addiction" until I'd lived like a junkie. Everyone's just trying to keep them from dying and off the streets, to "reduce harm."

Heroin is the most fucked-up drug to be fucked up on, but the meth addicts never stopped talking about theirs. Shelly and her gang called themselves "dope fiends" while the rest of us looked at them and thought, *Oh, come on. You're just another white trash methhead.*

The goddamn tweakers. They walked into morning art therapy all pockmarked, toothless, and talking talking talking, with wiry, frizzy hair and perpetually black-smeared eyeliner, telling us how they lived in a hollowed-out redwood with their baby daddy and two kids, turning tricks in the back of a van and dismantling microwaves in their free time until CPS closed the adoption case on the first six kids they lost but now they are *going to change for sure!*

I would look at them and think, *Bitch, you can't even form a sentence. What do you know about getting well? Maybe stop smoking battery acid and see how that goes.*

And then I would lean back in sweet superiority because I always chose cocaine, the rich man's drug, and hated meth, the white trash drug. Admittedly, I had tried meth once with Mac in some man's converted garage, because there was nothing else available. I felt like I had consumed ninety million cups of coffee and lit my brain on fire: a lot of action, no thought. I could not find the fun there. I wanted my brain to think excellent, comforting things, at least for a few seconds until it started wailing about the next line, or, even worse, grappling with the inevitable end of the line.

I had always hated tweakers. First, they never shut up. Second, they were dumb. Whether they started dumb or became dumb on account of all the cold medicine they smoked was a mystery, but the result was the same. Third, they hurt people. In the news and among my addict friends, I would hear stories of what the tweakers had done. I heard about one near my town who passed out alongside a river in winter with her baby tucked next to her, a baby wearing nothing but a cotton shirt and wet diaper, until the baby froze to death. I read about another one spinning out for six days and raping a nine-year-old girl while the girl's mother smoked meth in the garage.

To me, tweakers were the addicts without standards, the druggies without a single code of basic decency. If we were all Mafia members, meth addicts were the mob bosses who killed wives and children. The rest of us were Don Corleone.

Upon returning to my room after that first day, I met my new roommate, Alice, a woman in her fifties who I imagined had been smoking cigarettes for thirty-five years. She looked seventy-five, with deep lines around her jaw, which jerked to one side or the other at the end of sentences, and eyes beneath drooping lids—eyes that darted arbitrarily from one spot to the next. Her smile revealed missing teeth on the upper right and left side of her mouth and one missing tooth on the bottom. Her gums were yellowed.

Meth mouth, I thought.

Her laugh was cavernous and burly, and her voice was like sandpaper, rough and grating through years of smoke snaking through her throat. I forced a "hello" and shook her limp, tiny hand, then said, "Oh, I have to go get something," and left to gather myself outside. I wanted to figure out what sort of physical ailment would convince the house manager I needed a new room. Some sort of inarguable disease that required isolation. *Maybe I should tell her I have asthma and can't be around smokers.* As I took a drag of my cigarette, the fault in my plan dawned on me.

I heard the sliding door open, and Alice emerged onto the back porch. She sat down at the table across from me, pulled out a pack of Pall Mall cigarettes, and retrieved a half-smoked one from the pack. I offered her a light, out of habit mostly. She glanced at me, inhaled deeply, and looked around the yard. I found myself chattering.

"So how's it going?" I asked, adding, "Well, I guess that's a stupid question."

She cackled and said, "I'm better than I was a week ago. Guess that's something. Shit."

"That's the truth," I said. "I can't believe how weird this place is." I felt like a fraud, chatting with a woman I had just scrambled to avoid. But I couldn't find it in me to snub her. I could only judge from afar.

"Yeah, I don't know why I'm here," she said flatly.

"*Really?*" I sputtered sarcastically. It was rude, and I knew it, because what I was really saying was, "Lady, I can tell just looking at you why you're here."

"This is a waste of fuckin' time," she said. "I won't stay clean."

She talked less than most tweakers I had known, less than Shelly in group, less than the addicts I had met at various houses over the years. She was reserved, even shy.

"Then why come?" I asked.

"I'm here for my daughter. She won't let me see my grandkids anymore."

I told her that must be rough, and she asked me if I had children.

"Yes," I said, brightening. "Two."

"Are they still with you?"

My smile faded and a wave of humiliated rage poured over me when I realized Alice and I had both been relieved of the children in our lives. *This fucking tweaker and me. We had the same result.*

I stamped my smoke in the ashtray and mumbled, "I see them a lot," and left.

• • •

During one-on-one therapy, Ned tried to claim I hated tweakers because of what they represented in me, that somewhere I knew I was no better than them, and could have done any one of those things had I gotten hooked on a drug that turned my brain into soup as fast as methamphetamines do. I explained to Ned that I was in fact better than them because I didn't choose a drug that turned my brain into soup.

"You know, Janelle," he said during our third therapy session. "We hate the traits in others that mirror ourselves."

What kind of madness is this, I thought. "A mirror to what I hate about myself." That was the kind of bumbling nonsense

Ned used to throw at me during "sessions," but I knew he simply didn't understand my position.

In group over the next four weeks, I met all the other addicts and categorized them based on how much they irritated me. I met the pill poppers, who seemed less sick than the rest of us merely on account of their failure to shoot, snort, or smoke anything. The psychedelic drug types, who I didn't understand because acid is a thing you do in high school and then abandon, and the potheads, who everyone felt sorry for, because truly, *how do you need rehab for weed?*

Next to the tweakers, the most insufferable humans were the "dual-diagnosis" people, because they thought they were *very special*. I wondered how they felt so special when almost everyone in the room had in fact been dually diagnosed with a mental illness as well as addiction. We all had depression and addiction, or bipolar and addiction. We were all self-medicating. We were all super sick. We were all very sad. But they wore their mental illness like letters at the end of their names.

By the end of my time in rehab, the people who fascinated me the most were the straight alcoholics. The drunks. The boozers. The men and women who didn't shoot, smoke, eat, or snort drugs, and who possibly never had. The ones who woke in the morning at four a.m. to take a shot of whiskey from a bottle in the hall closet simply to kill the shakes and sleep again, only to shuffle to the shower at eight a.m. after a quick swig of vodka (because it's "odorless") and make it to work red-faced and sweaty, to sit in a cubicle or run a business or sell a car, to run across the street and have another shot at lunch, to smoke hasty cigarettes behind the garage, to scream at their kids and beat their husbands and wives, to swear tomorrow they will quit, to carry on for ten or twenty or thirty years. And end up here, in group, with Ned and me, mumbling, "Oh, I never did any of the crazy things you all are talking about. I just drank."

At night, I'd wonder if they *were* perhaps the sickest people in the room, people who would die under the radar of "functioning alcoholism," lacking the flash to get noticed, failing to pose sufficient threat to society to get locked up, dying by a rope in a closet one day, or a car smashed into a tree, or down the road in the ER after liver failure, or old, tired, and miserable, in the park with a bag. Shuffling down the sidewalk, still sure they aren't that sick.

I loved them, every damn one of them, though I didn't know why.

When it was my turn with the talking stick, I either spoke in short, withholding sentences with my arms crossed defiantly in front of me, or dumped the most shocking version of my story into the room. I was always playing "Who's the sickest in the room?" I was so sick I was raging and cold and disengaged. I was so sick I would tell you about *my* diagnosis of borderline personality disorder—a diagnosis with an unofficial prognosis of "you are trash and there is no hope for you." After my first diagnosis of the disorder many months before, I learned that borderlines are so impossible many therapists flatly refuse to work with them. Borderlines ruin children through sick and twisted rage, harm themselves, generally exploding the lives around them plus their own. And the worst part was I actually did, in fact, *feel* borderline. When I read the collection of symptoms making up "my kind," I felt I read the first accurate description of the way I had felt since childhood.

I split. I saw people as all good or all bad, and sometimes that changed within an hour. I cut my arms to watch the blood rise. I cheated, lied, and manipulated. I raged. Oh, God, the rage. Psychiatrists had also diagnosed me with bipolar II, but that was nonsense, because the doctor would ask, "Do you have mood swings?" And I'd say, "Yes, yes I do. I am a cocaine addict. Of course I have mood swings." But nobody explained how they differentiated between the two.

Then he'd ask if I went on drug binges, which I explained was affirmative. And then he'd ask if I went on spending binges, which was obviously a yes as well. In fact, I used to fill whole carts in stores like Marshalls and Ross Dress for Less and Target, but then I'd look around the store and at the cart and realize I couldn't handle the gravity of the situation. The cart. Checking out. Continuing to push it. So I would make sure no employees were watching, and I would leave, walking away from the whole damn fiasco, to sit alone in an aisle somewhere. Sometimes I would obsess over one item in particular, like gift bags or candles or embroidery thread. I would buy fifty. They thought this was "manic." I thought it was simply "confused."

Then the doctors diagnosed chronic depression, which seemed accurate. I mean, *wouldn't you be depressed if you couldn't stop buying gift bags?* They also diagnosed me with PTSD but never explained the trauma that damaged me, which made me wonder if they simply drew diagnoses out of large, expensive wool hats.

No matter what they said, I knew the depression and mood swings and binges and erratic behavior were somehow related to the drinking and drugs. The borderline, though? That was me to my bones. That was me before I started drinking, and in the dark when nobody was looking. My doctors talked about borderlines having so sense of self. No sense of identity. They were shells of people.

I felt like that. I could never figure out if I actually loved *anyone*.

Do I care if you live or die? Why do I hurt everyone? Why am I not showing up again? Why am I slicing my arms with little blades? Why am I so afraid you'll leave when I'm not even sure I want you here? Why am I devastated you are suffering? Do I want to die for you? Does your pain erase me? Can I fix it? Why am I screaming "I hate you?" Why am I shoving you away when I wanted you here? Why do you not see what I see? Why am I still drinking? Why can't I cry?

I studied that bulleted list of borderline symptoms and found inarguable evidence that I was, in fact, born without a moral compass. At least I was right about that.

• • •

I don't think Alice moved when she slept, and she made almost no sound when she walked. It was as if she were trying to take up as little space in the world as she possibly could. She only talked if you engaged her first. Well, except one night at dinner when Shelly the chattering tweaker was complaining about her kids. Alice stood up, shoved her chair in, and said, "You shouldn't let those babies go."

We became friends, Alice and I, and we'd laugh at Ned's endless positivity, and theorize who was going to sleep with whom and get kicked out. She told me about her Chihuahua, and we spoke of ridiculous, simple things like pizza and swimming pools.

When Alice was twelve, she was traded to a fifty-year-old man by her mother for a bag of heroin and a case of beer. She escaped him when she was fourteen, and survived on the streets until age eighteen, when she met a man who would "take care of her." She had six children, all of them taken by child protective services, and got sober for the first time when the man died and she went to prison, where she birthed her daughter.

When her daughter was nineteen, Alice relapsed, and couldn't afford heroin, so she landed on meth. She lost her teeth and face and mind, but probably not her heart, because when I asked her what her favorite song was she said, "Boots of Spanish Leather" by Bob Dylan, and I thought, *Well, damn.* I had been singing that song for as long as I could remember.

She had given up. She had not a single thought of change in her mind, not a shred of power at her fingertips, but she loved a song like that. She still flipped over a single cigarette as a "lucky." I teased her, saying, "Alice, nobody does that past the age of fifteen."

She flipped me off and said, "They would if they had my luck."

She ruined everything I knew about tweakers.

Two weeks after she arrived, Alice left, because her daughter could only afford two weeks. I was glad to have given her my Buddha statue, because it was a little thing I could remember her by.

• • •

On my twenty-seventh day in rehab, I received calls from my father, mother, and mother-in-law, all letting me know Mac hadn't been seen in three days.

Their voices were urgent and severe. "Do you have any idea where he is? Can you guess? This is just insane!"

I was unconcerned, irritated, and marginally jealous. *He's fine, people. Just on a drug run. Calm the fuck down.*

"Not exactly," I told my mother-in-law. "But he's probably somewhere near Charlie, the drug addict who is not actually named Charlie and likes to spray paint kitchens." I tried to think of the street where Charlie lived but only recalled the alley where we used to park. I told her about that and the coffee shop a couple of blocks down from his hovel.

She paused, and asked slowly, "Well, what is his actual name, Janelle?"

"I have no idea, but you don't need his name. Just go see if Mac's truck is in the alley, then wait, and if he isn't there, he's probably around there somewhere."

So Mac's older sister went looking for him, and found him wandering the streets of downtown Sacramento, just where I said he'd be. She found him at five a.m., walking barefoot, without his wallet or keys.

The next day, on day twenty-eight, two days before my scheduled rehab departure, Mac and I spoke on the phone. It turned out he was sitting alone one night in the adorable country house we had just rented to begin our life anew, and in a flash of brilliance remembered the abandoned cocaine baggie from the day God spoke to me. So he took it, and drank a bottle of rum, and got lost on the streets of Sacramento after hanging out with Charlie.

While I could relate from a past life, I was healed now in rehab and therefore outraged at his poor choices.

"WHERE WERE THE KIDS, MAC?" I screamed into the

phone, sitting on the couch beneath a watercolor of a snow leopard. My privileges had been upgraded to use of the portable house phone as opposed to the pay phone, but we weren't allowed to use it in our rooms. Consequently, everybody squealed at their spouses in common areas, and absolutely nobody cared. "WERE YOU FUCKING SOME BROAD, TOO?" I thought of that night in the Thai restaurant parking lot.

He was quiet and sounded tired, with a shade of guilt and the slightest wash of shame. "What? No. What? What are you talking about? They were at my parents'. I'm sorry, Janelle."

"And now you're going to rehab for ninety days on a goddamn beach in Southern California to find your inner child while I come back to pick up the pieces of our family?" In twenty-eight days, I had transformed from mentally ill cocaine addict to doting savior.

"Janelle, aren't you just coming back from a rehab?" He was growing irritated.

"Mine was only thirty days, Mac!" I hung up to call my mother and tell her she needed to come get me, right then, so I could go home and clean up the mess my cosmic disaster of a husband made.

When I heard Mac and I would be in rehab at the same time, I decided my in-laws and parents were going to try to steal my children. I envisioned long, drawn-out, vicious court battles between them. I had no evidence of grandparents or anybody else for that matter vying for possession of our kids; in fact, I had no evidence of anything but support from all of them, but I felt untethered. I was convinced that if I stayed the last two days of my program, I would lose them. *One of us has to be with them*, I thought.

The counselors advised against leaving early, saying, "Janelle, in your new life you must start following through on commitments." But I had done twenty-eight days out of thirty, and that was good enough for me. So I thanked them for their service and convinced my mother to retrieve me. Once again, she believed I knew best and agreed to come that very day.

"Will you bring the kids?" I asked, holding my breath.

"Yes," she said, and I could hear her smile. "They're sitting right here." I felt my heart jump.

I packed my clothes in fifteen minutes, and the two hours I waited for them to arrive felt like Christmas Eve when I was nine. They ran to me in the front yard of the rehab house, and I got on my knees to hold them. I couldn't believe they could be so beautiful. In the car, I tried to nurse Rocket, but he had no interest. He turned his head away and sat up, and for the first time, it occurred to me that there were two children without their actual mother, and that they missed her in a material, clear way, and would create their own defenses to protect themselves. I thought again about the nursery I had made for Rocket, the clothes all lined up by size, the morning I brought him home, and the morning he left. I shook my head right and left to knock the images out of my skull.

Then I reminded myself how very sick I was, and I asked my mom to please drive, because I had to get home.

10

MAINTENANCE WHISKEY

One week after I left rehab, my mother and I sat in her living room in big, soft easy chairs with the footrests kicked out, constructing plans to prevent me from detonating my life. My plan was that I would live in the house Mac and I had rented before I went to rehab. Mac had moved our belongings from the big Natomas house to the new one, but didn't get beyond dropping off furniture and stacking unmarked boxes in every room. This was the extent of my plan.

Her plan was: "Devote your life to recovery."

"Don't your counselors say you should take time to just focus on recovery before trying to do life again?" It was not an actual question, but I answered anyway.

"Yes," I said. "And I have, right?" I narrowed my eyes at her, sensing she had an opinion on my life that differed from my own.

"You have, but I think you need to get all this psych stuff in order before you get back with the kids." As if cued, Rocket bolted out of the bedroom holding a wooden screwdriver and a brown-headed doll with matted hair. When he passed me, I leaned over and grabbed his shirt, yelling "Hey!" and demanding a hug. He spun around in smiles and folded into my arms just long enough for me to get a whiff of the sweet honey sweat of his chubby neck before he ran off.

"I need to be with the kids, Mom, and Mac and I just rented that house. Have you seen the porch? It's amazing. Right next to a horse ranch."

"Yes, it's nice, but you rented that when Mac was still working. He's in a ninety-day program and you're out of money. You're on mental health leave for two more months."

"How do you know that?" If I told her that, I had forgotten.

"Because your boss and I talk, Janelle. Everybody talks about your health now." *Good Lord*, I thought. *Everybody is so earnest about everything.*

"Weird." I rolled my eyes, pondering how they all couldn't see how I had my life handled now.

Since she seemed to make a decent point, even better than mine, I turned my attention to the show we hadn't been watching but that played in the background because it was comforting—the way it droned on, the hum of canned laughter and commercials with all the happiness they promised. All those beautiful people. All the beautiful things to buy. Like candles and gift bags.

She lowered the volume with the remote, looked at me, and asked, "So, you think all those diagnoses are true? Your dad wonders about them."

"You talk to Dad?" I asked, surprised.

"Of course. He's been helping me with the kids."

"What do you mean?" Now I was utterly shocked.

"What do *you* mean? I have to work. Mac's parents work. Your dad works. Everyone works." She seemed mildly exasperated.

"Wow, that's really nice of him. Too bad he didn't do that for me when I was a kid."

"Well, he's doing it now," she said dismissively as she shrugged her shoulders, clearly on his side. It was strange to think of all the life going on behind the scenes while Mac and I hid out in motel rooms. I had a fleeting thought of all the trouble I had caused, of all the grandparents scrambling to compensate for our deficiencies, but I shoved it out of my mind with the thought, *Well, I am very sick.*

"Mom," I said. "If you don't think all that 'psych stuff' is true, why are you telling me to take care of it?" I had spotted a hole in her argument.

"I didn't say that. Your dad and I were just saying it seems a little *excessive*. I mean, you weren't ever like this before."

I turned to face her. "You sent me to my first shrink when I was in high school. Remember that dude with the beard who hooked my fingers up to some machine and talked to me about chakras?" I lifted my eyebrows and smirked, knowing the memory would make her laugh. We loved making fun of new-age hippies.

"You were sixteen and wild and very angry. I didn't know what to do with you."

"I loved that guy," I said. "What was his name?"

"Sergio." She smiled, and I laughed.

"But I've kind of always been crazy, Mom." I said, wondering why it was suddenly so important to me that my mother understood I was *definitely mentally ill.*

"Well, what do you think about what the doctors say, in your heart of hearts?"

"Please don't say 'heart of hearts.' I can't talk to you when you say things like that." I was not joking.

I stared at the television, though I was, in fact, thinking of a real answer. "The borderline seems true. The rest I don't know. Bipolar maybe. But not really. Hard to tell when you're a coke addict." I watched her flinch at my last two words.

She looked away, and I continued, "I get really depressed, but maybe that's the drinking. And Mac and I fight all the time."

"I know," she said, and paused. "I think you should go into one of those 'sober living environments,' Janelle, and do an outpatient program, just to be safe, so you can really get well. We can take care of the kids." She looked at Ava sitting at the kitchen counter, coloring in a Hello Kitty coloring book. Rocket came darting back into the room, launching himself onto a couch cushion on the floor. He distracted my mother, so I didn't answer.

"Pick that up, Rocket. It's not a toy. It goes on the couch."

He turned around and looked at her, deciding whether or not to obey. She looked at him harder and he kicked the cushion, then set it on the couch. "Thank you, sweetie," she said cheerfully.

He didn't respond.

"He's still not talking, huh?" I asked, making sure I didn't sound too worried.

"No, but he's barely eighteen months!"

"Ava had tons of words by this age. Do you think he's okay?" I watched him drag a wooden frog pull toy around the room.

"He's fine. Boys develop slower than girls. Your cousin Benjamin didn't speak until three, and then he spoke in full sentences." She was relaxed, and got up to make dinner.

Still, I wondered if I had broken him. He was so silent. *Why is he so silent?* I thought of Alice and wondered if she was still alive, and if she got to see her grandkids.

"Where would I go to outpatient, Mom?" I yelled from over my shoulder while she opened the refrigerator.

"I was thinking Marin County. Found a great place there!" She had obviously been doing research.

"I don't know. Maybe," I said under my breath, flipping to a new channel to vacate my mind for a few seconds.

I considered my situation: no job, home in boxes, husband in the drunk slammer, and little money. I had spent three nights alone at the cute house in the country and was sure I was going to get cut up into small pieces by some Republican on a horse. It was dark and quiet out there. Nobody would hear my screams. An actual clown lived across the street. She seemed friendly, but still, she was a clown, and sometimes she walked down to her mailbox in her clown suit.

Perhaps this is what happens when you choose a new rental in between coke binges.

At the thought, I told my mother, "It *is* already feeling a little impossible."

"Let's check out that program," she said.

•   •   •

A week later I moved into a house I found on Craigslist that was forty-five minutes away in Petaluma, California. It was occupied by two sober, friendly men. One was about twenty-five and had recently kicked heroin for the fifth time. This time, he was doing it through Suboxone. The other was "old" in age and sobriety—forty years old and one year sober. He was an alcoholic.

I brought my red embroidered blanket and a new Buddha statue to my new room and enrolled in the most highly esteemed outpatient rehab in Marin County, which is one of the wealthiest counties in northern California. My family and I were under the impression that if you paid more, you received better sobriety, so my parents and grandparents pooled thousands of more dollars in cash and credit to help me, again.

In addition to the outpatient program, I signed up for a dialectical behavioral therapy group that involved weekly meetings with a group plus individual therapy. I got a psychiatrist, worked out, and stopped eating sugar. I took up running, kickboxing, yoga, and meditation, began shopping only at the co-op and Whole Foods, and hired a personal spiritual advisor/holistic health practitioner. I woke every day at seven a.m. to meditate, shower, eat bee pollen, and head to the rehab, where I sat in group listening to forlorn white addicts express how dejected they felt. One of them lived on his yacht off Tiburon. Another owned the winery that made my favorite cabernet. Millionaires. They were actual millionaires.

I thought of Alice and how she couldn't even stay for the whole month, and how drugs were the great leveler until it came to outcomes. To treatment. To the world opening itself to help. Nobody cared if Alice lived or died. Nobody would even notice if she were gone. I wished she could have come with me.

I met with a therapist at the rehab—in addition to the dialectical therapist and psychiatrist—who was staunchly devoted to Jungian psychology. We began a long and meandering exploration of my unconscious and deepest longing, the needs I had but didn't know I had, but had better figure out how to satisfy, and soon.

After our sessions I felt emotionally heavier and remarkably more confused, especially when the topic landed on my mother. Apparently, somewhere deep down I had always yearned for a clearer, healthier relationship with her, but never got it. She gave me nothing to "bump up against" because she was nebulous and blurred herself, and that was why I had no "self." When I left the Jungian's office, I felt a bit like a fraud and a liar, as if I were saying things that weren't quite true, because sure, all those problems with my mom were real, and we had endured dark times when I was a child, and I found myself entwined and obsessed with fixing her marriage, finances, and heart, but her love for me was warrior-like—brave and firm and wild—and she was my unequivocal best friend. Talking about her like that felt wrong, and I couldn't make the therapist understand that we were *dysfunctional* and *perfect*. I couldn't make the therapist understand that I was heartbroken and infuriated by her, but she was the only human I feared I would die without. I didn't understand why we couldn't be batshit crazy and woven through each other in the crispest, purest, and sanest love.

In the Jungian's office I learned about dissociative behavior and "sober blackouts" and practiced deep belly breathing. After group, I would go to the gym and kickboxing class. In the evening, I would attend my dialectical behavior group, or go to my psychiatrist, or sit at home and read Thich Nhat Hanh and Jon Kabat-Zinn.

I was living, breathing, thinking, and eating recovery. I got stronger. I lost weight. My mind grew clearer while my family delighted in my "progress." I had a whole army of activities, mental health workers, family, and friends encircling me, blocking me from the siren song of alcohol. I bought a lottery ticket one day at a gas station and won eighty dollars, which I took as a sign of God's pride in me. Yes, the God I didn't believe existed.

When I was sober almost sixty days, at the peak of my wellness, Mac invited me to "family weekend" at his rehab. *Of course!* I thought.

I booked a flight using a high-interest-rate credit card I had somehow been approved for and set out on my journey to Southern California. But while sitting in a restaurant in the San Francisco airport, waiting for my flight, the thought occurred to me that I was afraid of flying. In fact, I hated flying. At some point, while darting around Europe in airplanes, I'd realized that each flight I boarded increased my chances of dying. *The more I fly, the more likely I am to be on a plane that malfunctions midair and spirals desperately into the ocean amid screams of mothers and children.*

At the airport in San Francisco, the thought that followed this recollection was, *You know what would make me feel better? A glass of wine.*

I failed to remember the Xanax in my purse, and without another thought, without a whispered word from my conscience, therapist, God, friend, or enemy, I rose and floated to the bar across the concourse, stood for a few moments waiting for the bartender, and when he placed his hand on the bar and nodded to me, I smiled and asked, "May I have a glass of chardonnay, please?"

The next thing I knew I was driving a rental car with a handle of Captain Morgan on the passenger seat.

I had sipped two glasses of wine before my flight and switched to cocktails on the plane. I then picked up my rental car and drove immediately to Safeway for booze, but in my hotel, I had one drink and realized what I had done. By then it was midnight, and I had to get rid of that bottle. I grabbed the rum, took the elevator downstairs and looked around the lobby for somebody who looked like they needed a handle of Captain Morgan. Nobody was there except the front desk clerk, but he was perfect. He looked about twenty—a surfer type with long sun-bleached hair. I walked up to the counter and set the bottle down in front of him.

"Do you want this?" I asked, without introduction.

"What?" He asked, confused.

"This. The rum." I smiled, realizing my behavior was a little odd. But he was so young. *Of course he drinks*, I thought. *This is Newport Beach. Everyone drinks in LA.*

"Um..." He looked around nervously.

"Do ya not drink?" I asked. "Because if you don't drink, I seriously misjudged you. Maybe more of a weed guy. I could see that." I laughed the laugh of the sweet spot of drunkenness.

"Yeah, I totally drink. Alright! Thanks!" He grabbed the bottle quickly and smiled.

For some reason, I added, "I don't fucking want it." This made him laugh again, and he thanked me again, and I could see his after-work plans had instantly improved.

"Noooo problem," I said, leaning against the counter for a moment, gearing up for the walk back to the elevator.

Back in my room, I fell asleep immediately.

. . .

The next day, while walking down to the beach, I told Mac about the rum.

"It was a terrible mistake. But you know? I'm glad it happened. It taught me the power of alcohol. I mean, I really get it now."

I was prepared to grovel, but he listened to the whole story and said, "Well, you learned from it. Sounds like it had to happen." He put his arm around me. He and I believed my declarations of sorrow and a new start.

When I returned to Petaluma, I told my sobriety army about the relapse, and all of them suggested I go to one of those ridiculous meetings in basements for low-bottom drunks and other nondescript failures. At the first sign of my weakness, both roommates launched into passionate diatribes regarding *the only way they could stay sober*. I told them I thought it was a cult religion, but as I was saying it, I knew it was a lie. I had family members who got sober at those meetings. They were neither cult members nor religious, but I had *opinions*.

I *knew things*.

But they were right. I had gotten drunk again. I drank again in spite of all the money, work, focus, therapy, and talking I had done specifically to avoid drinking again. All that talking, examining, deconstructing of emotions. It all failed me when I needed it. I couldn't even explain how or why I drank that night. It just *happened*, and it frightened me. I agreed to try something new.

The next day, I drove a few times around a gravel parking lot trying to delay the moment when I had to walk into what looked like an abandoned church hall with homeless people and fifty coffee-can ashtrays around the perimeter. Finally, I parked and meandered inside, choosing a seat in the back of the room, behind a mass of what felt like twenty thousand people considerably too happy to be sober. They were clean and well-dressed, laughing and eating cake. They surrounded the ones who looked like small wet dogs with matted coats, and I hoped to God I didn't look so sick they thought I needed love, too. I avoided eye contact and sipped my coffee out of a Styrofoam cup, thinking, *Now I really have hit the bottom of the fucking barrel.*

When the meeting started, somebody started talking up front about how they now didn't have to drink against their will, and I rolled my eyes. *How does one drink against their will? Is somebody holding a gun to your head? Idiot.* It did not occur to me that I had done exactly that in the airport a mere week earlier. There were lists of twelve rules on the wall. Apparently my coat was also matted because immediately after the meeting a woman pounced on me before I could escape. She was relentless with her offers of help as my "sponsor," so I mumbled okay to get rid of her, but later realized when telling my mother about her that a sponsor could be my new move. My new bulletproof plan.

It's fine, Mom, because now I have a sponsor.

The woman and I began drinking a lot of coffee together, and we talked and talked and talked. She gave me a large blue book and took me to a Native American event in a teepee—or, more accurately, an appropriated event by a bunch of white woo-woo types—where we all took our clothes off, got smudged by sage, chanted, and sweated together. It was supposed to be spiritual, but I mostly found it interesting that people who were menstruating weren't allowed in. Because none of the people were actually Native American, nobody could tell me why.

Once again, I had no idea what the hell anybody was saying

in the teepee or in those meetings. I sat foggy and bored, watching the drunks around me, growing irritated when they talked too much, waiting for my turn to explain how it's done, shunning suspected tweakers as well as anyone with serious grammar deficiencies, and departing before they launched into their weird prayer circle. My understanding of the program was that you sit and drink coffee until something happens that makes you sober.

It also had something to do with God.

At home, I read the big blue book my sponsor gave me and highlighted the parts that resonated with me. I read it like a novel in college. I read it like I was going to write a paper on it. More information. More ideas that were going to kick in *any minute now*. Ideas to keep me sober, to stand between that drink and me. The meeting people had slogans: "Remember your last drunk," and "Think it through." I agreed to believe them. I did everything I could to fill my brain with a million defenses against the moment I'd once again realize I'm afraid to fly, or think, *It's been so long since I took a drink, surely* one *would be fine. Just one.*

After the relapse, I increased my exercise and therapy even more. Rocket and Ava came to visit me on my birthday. They brought me gifts and asked when I was coming home. I realized it was time. I must get back with my children.

"I am so grateful for that relapse," I told the meeting on my last day in Petaluma, "I learned my lesson. I am terrified of alcohol now."

• • •

Six months later, I narrowly avoided inpatient psychiatric care.

I had been on a ten-day bender, drinking whiskey in the

apartment I had rented to "find myself" before getting the kids back, with my plants all dead on the back patio; Morgan, the little dog I had acquired as my companion, and the laundry in a giant damp heap at the foot of the bed; and me on the couch, in the habitat meticulously constructed to avoid that exact moment.

A few weeks prior, I had found it necessary to make a trip to my mother's house at nine a.m. to steal change out of Ava's Hello Kitty piggy bank so I could buy some whiskey to come down off the crack I had been smoking all night. After that, my mother found it necessary to take away my key to her house.

The next day, I walked into work late. I had found a little job at a chain tutoring center in my town, and they told me I was excellent, definitely managerial material. But my boss didn't say a word when he saw me that morning. As soon as I stepped over the threshold, he looked at me, shook his head "no," and pointed to the door behind me. I guess I had called in sick one too many times.

I was then locked out of work and out of my mother's house. I hadn't seen my children in a month. I didn't try to call anymore. When Grandma Bonny called, I avoided her. When Grandma Joan called, I avoided her too.

Meanwhile, Mac was a beaming light of sobriety, living back at the dome and apprenticing as an ironworker. Without me, he found a new career. My father was still sober and spending more and more time with my children. Everybody seemed to be getting better except me.

I had met a new friend at a shadowy party of misfits who still lived like they were twenty even though they were all in their thirties. She drank like I drank, and we passed hours in my apartment guzzling Maker's Mark whiskey (when we could afford the good stuff) and listening to old country music. I wondered how I had ever survived without whiskey. In the past, I thought it tasted like stale fire. With her, though, at that time, it tasted like truth.

My days became Waylon, Johnny, and Hank. I thought I had finally found my people. *I am an outlaw. That's what it is.* Since I had no job or family, the drinking turned from night to all day and all night, without end.

One day, Mac knocked on the front door while I sat on the couch, immobile, pretending I wasn't there. He could hear the music. He could see my car. He pounded on the door, growing angrier with every smack of his fist against the wood. Eventually he left, roaring as he walked down the stairs.

The next day, I told my outlaw girlfriend that he broke the door down and came at me physically. This was an outright lie, but I wanted some sympathy. I wanted people to understand I was the victim here.

• • •

Sitting across from the hospital psychiatrist, I tried to explain that it was just Morgan and me in the apartment, and due to the drinking situation, I couldn't manage to get him outside anymore to pee and poop. The apartment manager, I explained, was overreacting.

"Plus, I covered it with paper towels, doctor, so I didn't have to step in it." I didn't tell him I had lived that way for weeks, covering every stain and hopping around them like a child trying to avoid the cracks on a sidewalk.

I thought this would clear it all up for him, but he said, "Nobody sane would live that way."

This startled me. *I am not insane*, I thought. *I was just drinking! It was a lot of drinking.*

I got off with a month of intensive outpatient treatment, so each day I drove to Sacramento to sit in the corner of yet another group therapy room with my hood up, promising not to drink and trying hard to schedule psych appointments that conflicted with art therapy. I hated art.

This place was not like the rehabs of a year before. This place was for the poorest people, the crazies on the street, the ones chattering to themselves in Central Park.

But the psychiatrist was not done with me.

"You know, Janelle, you went from living a good life to fired and in a mental healthcare facility in eight weeks. Why did you start drinking again?"

"I don't know. I thought it would be different this time."

"What led you to that conclusion?" I looked down, and I watched his hand move across the yellow legal pad in an open manila folder. *Who knew what kind of lies he was telling about me.*

I thought about the way I had started drinking after that stretch of sobriety between the sober living house and my new apartment. I thought about living with my mother, and deciding with her that I shouldn't yet return to Mac and the kids, and how I went to meetings every week and exercised, and how my job at the law firm said I could take a few more months off to "get well," so I got a job at the tutoring center. I thought about the night I picked up a six-month token from the cult meetings, and stood in front of them declaring the miracle of sobriety, and how they all cheered for me. I thought of my sober friends asking me to ice cream after the meeting, and me saying no, and how I fully intended to drive home, but by the time I got to the freeway, I remembered that alcohol was never my problem. It was *cocaine* that turned me into a blithering idiot. I recalled the words of my friends in the meetings, "If you aren't sure you're an alcoholic, go try some controlled drinking." And I knew what I needed to do. I needed to try some controlled drinking.

How do I explain all that to you, normal doctor guy?

I couldn't, so I said, "I thought because it was so bad before, I would drink differently this time. I wanted to prove I wasn't an alcoholic." It was the most honest answer I had ever given a doctor. I yearned for help this time. I was so tired.

He didn't respond to my answer, but instead asked, "Are you med-compliant?" which is code for "Do you take what's prescribed?"

"Yes, I am." I said, resigned. *This fucking guy doesn't care.*

He scribbled more lies on his page and looked right at me, stating, "You were living in a house full of dog feces and urine." He seemed to desire an explanation, again.

"I know. It was raining a lot. I told you. I couldn't get outside."

"Why are you cutting your arms again, Janelle?"

"Because I like watching the blood come up," I said, pausing before saying, "It feels *manageable*."

"Are you still drinking, Janelle?" He was simply moving through his checklist of questions. He didn't respond directly to a single one of my answers. I wondered why I bothered with these doctors.

"No. Yes. Well, I didn't today." And that was true, although last night's alcohol was probably drifting out of my pores.

He snapped the file shut, leaned forward, and asked loudly, "Are you always this difficult?"

I sat stunned and terrified. I knew I was in bad shape, so I had promised myself to tell the doctor the absolute truth. I did so. *And now he thinks I'm crazier than ever. He hates me because he thinks I'm messing with him, and yet, I am being honest. I am trying to get help.*

Is my truth more horrible than my lies?

His reaction confused me, and I began wondering if I was telling the truth at all.

Maybe I thought I was being honest, but I was actually lying? Maybe I am truly insane? The truth was melding with the lies, and I couldn't tell him what was happening in my mind because *I just told him pure truth and he's asking why I'm being so difficult.*

He prescribed more and different pills.

· · ·

On my way home from the loony bin that night, I bought a pint of Ancient Age whiskey and a pack of Pall Malls, just like Alice used to smoke. I paid for them with the twenty dollars my mother had given me. The next morning, I started thinking of my mother the second my eyes opened. I saw her face and smile and felt her hug as she handed me the twenty dollars I had said I needed for groceries. I thought of my children. *My mom, she was always so kind.* I promised myself I would visit them that day.

When I opened her door, Rocket, who was two, ran to me as fast as he could, and I went down on my knees again to hug and kiss and hold him. He grabbed my face and declared, "Mama, home!"

I couldn't even respond. I couldn't tell him I would stay. I could not tell my boy when I'd be back again. I didn't even bother.

Ava was six. She kept a box by her bed of trinkets and notes I had written her, from rehab and elsewhere. When she missed me, she read them, and maybe cried. Mac told me about the box to get me to sober up and come home.

Instead, I drew pictures during art therapy and sent them to her, pictures of rainbows and houses and suns, the same stupid drawings I'd made as a kid when all the other kids drew more interesting things. Those birds that were just two curved lines connecting in the middle. The house with the flowers along the outside and a tree in the corner and a big yellow sun with lines of orange.

I fucking hate art, I thought. *But I'm glad I can send her pictures of the home I can't make.*

During breaks at the outpatient center we stood outside in total silence, smoking. The victim Olympics were over in that place, the pecking order gone, the hierarchy of sickness no longer fun. Nobody cared anymore. The souls around there were too lost, too poor to posture, too tired to fight. We showed up unwashed. We showed up stained, dosed on legal drugs, to tell them what they needed to hear. When we talked, it was only to compare release dates.

Every day I watched with agitated jealousy the people who got out. The staff there had no personal stories of salvation, no hopeful anecdotes or phrases. In fact, I was convinced they preferred us dead or in jail. They recited canned platitudes and worn-out "inspirations," checked little boxes, and fed us out of Styrofoam trays on a pushcart. I refused to eat anything except Snickers from the vending machine. I never took my hood off.

• • •

On the day I graduated Lightweight Loony Bin, I headed straight to my outlaw friend's trailer to celebrate.

Six days later, I took a shit in a bag and put it in my trunk. The toilet in her trailer was broken and I needed to go to the bathroom, so I placed the bag in the toilet and went. Then I found myself in possession of a bag of shit, but telling people around me I was carrying such a thing was out of the question, although perhaps they would not have found it so odd. Absolutely stranger things had happened in that trailer park—for example, the man who wore masking tape on his head, or the man who stood in his parking spot directing nonexistent traffic and protesting capitalism. Still, the situation struck me as rather difficult to explain, so I concealed the bag in a larger bag, and then hid it in my trunk.

I then got *distracted* and left it there for probably two days, which is two days longer than anyone should have feces in her trunk.

I could have walked four minutes down to the gas station to relieve myself, or the fast food joint right next to the gas station, or I could have even shit in the dirt. I could have thrown the bag away in the dumpster twenty feet from the trailer. Just about any plan was better than the one I came up with, but after six days of what I called "maintenance whiskey"—which is when you're drinking around the clock simply to kill the shakes—things get weird.

Every idea was a three a.m. idea, and nobody was left to question them.

• • •

My days became maintenance whiskey and trips between my apartment and the outlaw's trailer. At her place, hippies and Hank III fans with questionable dental hygiene occasionally showed up with drugs I couldn't afford, and I would marvel at their generosity. They would show up with soma and ecstasy, and I would take all that was offered. If I had recently refilled my Xanax and Ambien, I'd take that too. Somebody would come by with Percocet or cocaine, and I'd take that as well.

I drank every day to kill the shakes. I did drugs when they came around but I had no money or energy left to find them. I was on a pure Ancient Age and Pall Mall maintenance plan.

Yet no matter what I consumed, I got no relief. I found no calm. I was driven by a compulsion beyond my mind, heart, love of my kids, or life itself. I held on each day to a vague memory of the peace alcohol once brought, of the way it blanketed my throat and belly with warm relief, my whole heart, actually, the way it connected me to others and my life and future. The way it took me straight to serenity, to comfort in my mind, in the universe. In those meetings they told me, "One day, alcohol will stop working for you." I scribbled those words in the front of the big book they gave me, thinking, "My God, that cannot possibly be true." In that trailer, I learned it was true. I learned that one day, I would grow physically drunk—stumbling, vomiting, slurring my words—but my mind would remain clean, stripped, and still starving. The relief alcohol once brought would never return. Like a rat on a wheel, I would frantically chase a drifting memory.

On the morning I woke up in my apartment with not a single

dollar or drop of booze, I took a swig of vanilla extract from my kitchen cupboard and shuddered, thinking, *At least it isn't face toner.* While I was sleeping, my mother had dropped off on my porch a package of sliced turkey breast and loaf of bread, with a note attached that read, "I love you, Janelle!" With a smiley face. I couldn't eat the food. The smiley face broke my fucking heart. I detoxed and shivered until I got my unemployment check, then went back to the trailer.

· · ·

Four days later, my eyes rolled back in my head after I took a pull of Ancient Age. I was back on that maintenance plan. Someone put me in my beige Ford Taurus, a gift from Grandma Bonny, who, at that moment, was dying of dementia and old age without my attention, two counties away. They drove me to the emergency room and dropped me off, leaving me with my keys and car in the lot, finding their own way home so I could leave when they released me.

I fell asleep on the hospital bed, and when I woke, disoriented and restless, I looked around at the patients next to me, at the people surrounding them, and I noticed my only companion was a new bracelet around my wrist. I tried to rip the oxygen tubes out of my nose, but a nurse materialized and leaned down right in my face, slowly articulating in one long, compassionate snarl, *"Do you want to live?"*

I nodded. "Then focus on your breathing," she said with equal severity. "Because your brain is not getting enough oxygen." She was about fifty years old and quite apparently fed up with my kind. Her tone was bulletproof. It didn't even occur to me to disobey her. I nodded and lay back and focused on deep breaths and the people bustling around me. I was in a spot in the hospital where they didn't even close the curtains. I looked down and noticed I had no shoes, and my skirt was ripped.

Eventually the doctor arrived and announced he was sending me back to the loony bin because I had so many substances in my body it was "obvious you were trying to commit suicide."

"Oh no, doctor, I'm not trying to kill myself," I explained. "I do this every day."

He gazed at me in silence. I thought he was going to say something, but he only looked at me with resigned disgust and signed my release papers. He handed them to me and walked out. On my way to the exit, the nurse approached me in the hallway and said, "You know, girl, you're gonna die." I nodded and kept walking, as did she. It wasn't news to me.

In the parking lot, I looked down at the bracelet and wondered when I had become a person without companions in an emergency room. I had a mother, father, husband, and children, but they had no idea where I was and had long since stopped expecting such information. I called my mother yet again.

"I almost overdosed. This has to be the end."

I meant it no more or less than every other time I meant it.

My family rallied and booked me into St. Helena, one of the oldest and most revered treatment centers in California. My mother and her friends from church cleaned up the horrifying mess of my apartment and wrote me encouraging notes in a little red book of thoughts and prayers. My mother gave me the little book on her first visit, telling me how when she was cleaning my apartment she had found some little shoes and a shirt I had bought at the thrift store for Rocket, carefully folded on my counter, and when she saw them she had dropped her head into her arms and wept, because she knew in that moment how hard I was trying, and how I was dying.

In the new rehab, I didn't care how I compared to you, and I didn't care if you were sicker than me or not, and I didn't care what you did in the 1980s. *Just leave me the fuck alone.* The doctors there explained that I was in "late stage alcoholism" and my liver was not looking good. *Ah, whatever. Where can I have a cigarette?* It was a nonsmoking facility, so I had to walk up a hill behind the hospital and hide in the bushes to smoke as often as I could. I hung out with a dude who drank hand sanitizer once in jail. At our first AA meeting in the town of St. Helena, I considered making a break for the Chevron across the street, thinking I could hitchhike home, before recalling yet another glitch in my plan: I had been evicted and thus had no home. I figured the outlaw's trailer was most likely still standing. *I'd always be welcome there.* Like Alice, I had no real hope of recovery.

But on the second weekend, my mother brought Ava and Rocket to visit me, and Ava handed me a piece of paper with a poem she had written. It read:

March 8, 2008
The skies are so blue
The sun is shining.
I want to see you.
I miss you so much
I really do
Why do you ever want to leave me
ever in these days?

We do not have to be in this world.
We can be flying on unicorns every day.
It seems so difficult every single day.
Why do you have to be gone?
I love you so much.
It seems I haven't seen you for three years.
I'm so happy
I don't want to leave you ever.

I read it and knew there was no choice but to stay. My attitude transformed with the words "We do not have to be in this world." My baby was willing to go anywhere, anywhere to be with me. How could I not listen? How could I not go with her? My heart ached for that place, too.

My mind circled my children's faces every morning when I awoke, and each day in group, and when we sat in the cafeteria pushing food around our plastic trays. I wrote my children letters and completed every soul-searching therapy assignment. I attended the mindfulness meditations, wrote in my journal, and the whole rehab knew I was going to make it. If rehabs gave a "most likely to succeed" award, I would have won it. I left healthy and energized, with my counselor's words echoing in my brain: "I've been here a long time, Janelle, and I know who's going to make it. *You* are going to make it."

Mac picked me up on my last day. Each night in rehab, I had stood in the hallway leaning against a wall, discussing with him on a pay phone my great turnaround—fighting, crying, planning—until we agreed to reunite our family at his parents' ranch. He and his friends finished moving my belongings out of the sick apartment and into a storage unit, and on the evening Mac and I drove to his family's home, where he was living and we had lived many years before, I realized I was as happy and clean and full of love as the day we brought our first baby home.

Six days after that night, six days after the night my children squealed and laughed and jumped into my arms because we were finally together again, a family, I told Mac I needed to go get some bread.

I returned to the trailer where I nearly overdosed. It was my twenty-ninth birthday.

• • •

Nine months later, in December of 2008, Mac let me know he was finished. With me, with the marriage. I knew it was true. While he spoke, I drove north on Highway 5 on my way home from the Anza Borrego desert. I had gone south with a friend in a three a.m. idea, but I drank all my money and expended all my gas. I considered pawning my laptop, but instead called Mac. He deposited fifty dollars in my account, just enough for gas to get home. On my way, I called to thank him.

I tried everything, but he was done. I groveled. I cried and begged, but the more I scrambled, the more calmly he spoke. "Janelle, I'm done waiting for you." I wished he would at least rage. There's room for negotiation in anger. But there's nothing in neutrality. There's no game in surrender.

I had lost him.

He had not taken a drink since March of 2007. When we would have lunch together, I'd suggest we order Coronas, and he'd say "No, thanks. One is too many and a thousand never enough." He had now found sobriety in those rooms for drunks I knew were full of lies.

Too bad I'm not like them, I'd think.

Back in Woodland, I weaseled into my mother's house through lies and manipulation, convincing her I was sober. She posted a list of house rules on the refrigerator as if I were seventeen years old. Curfew, medicine compliance, abstinence from alcohol. I wasn't doing drugs any more, and my outlaw friend was forced to return to *her* parents. They too thought she was going to die. From my mother's house, I managed to pull it together just enough to return to my job at the law firm.

No longer drinking daily, I clenched my fists through three dry days, then drank again. I'd drink for two or three or four days straight, then, after a night of withdrawal, I'd maybe make it to work. Then I would swear it off. Then three more sober days would pass, and it would all start over again. I emerged from each binge in confused, gray hopelessness, but soon I didn't care anymore.

I couldn't get relief. I couldn't help but try.

My neighbor, a young man whose kindness seemed limitless, offered me a shot of Dilaudid one day. I watched him flick the tip of the needle. "Why do you do that?"

"To remove air bubbles. If one gets in your vein, it will kill you." He laughed, as if that were funny.

Here was the suicide rock star vibe I used to admire from afar. *How tough. How cool.* I didn't feel tough. I didn't feel cool. He tied my arm and pulled it and plunged the syringe. Red-orange light coursed through me. I dropped onto the couch and didn't move for three hours. I understood the appeal immediately, but I didn't want to die.

I did it only three more times.

• • •

I saw my children for a few moments two or three days a week, but only at my mother's house. I didn't take them places. I didn't make them meals. I didn't stick around.

I have reasons to go, kids. I'm sorry. I have reasons I can't be there. The alcohol has stopped working. I have to keep trying.

I never bought the replacement silk streamer. Ava never asked. She still had the box by her bed. I missed her graduation from primary school. My mother sent me photos, and I showed them to the people I was with. "Look at my little girl!" I beamed.

In the throes of the morning, I heard Rocket's voice again.

"Mama, home."

But I knew I couldn't stay.

11

I FOUND GOD IN A LEAF BLOWER, AND I FUCKING HATE LEAF BLOWERS

Nothing happened on March 5, 2009, that had not happened a thousand times before. I woke at nine or ten or eleven a.m. in a bed in my mother's house, where I was still living, under a big window with no screen and blinds that didn't shut all the way because I had broken them. Sometimes I needed to crawl in through the window because I smelled like alcohol and was lying.

The sun beat me through the blinds that wouldn't shut, relentless against my pounding head. I was supposed to be at work, but I had called in sick again. They were probably going to let me go soon. I could feel I was riding the last few feet of their tolerance. My mother drove Ava and Rocket to school that morning. Mac, my mother, father, grandparents, and in-laws were working. Everybody was working. Everybody was away in the world, living their day.

I sweated and shook, closed and opened my eyes in the fog and pain behind them. It was nothing. One more time. One more day. *Here we go, old friend.*

I rolled over and looked at the pile of books on the bedside table—literature, some self-help stuff. An AA book. A glass half full of water. A journal I hadn't written in for years. I rolled over and stared at those books and felt a burn in my eyes and brain as something sunk into the realm of knowing. I closed my eyes, flipped onto my back, then to the other side, and back again— enraged, desperate, and agitated, moving for the sake of passing the time, to shake the frenetic feeling from my blood. I stared at the pile of books again, and when I saw them this time, for some reason, I saw the end of my life.

I saw it roll out in front of me like a carpet might unroll, the years unfolding one at a time down a street or giant hallway, and I saw the end of it. I saw it with my whole body and felt it with every shred of vision I had in that condition.

I would die a hopeless, useless alcoholic, and there was nothing I could do about it.

That was the part that killed me right there: I had no defense. I was out of ideas. I had no strategy, and I had no person or thing left to blame. I was dying. Or dead. My children and family were gone because they should be. My family had disintegrated, my life was in ruins, because I had no idea how to *live it*. I couldn't take one more step sober, and I couldn't take one more step drunk. I accepted that end. I accepted it in my bones.

I always had a next move. As soon as *this one thing* happened I would be happy, and my life would work, and I would stop drinking. As soon as *this one thing* happened, I would manage my drinking. But I had exhausted every plan, every move, every belief. Every therapist, every geographic rearrangement, every theory, every book, every rehab, every medication. I tried love and unlove and job and no job, rock-n-roll and hiding out, desk jobs and grad school and no school. I tried babies and friends and no babies and no friends. I tried living alone and living with others. I tried talking through it and living lies in silence. I tried churches and swearing with oaths and getting naked with women in teepees. I tried cutting it out of me with blades. I tried begging the gods. I tried retreats. I tried gurus. I tried pills.

And it all failed.

I failed.

I drank. That was my future. No matter what, I would always drink again.

Leveled under that window, I wanted nothing back. I knew I had no footing to demand a return of the people or life I loved.

I suppose the bottle killed me that day—the fighter, the one who kicks and screams and rails against powerlessness. It killed the one who hated the tweakers, who wanted to be better than others, who whined and cried—postured and fought—about what she "deserved." Those Nikes. A more intellectually challenging job. Respect. It killed the one who resented my father for being gone those years, and it killed the one who strategized, polished things up, set it up *one more time*. Above all, it killed my self-pity.

I saw in that moment I had already received everything I "deserved," everything I had built, brick by brick, one day at a time.

I would always drink again, and alcohol was my God.

The truth descended like a veil of black around me, pushed out in every direction of my mind and the room. I heard lawnmowers outside, people tending to their yards, leaf blowers—those fucking things—people driving by. I heard a dog yap here and there, somebody's pet that was cared for, fed, walked. People on their way to work, maybe visiting a friend, an errand, a quick stop home for lunch. I heard the world right outside that window. I heard it happening, moving, bustling, alive, and for the first time in my life I wanted more than anything to be a part of that world. I wanted to wake up and know where I would be that evening. I wanted to pick my children up from school. I wanted to take my trash out, answer mail, get up and make coffee, go to work, and have it all mean something. I wanted to find some satisfaction in these tasks, these tiny stupid life things we do.

I wanted to be a wife. Mother. Employee. Friend. I didn't want my kids back, my family, my husband. I didn't want anything but to live one single day free. I wanted freedom.

I wanted freedom.

The bottle killed me that day. I found God in a leaf blower, got up, and walked into the sound.

•   •   •

I never would have thought to look there, in total defeat. I never would have thought giving up would bring me to life, that surrender would be my hope. It's almost funny. All those rehabs were about bolstering me, telling me I was capable and smart and worth more. It was always about arming myself and fighting, *beating this alcoholism.* We talked about my childhood and what I deserved and didn't get and how that wounded and broke me.

Well, that's nice, but it still doesn't give me a solution, does it? I'm still not showing up to my kid's birthday celebrations, and I'm still somehow unable to silence the voices that insist, "Go ahead. Take a drink. It's going to be different this time." I still can't seem to make myself change no matter what I throw at it or how hard I want it. I always go back to the booze, and the drugs, and the same nonsense of my entire life. I know my problem inside out and backwards and all the catch-

phrases, and Jung and I are best friends and DBT and CBT and all the rest. I get it all, I know it all—I am no fool. But you're trying to fix a broken brain with the broken brain, and if that isn't insanity then I don't know what is.

When I died at the bottom of that bottle I abandoned the fight. I stopped caring what my brain said, realized my life was what it was because *I was running it*. My ego, my thoughts, my plans, and my "needs." I spent years trying to manage it all, trying to control and fix things. If I thought it, it was true. Even though the results of that reliance were disastrous, it never occurred to me I could ignore it, that I could rely on something else, something outside of me, something that perhaps wanted better for me than shitting in bags and loneliness.

Of course I did not figure these things out on my own. From that bed, I went to the only place I knew would accept me, the only place that might understand, the place I had gone for two years without ever staying sober, the place I'd go on cold nights after a bottle of whiskey, where I would bang on the table and tell them they were full of shit, the place where the people put a hand on my shoulder and said, "Keep coming back, Janelle."

I was taught these things by a washed-up ex-gutter drunk who had spent a good portion of his life shooting cocaine in a refrigerator box. He was in his late forties, with a wife and two children. He had blond hair and glasses and shimmering blue eyes. I met him while I was smoking out in front of the alcoholics' meeting hall. He watched me tell my story of woe to a poor sot next to me, but when he got up, he handed me a piece of paper and said, "You need help? Call me tomorrow." And I did.

I was taught this by the group of drunks I had been hanging

out with for years but could never hear or see because I wasn't like them yet. I wasn't leveled yet. My ideas were better than theirs. Until that day I was rearranged, ran out of ideas, and lost faith in my ability to make new ones. I showed up broken, fumbling for words, and they didn't care. They offered me a new perception.

Universe, take it. Take it all. God, whatever. I don't know about God. I don't know if he or she or it is up there looking at me or sent me that desperation and surrender. I don't know a single thing about any of that, but I know when I died, when I stepped out of the way and my bones knew I was utterly powerless, help started flooding in like the man from Sebastopol who happened upon us on the beach on an island in the Caribbean, took us home, and didn't murder us.

I got some help from that washed-up gutter drunk because somebody helped him. He didn't tell me warm and beautiful things. He said I was a dead woman. He said, "We're all in various stages of 'my case is different.'" He said I was just another drunk.

He told me, "Janelle, in your case, if it looks like a duck and quacks like a duck, it's probably a fire hydrant." His words taught me I had an unreliable brain, and it would always lead me to another drink. For the first time, I realized my perceptions were wrong, and if I wanted to live, I had to get a new set of eyes. I called him Good News Jack, because he was full of news that sounded mean and awful except it was setting me free, and I knew it. It sounded like this: "If your ideas worked so well, what the fuck are you doing here?"

It sounded like this, too: "We aren't looking for another idea, another mental construct, more mind candy. We're looking for a rebuilding, access to a power that can save your sorry ass."

And I believed him, because I had nothing else. I decided I'd

give his suggestions a try because I had exhausted all other options, and I figured at least this way there was *potential* for change.

When I told Good News Jack I had a bit of a shady past with
God, he said, "Janelle, if you're sittin' there and your ass is on
fire, and I walk up with a fire hose, offering to put it out, are
you going to tell me, 'Hold up. No thanks. I don't believe in fire
hoses?' No, motherfucker, of course you're not. You're going to
say 'Yes, please' and hope it works."

I said "Yes, please" and hoped it worked. I did not think it
would. Why would I? Nothing ever worked. I fully expected to
drink again. I even told that room of ex-drunks: "Look, I'm going to do everything your book says so that when it fails, I can
drink again with a clear conscience."

•   •   •

Good News Jack told me that people trying to live on their own
and failing desperately is an ancient process, and some of them
are lucky enough to fail so badly they die while breathing, and
surrender brings them to God, or life, which is one and the
same. I'm not talking about Jesus or baptism or any other rit-
ual thing. I'm talking about really, truthfully not being able to
live, and somehow having the ability to recognize it, admit it,
and try something new. I'm talking about a rebirth that happens
from the bottom up, not as a great new belief, but as a complete
rearrangement from a flattening, when everything you thought
you knew to be true, that you thought you knew about yourself,
turns out to be wrong. A decimation. Leveled, and rebuilt. With
new eyes. New ground. New power.

They say many of the mystics had that experience. I was not a mystic. St. Francis was, and he was something of a drunken loser. He too found himself miserable. He wrote that when you "die unto self you awaken to eternal life." Not heaven. Fuck heaven. Fuck the afterlife. I had enough of that as a kid in church wondering if the Big Guy could ever overlook last night. Eternal life, as in literally the element of life that is eternal. The power. The energy. The pulse holding the stars. The pull of the planets. The universe beyond human comprehension. The thing that makes me alive beyond breath.

Maybe we are just masses of meaningless flesh and blood, but it sure as hell doesn't feel that way when I really feel deep into my gut, or look at the ocean or a redwood in Mendocino County, or smell the breath of my baby. Those damn stars glaring down at me. All the clichés. Tell me we know how it works. Tell me science explains it all. Tell me we haven't just chosen the God of Reason over the God of Mystery and that we're stronger and braver and more intellectually sound because we don't have "faith" like those pathetic believers. We're stronger, I know. But that faith simply has a different polish.

And anyway I didn't have faith in any damn thing other than that I was not God, and my brain was not reliable for a whole lot beyond making a cup of coffee or doing a math equation or planning my day or a trip or solving problems of the intellect.

But my problems have never been of the intellect. Mine were of the heart and bones.

My brain can't bring peace. It can't bring life. For that, I had to let go and hover over the reef, traveling into the black—a nothing, a tiny nothing paddling and kicking across the expanse of blue, taking deep breaths and heading for the shore, all I know of safety, buoyed by ancient waters pulled forever by a cratered moon.

PART THREE

12

THERE ARE THREE TYPES OF MOTHERS IN THE WORLD—I AM NONE OF THEM

Alcoholism killed me three weeks before my thirtieth birthday. Rocket was three and Ava was seven, and I had no idea how to drive either of them to school. They attended private schools in Davis, my old college town, the one I used to frequent with my rhinestone Playboy bunny diaper bag. I neither chose nor paid for those schools and had visited them only a handful of times. Perhaps this should have embarrassed me, but two months before that I was drinking bottom-shelf half pints and smoking Pall Malls alone in a beige Ford Taurus (the very same Taurus I now drove to pick up my adorable kids at their adorable schools). I knew embarrassing, and *this was not it.*

The front doors of their schools were kept locked, and I always wondered if it was to keep the kids in or the riffraff out. Except there was no riffraff. This was Davis. There were merely "nice" people in sustainably sourced shoes. On further thought, I realized I was the riffraff.

We had to use a code to enter the blue-trimmed, glass-walled fortress, but I didn't know it the first time I tried to get in. I stood at the door of Ava's school yanking and observing the button box until the receptionist took pity on me and opened the door, deciding, I suppose, to let the riffraff in. "Hi! Thank you," I said. "I'm Ava's mother."

"Oh! Hello! Heard so much about you!" She smiled. I smiled too, thinking about the layers of potential meaning in her sentence.

"Yes. It's nice to be here," I said.

"Very nice to meet you," the principal said, peeking her head from around the corner. As she shook my hand, I thought for a moment she was gaining a visual on the dirtbag absentee mother. *Fine with me. Take a look.*

I had never signed the attendance forms on the front desk. I didn't know where to park, or where their classrooms were, or what the hell "car line" was. I didn't know about cubbies and folders. I had never met their teachers.

And there were other parents *everywhere*, specimens in capris and cargo shorts who had been navigating Scholastic order forms for a long time. Moms and dads who had never missed a parent-teacher conference, let alone a kindergarten graduation, and certainly not because the bottle rendered them useless. But I didn't feel shame, even when the best of them strolled past me. I was too busy enjoying the scenery, a thousand things I'd never seen before.

Until then, I had spent my entire adult life drunk, in the aftermath of drunk, in the pursuit of drunk, in the avoidance of drunk, or in the precarious hell of in-between drunk. In this condition, life is not "dealt with" or "worked through" or "handled," even during periods of "sobriety." There is no sober.

There is occasional physical detoxification, but there is no mental function of the un-addicted. Or there is, but it's on the primal instinctual level—as in, eat, pee, shit, work, bathe.

Basically, I was alcohol's bitch.

This makes for a rather exciting life if one manages to not die and stay sober. The world around me was cast suddenly in Technicolor, and for a moment, the dull grays turned into vivid light.

I was a child those first few months of sobriety. I was a child skipping through the halls at recess, doing cannonballs into a swimming pool, or crawling into bed on Christmas Eve. I was a kid in fucking Disneyland.

Mac and I saw each other often, but I wasn't toiling for our reunification. Instead, I was chasing sobriety like a desperate lover. I knew I had no ground for demands on Mac anyway, though I yearned for our family. I remember watching him with our babies in those early weeks of sobriety—the way he hoisted Rocket onto his shoulders, and brushed Ava's hair—*this is my family*, I'd think. And it was so fucking beautiful. The way he held their hands and tied their shoes and sat with them at night on the couch for as long as they wanted. I was watching a father with his kids. How pure it felt after the life I had been living. How warm, like coming home, like crawling into your own bed after two weeks in motel rooms. I wanted in with my whole heart, but it was not for me to decide.

Mac held me at a safe distance, dropping by sometimes, meeting me for coffee. He came by my mother's house on my birthday after I got sober. He sat at the other end of her dining table, observing me quietly. He had picked me up a couple of Grateful Dead patches from a record store in Monterey. "I thought you could sew them onto your hoodie," he said. He didn't stay for cake, and I felt a little slighted.

When I asked him about it, he said, "I don't know if I want anything to do with you, Janelle." I understood that. I wasn't sure I wanted anything to do with myself.

Two months later, Mac agreed to take the kids with me to Half Moon Bay, a heavenly coastal town near San Francisco where the cypress trees and dunes turn life into the soft roar of merciless waves. When we were almost to Highway 1, I mentioned I couldn't see well through the dirty windshield. Mac suggested with brilliant nonchalance that I "use the washer fluid." When I curled my lip at him to say, "God, that's rich," he informed me he had added fluid to my car when we stopped for gas. "Holy shit!" I said, forgetting entirely this was a typical adult activity.

I clicked it on, and it worked. I clicked it on, and it *worked*! I turned the dial and water came out, and the wipers moved, sweeping the bug guts and dust right out of my way.

"Hey kids! It's *raining*!" I yelled. I thought I was damn funny, and so did they, and I remember our delight. I remember feeling capable and alive and real. I had a car with working parts. I had a family. I had a body and air to breathe and I was free to drive to the beach and make stupid jokes and my kids would laugh, because I'm their mother and they think I'm wonderful and funny and nobody cares.

Nobody sees me. I am unseen. I'm just one among all of you. I can use a lawnmower on a Saturday morning. I can punch the numbers in the fancy school door. I can show up for parent-teacher conferences—but more importantly, I can miss them sometimes and still look you in the eye, because I really did forget. I was not taking lines of cocaine off the hallway mirror and remembering the meeting in the quicksand of the morning.

I knew when he told me about the washer fluid that he was going to try, that he was still willing to help me, to show up for us again. He had told me once, "Janelle, I will always help you again," though I thought perhaps that promise had expired. That we, I suppose, had expired.

We never formally reunited. That was not our way. After we met for the first time, we were *together*. When were apart, it was only in body. And when he said, "I don't know why, but I really believe you're different this time," I knew we had never left the domain of our love. Although it was twisted up and weird and unspeakable—built on bad decisions and slightly better ones—it was ours.

And for people like us, who have shivered in the emptiness of stone-cold addiction, the warmth of a family bed need not be discussed. Its existence is enough. One simply crawls in.

●   ●   ●

Good News Jack and I met three or four times a week either in his backyard or in the tiny office at his house, where I would sit facing him alongside the family computer and an abandoned treadmill. He would wedge a chair under the doorknob while his five-year-old daughter body-slammed it trying to get in, and I tried to understand the strange things he'd say, like: "If nothing changes, nothing changes," and that I was "wrong until further notice."

Under normal circumstances, I would have told him to go fuck himself, but I was fresh out of comebacks. So I took actions

I may or may not have agreed with, and often barely understood, because Jack stood in front of me a free man, and I knew he drank like I drank and for the same reasons. I would have followed him anywhere to gain what he had.

And yet, we seemed to speak little of alcohol, and he only mentioned the "tools" I learned in rehab to cackle about how they "never work for chronic alkies like us." He had no interest in "phone lists" (which, for the uninitiated, are lists of phone numbers of sober friends we are supposed to call when we're about to relapse. The idea is that we never leave home without the list, and just when we're about to catapult ourselves into sheer disaster, we call somebody to talk us out of it. My problem was I never believed I was about to catapult myself into sheer disaster. I believed I was going to *prove I could drink like a lady this time*, whatever the hell that meant. While I did not see a need to trouble my rehab friends with my own innocuous drinking, I did occasionally wonder if I should give them a jingle to help them learn how to drink better).

Good News Jack wouldn't even feign interest in my "relapse triggers" or complex emotional pain rooted in the tenuous attachments of my inner child. He did, however, grow giddy at the prospect of dissecting at an atomic level the manifestations of my self-centeredness. When I'd protest, he'd say, "Do you really want your life to change, or do you want to remain an asshole with better consequences?" The most shocking part was I found myself admitting I wanted to remain an asshole, and in fact had never heard myself articulated so succinctly.

Saying it out loud felt like cold water on a hot day, some longed-for honesty in a parched mouth. And when I admitted such things, his face would beam, and he'd shout, "Yes! Janelle!

That is the honesty you need to stay sober. No more self-delusion. No more bullshit. You're a selfish fuck!" He'd roar with laughter, as if being a selfish fuck was the happiest thought he'd ever entertained.

"That's what's killing you, you know? All of us—we're all whistling past the graveyard, sayin', 'Well it ain't gonna happen to me.'" He took a drag of his Marlboro Red while I visualized myself in all those rehabs—the throw blanket, the Nikes, the promises to my children—whistling how I was "fine," pretending, posturing, but truly believing my own lies. *I was in the graveyard setting up a Buddha statue and judging tweakers.*

"So what do we do?" I was on the edge of my damn seat.

"Recognize that you, *you* are the problem. You! You're the problem! You've always been the fucking problem! Isn't that wonderful?"

"I have never heard anything more wonderful, Jack," I said flatly, rolling my eyes.

"Because there is power there, you fool. Power. That's what you need, what you've always needed, right? You aren't a victim! You try to arrange your life and control everyone to fix your inner self. It never works. You try harder. People hate you more. All the while you're looking at the damn problem!" He laughed again.

When he spoke words like this, it sounded like a symphony, as if every word was a note falling one by one into a song so painfully beautiful I would sometimes sit silently across from him with tears falling down my face. I couldn't explain it—what his words meant, how they pulled the truth from me, or how they cracked open the catacombs of my soul. They seemed to send bright light into my most hideous corners of shame and deceit. He was right. It felt like hope.

"You never said what we do," I said.

"Get the fuck out of yourself, Janelle. That's what we do."

In therapy, it had always been about me—my childhood, my parents, my thoughts, my goals. But when I told Jack my perception of things, he'd say, "You know, Janelle, you could just jump off the crazy train rather than riding it all the way to the bitter end." And then he would say that thing about the ducks and fire hydrant and tell me *again* to think of others, which was another shoddy plan as far as I was concerned.

One day, when the gleeful dust of new sobriety had settled, I was trying to make Ava and Rocket sandwiches but was somehow failing. I stood in my mother's kitchen behind a cutting board, staring at bread and turkey, feeling like I might explode from restlessness. I told the kids I'd be right back and went outside to call Good News Jack.

"I just feel like shit, Jack. I do not feel 'good' at all." I was angry and accusatory, as if his sobriety plan had already let me down.

Without hesitation, he answered, "I never promised you'd feel good. I promised you'd never have to drink again." I thought about that, about not feeling good and simply dealing with it, about diminishing the importance of "feelings"—as in, sometimes you feel like trash, and you carry on without fixing it. He was a well of revolutionary information.

"What the hell are you doing right now anyway?" he asked.

"I was supposed to make the kids lunch, but I freaked out."

"Go fucking make them lunch and stop thinking about yourself." Then he hung up on me. He had a way that really made me feel loved.

Over time, I realized Jack had given me a job: be in the world, try to be of service to others, and clean up the damage of my past. When I hung out there, I lived in the sunshine. I lived in the knowing that I had been rearranged, and the booze obsession had left me, and I was free to go about the world, to live like any other semi-functioning whacko on the planet.

• • •

"So, did your daughter get into G.A.T.E.?" she asked, stopping me in the hallway as I headed to Ava's second grade classroom.

I had recently learned that standard behavior around Ava's school was to move from the fancy private school to a fancy public school when the child reached third grade, to take advantage of "Gifted and Talented Education," which was where all the superior kids were headed. The woman standing before me was their captain. She had adopted *her* children from another country, which also made her captain of the white liberals. She was around fifty, with black, gray-streaked hair, and owned an impressive array of Tevas. She had dark brown eyes and a brow that threatened to destroy me if I said something out of line. Sadly for me, I rarely knew where that line was.

"No, she didn't," I said, shrugging.

She jolted, tilting slightly forward and raising her eyebrows in shock, as if I had just told her my dog was bleeding to death in my car. After the initial blow wore off, her face registered thinly veiled disgust, but it wasn't until the pity settled into her eyes that I felt her derision, and thought with a stab that maybe my daughter wasn't as smart as I thought she was. I recalled the day my mother took her to the exam, and how I didn't go with her, and I wondered if I should have. I considered having her retake it, and then remembered I didn't care.

My kid is fine. I am fine. She's smart, and I'm sort of smart. For whatever reason, she didn't pass the test. I looked up and shrugged again.

"Oh, well. That's too bad," the lady stammered, straightening her North Face vest.

"Is it too bad?" I answered, smiling, before I turned and walked away.

I signed my daughter out, chatted with the receptionist, held my girl's hand on our way to the car to make sure she was safe, and all these actions felt like tiny miracles. I gave a death glare to the woman when I saw her in the parking lot, because I was sober, not Jesus.

On my way home, I realized with a sort of stunned despondency that the only purpose of that exchange was for Captain Gifted to determine if I was as respectable a mother as she was. I had temporarily forgotten adults acted like that, although I should have recognized it immediately as the "healthy person" version of "Who's the sickest in the room?"

After that day, I began to notice that mothers were an extremely strange bunch, and for my own amusement, I began categorizing them based on money, parenting choices, and politics. Captain Gifted was Type I: The Put-Together Enlightened Mother Who Is Definitely Better Than Me. This type of mother is a living spreadsheet. She's read all essential theories of parenting, her spice cabinet is alphabetized, and her bottom sheets are folded in the linen closet. She probably has a PhD and drives a Prius. She definitely composts and wears a lot of fleece purchased from REI. She looks at motherhood as a complex responsibility to be calculated and controlled to achieve optimum outcomes. If I were *as proficient as she is*, my outcomes would also shine like beacons of hope in a dark forest. She will remind me of this frequently, but not directly, through earnest and heartfelt "suggestions," which she will view as charitable and I will view as a direct assault on all that is good in the world.

Then there is Type II: The Why Is Everybody Making a Big Deal Out of This Mother, who stays at home with her two (possibly three) children and has any situation handled in her skinny jeans, strategically undone hair, and never-chipped pedicures. She met her husband while living abroad and posts a lot of photos of herself drinking red wine on a patio. She says things like "I make my own cashew butter" and "I never stop eating," which is confusing, because I wasn't as skinny as her during the skinny days I reflect upon with great yearning. One imagines this is made possible by her deeply spiritual attachment to yoga combined with a diet of kale smoothies drunk out of mason jars and vegan gluten-free zucchini bread—which she brings to our playdate at the park, where we sit on a handmade vintage quilt while she coos gentle directions to her children in one of the Romance languages.

And then there is Type III: The Children Are Everything, Harried Busy-Bee Mother. Under no circumstances may I drop an F-bomb in this one's presence. She's on every PTA, preschool, and church board of directors, and not to be helpful. She's in it to win. *You think this preschool runs itself?* she seems to ask. *Lady, they're just crafts*, I think. "Organize the pipe cleaners, bitches!" she screams, but only with her grim eyes. She will spend a solid hour discussing whether the teacher's gift card should come from Target or Nordstrom or Starbucks. At minute two, I will want to stand up and scream, "NOBODY FUCKING CARES," but I cannot, because she's always smiling. The smiling makes me wonder if she locks puppies in closets or sniffs Krazy Glue in the evenings. Then I feel bad again for thinking these things because she's so goddamn "nice."

Alright, there are more than three. There's the Super Political Wounded Mother, who's been gaslighted since birth and complains constantly but can't change on account of internalized misogyny. She barely makes it through the day because *life is harder for her than the rest of us.* Her degree in gender studies compels her to suggest at every meeting that we "unpack our privilege," but later she will instruct people of color on Facebook how they can fight oppression more pleasantly. Her children are very deep. The entire planet wants to pass her a note reading: "Hey lady, stop talking. Or at least move to Portland."

Incidentally, I am grateful I was not yet on social media when I was drinking.

There's also the Aloof Badass Mother, who doesn't give a damn about any of this nonsense because she's drinking Pabst Blue Ribbon and getting tattooed and *pretty much never showing up to anything because it's all too mainstream.* She and her partner are about to sell their house to backpack around Thailand. She has a Tumblr and a vintage typewriter. She is polyamorous and attends Burning Man in feathers, atop a unicorn bicycle.

And, of course, there's the Earth Crystal Sage Mama, who manages to incorporate the words "womb," "goddess," or "menstrual blood" into damn near every conversation and once told me that cutting the umbilical cord is a form of "violence." She has a shamanic weaving teacher, smells like Dead shows and garlic, and truly believes there is an ancestral warrior leading her life on a daily basis. Her kid is named Lotus Reef and never wears shoes but can absolutely kill it in Hula-Hooping.

Whether or not these categories existed in reality, what I saw was that I fit *nowhere*. I lived in a house with linoleum floors and spent my afternoons with an ex-cocaine addict so I could remain among the living. I had trouble keeping the floor of my car visible at all, let alone composting kitchen scraps. I couldn't read the group emails from the parent associations because nobody understood the "reply all" function and I got bored by email number nine in the string of nine thousand.

But when I made jokes about the email thread, the other mothers looked at me like I was a dead bird on the porch, and then a week later I'd realize I missed an event because in email number 347, *the event was clearly outlined*, but I didn't read it because it was past email number nine.

I didn't fit in with the "read the books and learn and do it right" mothers because I read things, implemented them in a fury of excitement and staunch devotion, then forgot about them entirely three days later. I'd look at an abandoned chore chart as it leaned sadly against the wall and think, *If only*. Then I'd yell at my kids to do some chores because "I can't live this way anymore!"

Maybe we should start another chore chart, I'd think.

Of course I didn't fit with the Etsy hipsters either, because I wore Target maternity jeans six months after I had the baby. I knew I was wearing the "mom jeans" we're all taught to avoid like Red #2 dye and simple carbs, but *I never got around to buying other pants.*

But even when I tried to fit in with other mothers, my mouth would ruin it behind my back. One little ill-timed expletive and the whole thing would go to hell. We'd do fine at the sandbox until I dropped a "fuck," thinking it added to the moment, then feeling the wrath of a woman who believed nobody should swear on hallowed kid ground.

Oh, they couldn't hear me, I'd think, and mumble "Fuck" again, only this time in my head, because *I am in trouble now and I made it weird. Do I attempt to salvage this relationship? Nah. Move on. It was based on lies anyway.*

Motherly small talk was complicated because we were not actually talking about the thing we were talking about. We were both supposed to know this and stick to the rules, but I've been bad at that since the sixth grade, when my teacher duct-taped my mouth shut because I wouldn't stop talking.

It didn't even occur to me to censor the audible version of my thoughts *at all* until I had a certain epiphany at age sixteen, when I realized girls were getting the boys because they *act differently around them* and *you, Janelle, you're still admitting you prefer the All-man Brothers over Nirvana and it's 1996.*

I tended to say the thing that was true as opposed to the more palatable alternative, and this really concerned people, particularly when it involved raising America.

(Mothers don't admit that. Especially at the park.)

"What exactly do we have here?" they seemed to ask. "Do we eat it? Kick it? Counsel it?"

Probably.

I knew the game. I knew we were supposed to talk-not-talk about whose partner was the best and wealthiest, whose preschooler was the smartest, and whose baby was the most advanced, but I couldn't play. I tried a few hundred times, but eventually I focused on getting it over with by saying something like "Yeah, my son is three and barely talks," or, "My daughter refers to her vagina as a 'wiener shooter.'"

You win.

Your kid is smarter. The end. And yes, you have more money and, yes, more education, and your baby, I know! Your baby crawled at three months and talked at six months and slept through the night at twelve minutes—what a miracle! Must be superior genetics.

Now can we just hang out? I'm bored.

Can we talk about the way these kids give and suck life by the minute, day by day, and how sometimes you're sure you've ruined your life through the reproductive process, but five minutes later you're in tears as you pack the newborn clothes into the giveaway box? The way the years mock you with their passing, lull you into the safety and surety and vague comfort of knowing your children will always be small, until you realize it will soon be over? Done. Your time is done. Sorry. You should have paid closer attention. Should have held on tighter. Try not to fuck it up with the others.

But you already are. You're always already fucking it up. Can we talk about that?

Let's not talk about how we all became better versions of ourselves the day we became parents, and, please, would you stop pretending you did? Because your holier-than-thou shit makes me worry you watch dinosaur porn after the kids go to bed. Your steadfast focus on seasonal cupcakes and organic kombucha concerns me. Look, I've got some too. I know all about gut flora. But please. Is that all there is?

You didn't become some G-rated version of yourself and you know it.

But let's not talk about that either. Let's make a couple of jokes, chill out, and make fun of "man colds" or "wife colds"—do those exist?— and how hard it is to get kids to do chores when they're bickering and awful and you think, "I'd rather do it myself than listen to this!" No, but seriously, husband, you're fine. Why are you on the couch whining? Call your mom. Maybe she cares. I've had a cold for nine weeks, asshole.

Let's talk about that. Let's talk about sleeping babies and newborn breath and how I once wanted to kill myself after I had my baby because it seemed the only or best solution to the pain.

Maybe we won't talk about that at the park. Let's talk about something else.

Let's talk about coffee. You can talk about wine. I don't drink wine because I drank all the wine and alcohol has a tendency to turn me into a homeless person, but we can talk about it anyway because I understand. We don't need to pretend.

Let's talk about how we haven't seen the floor of our cars in months, and how it smells oddly, always, of apples (but where are the actual apples?), and how the sound of nonstop kid chattering makes my head spin, but I still lie down at night wishing I had listened because they won't be chattering forever.

Let's talk about my son, the quiet one, who squeaks and yells and screams and runs, all the time. I get so frustrated with him for the stomping and incessant movement and it's so hard to listen to him talk sometimes. He can't think of the word because he's dyslexic. I know he is. His father and grandfather are dyslexic. What kind of shit human gets impatient with a boy with dyslexia? What kind?

Let's talk about that. Let's talk about the fact that I am that mother. I am already that mother. I was the worst one, too. I let my children go one morning, and my boy, he was only sixteen months old. Don't you think he wondered where his mother went? Yeah, I hate me too, lady. I hate me too for the things I did, and when these memories come, I throw my head back and forth like a motherfucking lunatic trying to shake them out of my brain. I think perhaps I'd rather die than live with that shame.

Maybe we won't talk about all that. That's a little heavy.

Let's talk about how sometimes, by the end of the day, I

understand—just a little—how parents snap and hit their kids. I haven't hit my kids. I would not. But sometimes when combined with lack of sleep, and my husband working six days a week, and the times I drove intoxicated with my child in the car and poisoned breastfeeding, nearly overdosed in a trailer, and my sagging belly and gray roots, self-hatred, and joy that I'm free (from alcoholism, today), I wonder if I may break, just fucking break, so I come here to the park, and I sit next to you because you're a mother like me, right? And we can talk about it. We can talk and talk and talk.

"Is she sleeping through the night yet?" you ask.

No.

"Oh, where is she?"

In my bed, with me.

"Oh, you co-sleep?"

I guess.

"My baby slept through the night at two months because I did sleep training. Why haven't you sleep trained?"

Oh yeah. Okay. Talk to me about that, I guess. If that's all there is.

• • •

In August 2010, when I was seventeen months sober, our third baby was born, in a water birth at home, as the morning sun splintered across the faces of Mac, my mother, children, and midwives. They were circling me as our ten-pound, dimpled baby Georgia with a cleft chin and bald head opened her eyes against my chest, and I watched her body flood pink with our blood, from the center to her fingertips. Just like Rocketship.

At night, I would hold her in the crook of my arm and see only love, and I'd wonder how it could get like this. It was just me nursing her in the gray dim of a little nursery I decorated with Ava and my mother when I was pregnant, in the house Mac and I bought together, *where all our children live, and we are a family.*

How wholesome life had become, not in that church way, not in the way that made me feel unworthy, but in the meatiest, grittiest way.

Not beauty in the clouds. Beauty on the ground. Beauty in my hands.

Six months to one year to one year and a half sober. *I should be in a gutter somewhere, but I'm here.* With the thought, while I rocked, I'd turn my head up to the ceiling and close my eyes as the warmth of the day rushed over me.

I am none of those other mothers, I'd think. *I am all of them.*

I realized we are all a bunch of fakers. We've got too much past to remember, too much on the line to forget. We become some mother. We show up. We work and drive and love. It all feels like a tiny miracle. It all feels so boring we could puke. For some of us, that becomes enough, and we don't have to dance anymore.

Maybe I don't care quite so much about being better than you. Sometimes I want to be better than you. But in the end, I have nothing left to prove: to you or myself. I have no polish to fix what I am. I am a woman who lost her children, and I am the woman now standing here in this hallway bright-eyed and motherly while you size me up. You don't even know what it means for me to have this stupid fucking G.A.T.E. interlude with you.

Sure, I hate you, but I love that I get to hate you. I love that I get to be just another mother pissed off because a woman in Teva sandals condescended to her.

Because look at these wiper blades. All you do is turn this dial and swoosh—problem solved! Do you not see how funny that is?

Don't you think that's cool?

No? Alright. Guess it's just me.

And that's fine, because I'm just happy to be here.

13

FAILURE THAT ISN'T FUNNY: SOBER EDITION

Is that your boy up there?" I recognized the tone in the woman's voice as that of the inordinately concerned. Though she was smiling, I could sense I had offended her, and would soon discover how.

"Yes," I answered, joining the game of fake civility.

"Oh, okay! Well—I just have to say! It makes me nervous! Seeing him up there!" she said, pulling her shoulders up and making a face like, "I just can't help myself! I love all the children!" She seemed to punctuate every pause with unwarranted jubilation.

I spun through the mental Rolodex of the situation's features to determine which one of us was more irrational: *He is standing on top of kid-level monkey bars, over a sand pit. If he fell, he would fall into sand, notably soft, and if he fell and managed through some miracle to hurt himself, it would be a broken or sprained ankle or wrist at the very worst.* There wasn't even a damn rock around.

Sometimes kids need to climb, I thought. *Sometimes I need to let them climb so I can sit on a bench and play on my cell phone, pretending I don't have children.* Of course I didn't say that. She was quite obviously not the type of person who enjoys that level of honesty. Instead, I tried: "Well, I figure if he can get up there, he can get down!"

I smiled and shrugged my shoulders as if to say: "Kids will be kids!" I was attempting to connect with her, to be two mothers at the park, although at that point I would have settled with two humans sharing a planet. I thought my soaring charm might bring out the best in her.

Instead she looked at me as if I had just pulled out a meth pipe and hit it.

"Do you have *insurance*?" she bellowed.

"What?" I asked, thinking, *For sure she's going to kill me tonight while I sleep.*

"Health insurance. Do you have health insurance for when he falls and hurts himself? KIDS GET HURT, YOU KNOW." She said the last part as if she were leading a rally in the protection of all the children of the world who could possibly get hurt.

I lifted my eyebrows and mumbled, "Yep. I do," turned around and sat down, where I proceeded to think of all the piercingly witty things I should have said. "Actually no, I prefer to duct-tape my kids' injuries at home in the garage using a light dose of heroin to kill the pain." Ultimately I decided I should have just gone with, "Do you ever wonder why nobody likes you?" And then I should have stared at her. For a long time, until she grew so uncomfortable she cracked.

I glared at her from behind my sunglasses while my rage turned into an ill-defined shame. I watched Rocket play while the stranger's words repeated in my mind—"kids get hurt, you know"—and seeing Rocket stand up in the air sent my mind spinning back to a summer trip I took with my stepmother and friends to Lake Tahoe when Ava was eighteen months old.

On the way home, we had stopped at a restaurant with a full bar along the Truckee River. It was one of those funky Northern California motel/restaurant/bar places right on the river—an all-in-one establishment where you could eat, get drunk, sleep, and buy a small carved black bear that says "I left my heart in Tahoe." The patio and open-air bar were next to the restaurant, and above it was the motel, with stairs leading from the bar patio to the rooms. We had lunch in the clean high-altitude sun during one of those days that feels endless and so beautiful you could die right there without a single regret.

We had cocktails on the patio and it was all quite pleasant until somebody started pointing and yelling, "Oh my God," and then the whole restaurant was gasping and pointing, and I looked up to where they were pointing and saw my baby girl standing on the roof of the motel—a flat roof that extended from the motel, over the restaurant, to the roaring, maniacal river. From where she stood, wearing a little red gingham apron dress with a white blouse underneath, her favorite scuffed red leather Mary Janes and white lace socks—from where she stood gazing cheerfully at the people below, she was a few feet from death. If she took five or six steps to her right, there was no railing or edge or prayer that would stop her from tumbling down into the white water slipping and flipping over giant granite rocks.

I remember the blur of running up the stairs, three at a time, and stopping at the top, at the gaps between the wooden rails she had crawled through. She was in the middle of the roof, outside my reach—five feet from me and five feet from the edge. What I knew was that she could not run.

If I yelled or crawled onto the roof, she might bolt, startled, or thinking we were playing a game of "catch me," as we had done so many times before. I wanted to scream, to beg for help, but I couldn't frighten her—and yet, if I spoke softly, she might ignore me.

The terror pushed through me from my core—not in thought, not in sequence or data, but as a fiery heat in the center of me, rushing out into my arms and feet. My voice rose steady and calm, with all the power I had behind it: "Ava. Walk to me now." I smiled desperately to pull her to me. *Oh child, my dearest baby, please God come here.*

She walked immediately to me. As soon as she was within my reach I grabbed her, pulled her through the railing, and held her to me as my eyes burned. I rushed down the stairs and out the side door so nobody would see my face.

Back in the car, I didn't speak of it. If someone would have tried, I would have flatly refused to address it. But I knew I had almost lost my whole life, right there, and my child had nearly lost hers, and it was my fault. Again. I was drinking. I was not paying attention. I was chatting with strangers in the buzz of the day and sunlight.

Recalling that moment, of her little body hovering in the sun above an angry river, and me in my flip-flops, tan and half drunk, pulling her to me in burning desperation, I squeezed my eyes shut and flinched, noticeably. I knew I must have looked freakish sitting on a park bench, shaking my head with my eyes shut. But it was involuntary.

I drew a deep, quick breath at the crack of the image against my heart. When those memories came, they started like knives in my mind, and then sat like boulders on my chest. Like a thousand pounds of granite grief. It seemed they would crush me, so I called Good News Jack, my only source of new ideas.

"How do I live with the memories of what I've done to my kids, Jack? The images. How do I fucking live with the images?" I told him how twenty times a day they jumped in and out of my mind to thrash and stab and mutilate, and I told him how at night they moved in and set up camp. And how with them came a tidal wave of shame, of agonizing regret, of holy time lost, to never be regained, sweet innocence doused in kerosene— ignored, unrecognized, and by my very own hand. *How fucking could I.* That was the part I could not face. That I, I was that person. And I didn't see, but then I did, and then I could not look away.

"We call those nightmare memories. All sober alcoholics have them. Lot of people drink again over them." He spoke calmly, and I imagined he was out on his front porch, smoking a cigarette and watching his kids ride their bikes.

"I can't live knowing what I did," I said. "I can't."

"I know you can't. That's why we're not relying on you anymore. Remember what I said? If God only gave you things you could handle, what the fuck would you need God for? You can't handle anything. Look at yourself." His words were irritatingly factual.

"Why are you always so full of good news?"

"Janelle, the way you will survive is by using your experience to help other alcoholic mothers who did the same shit to their kids. *That's your job now.* We don't care what YOU think about your past. If you really feel bad, stick around and repair it, with your children and the world."

"But I'm a terrible mother."

"Of course you're a terrible mother," and he cackled in a way that reminded me what a long and insane road he too had walked.

"But you aren't gonna get any better by talking to me," and then he hung up.

I replayed Jack's words as I kicked a sheet of sand over the concrete, watching my foot slide around, making little mounds and knocking them over again. From that moment forward, every time one of those memories arose, I clung with all my strength to the idea that I might help another alcoholic someday with what otherwise seemed entirely meaningless destruction.

This was my version of "positive self-talk." It didn't erase the self-loathing. It didn't melt the regret. It didn't soften the blow of revulsion, the terror I felt at the mere idea of what could have happened or who could have been hurt, but it brought a microscopic surrender, another tiny letting go of my need to understand, control, and find relief—it gave me just enough to trust that someday, something will make those years worth living.

Jack's voice ran through my mind a hundred times a day. "We don't hang out in morbid self-reflection. It's self-pity with a better polish. Remember the duck and the fire hydrant? Fuck your beliefs. Focus on what's in front of you."

So I looked up at Rocket and watched as he balanced with his arms stretched out. He was concentrating on his feet and teetering on the corner of the monkey bars, and I wanted to tell him, "Be careful, son," but I didn't, for fear it would distract him, knock him off course. Plus, I knew he was alright, so I smiled, and nodded at that lady too, because my son was safe, and she would never know what that means.

• • •

One hour after my serene epiphany in the park and deep gratitude for my sobriety, I walked into my house with a screaming
baby on my hip, two bickering children, and approximately nine
bags of unknown origin hanging from my body. I set it all down
in the entryway, shut the door, and read a text from Mac letting
me know he was stuck in traffic and wouldn't be home for another hour, at which time I remembered there was some sort of
tee-ball nonsense that night.

Of course he's not here, I thought, feeling the weight of our offspring, a vague loneliness, and resentment as I walked into the
kitchen and saw a day's worth of dishes strewn across the counters and toys throughout the living room.

Good God.

My actual face ached from exhaustion. My cheekbones
throbbed and my eyes stung. The dog scratched at the back door.
Georgia was hungry and had just pooped. Ava and Rocket had
ignored me again, and I was alone in the maelstrom of kids at
dinnertime. As I looked around at the laundry on the couch, the
smear of jam on the floor, and the pile of Mac's tools on the
kitchen table, I felt that old familiar rush, the frantic sense of being out of control—and that if I didn't fix it, it would all collapse.

The next thing I knew, I was yelling in my children's faces,
"What is wrong with you? Why can't anyone HELP ME?!"

I saw red, as if a veil had fallen over me, casting the whole
room in shades of fury. As I screamed, my mind's eye hovered
in the corner of the room, staring down at the woman who was
so mad she was spitting. "Stop, Janelle, this is wrong." The voice
nudged, poked me in the ribs from a place that knew better, and

I knew the voice was right, but I could not stop. The more I yelled, the more I wanted to yell, as if the words weren't doing a damn thing, so I grew madder and louder, and the words seemed to get closer to exhausting the anger in me, but they never quite worked.

They did nothing but explode in quick, useless bursts.

Still, I thought I was going to get through to them, that my anger would change something. I thought I'd get some power and convince them to improve. I stormed around the house in a tantrum, barking orders. In glances, I noticed my children avoiding my eyes. I noticed their silence.

But I was *committed*. I was *angry*.

Or I simply could not find my way back.

The moment Mac stepped across the threshold in his five-year-old canvas beige overalls, patched with denim blue squares at the knees, all three children were squealing in delight and hanging from his arms in unchecked celebration of their *real* parent. I watched as they rejoiced in his arrival, while, I imagined, lamenting mine. *Well what do you expect, Janelle? You're such a goddamn yeller. But that motherfucker, he's never here. If he were here like me, he'd yell too.* But I knew our children would never see that. I felt wildly unappreciated and unseen, as if I were doing the grunt work while he stole all the glory.

Now I suppose he's going to want to shower, as opposed to taking over parenting so I can lie on my bed with the bedroom door shut.

Sure enough, off he went to the shower after giving me a kiss and eating something infuriatingly healthy, like an apple or raw almonds. While I turned the taco meat in the pan for dinner, I wondered why raw almonds were about the last food I'd reach for after a long day, and determined that if I incorporated more

Mac-style food choices into my diet, I too would stand lean and muscular before the bathroom mirror.

"Hey, Janelle! Come here!" He appeared to be hollering from the shower, and the playfulness in his voice gave me a rush of desire and dread, because damn he's attractive but also, *No way in hell am I having shower sex right now.*

"What's up?" I asked, leaning against the bathroom door, thinking there was nothing I wanted more in that moment than for *one more person to need something from me.*

"So," he declared, "I bought some go-kart frames from Phil."

"You did what now?"

Assuming I didn't understand the actual sentence as opposed to the content, he repeated himself, explaining that he had spent $600 on metal frames, which he and Phil would equip with lawnmower engines, and then the kids would ride them around in circles on dirt tracks. For fun, apparently.

Phil was a man who lived down the street and looked like a garden gnome. He was hands-down my least favorite garden gnome because he evidently had *very little going on*, and would invite Mac over every few days to stand in his garage and stare at things while discussing, I now knew, lawnmower ride-along toys.

"You fucking did *what*?" I understood the words coming out of his mouth, but I could not comprehend his decision to voluntarily add "build go-karts" to the never-ending task list of our lives.

I uttered confused bursts of total derision, then walked out of the bathroom, because he had turned off the shower and I couldn't bear the sight of his face.

I questioned how bare metal frames that might someday turn into "karts" (with a "k")—which, by the way, would never happen, because we could hardly manage to pick up the dog shit from the backyard, let alone complete arbitrary entertainment projects—became his area of focus while I contemplated my recent re-enrollment in graduate school, work, nursing a baby, driving two kids around the county a few times a day, bills, the house, the growing clarity of Rocket's dyslexia, the outgrown clothes in the kids' dressers, the dog's training, and the emotional and psychological well-being of our almost-tween daughter.

I dropped onto our bed and closed my eyes, leaving the ground beef simmering on the stove unattended, thinking, *Maybe, just maybe, if all goes well, the fucking house will burn down.*

I was two years sober, and while Mac and I worked to build a home, a chasm carved itself between us, growing more massive as my head cleared, as I got to know him, and myself, as sober humans. Life was opening for me in a thousand directions just as my marriage contracted into thankless redundancy.

I had barely known Mac without the dizzying balm of evening cocktails, and I certainly had never tried raising a family in such aridity. *What did it matter if we were horrible together before? I was drunk anyway.*

But now, sober, I felt the rift completely. The way his interests and sense of humor were not necessarily mine, the way his ambition and concerns were in conflict with mine, and the way he spent money, money I assumed he had stashed away. The way we made love, the way he glared at me on Saturday mornings when I suggested we do chores, as if I were a nagging mother.

I felt a deep and terrifying loneliness in our marriage, a descending awareness that I was becoming a servant to my family and nothing else, and I would spend the next twenty years in that condition.

I often thought of our "wedding" on the courthouse grass on that cold, gray day. I thought of the wedding dress picture I had clipped from a magazine when I was eight years old, and I thought of my friends' marriages, the way their husbands surely discussed monetary decisions with them and acted like grown-ups, investing in stocks and buying property and getting medical degrees. I assumed they made all kinds of choices together and were honest and clear with one another, and the thought made me think back to Mac talking behind my back to his mother and sisters (they were, for a time, understandably not elated about my existence), and the times he lied to me by omission—*You know, if I just don't tell her, she can't accuse me of lying.*

I felt a panic come over me, of distance, of not-real love, of un-love, even, of *lies*, of being left alone, of getting sober for what? This? I thought of the marriage that began on that dreary day—we were just kids—had there ever been real love? *Nah, we simply had a kid together and got stuck.* We didn't begin correctly. We wouldn't finish correctly. I mentally sorted through the freedom he had—to drive to work alone each day, to sleep while the baby cries, to not think about the things I thought about, to simply *not be the mother.*

Within moments, he morphed into a stranger.

Is this what marriage is? I want nothing of this.

I roared again, this time at Mac, and more unchecked than before, because he was an adult. He stood silently, leaning against a doorframe, still wrapped in his bath towel, for my thoughts had progressed from go-kart to divorce before he even had time to get dressed.

"Do you think it's *your* money and *my* money?" I shouted.

"No." His head was still slightly down.

"Well, obviously you do, since you think it's fine to spend that kind of money on useless fucking metal! I would never do that!"

He shifted his weight against the doorway, looking at me from under a furrowed brow. I knew the look. He was waiting it out.

"Do you have any idea how much I do every day while you are at work, Mac?" I reported in long form the play-by-play of each of my days, my voice growing hoarse from the yelling, my body intoxicated with rage. When I erupted at Mac, it only ended when he or I physically left the house, or a stranger came over, forcing me to behave on account of my pride. Occasionally Mac roared back. But mostly, he waited.

My rage would ebb, and I would apologize, again.

My family would just look at me.

You know, Janelle, you could just jump off the crazy train before riding it all the way to the bitter end.

• • •

That night, when the house was gray and quiet and my body untouched, my day became a nightmare memory: *Who are you, Janelle, thinking you can raise kids? Who are you, thinking you can be a mother and wife in a decent marriage?* I saw the woman's face while she yelled, the woman pathetically trying not destroy it all again, and I cringed. *Here I am again, hurting people. Here I am again, unable to control myself. Here I am again, the tiny psycho chasing her brother around with a kitchen knife.*

I thought of my mother's words, "You treat me like dirt."

She was correct. *She is correct.*

Lying there, I recalled daydreaming at school about how my mother was going to pay for Christmas, or the heating, or visualizing the violence I wanted to inflict on the bullies who were mean to my brother on the bus. He was huge, but so gentle. I was tiny, but insane.

In junior high we had a smoke-spewing minivan with wood siding. I'd ask my mother to drop me off down the road to save me from embarrassment—and the other kids from pollution inhalation. She always obliged, and it helped until after school, when the other kids' parents would show up, and I'd be sitting on a wall in front of the school as the sun went down and the principal left, concerned about me.

"It's okay!" I'd say cheerfully. "My mom is coming. She'll be here any minute." It was a partial lie. I knew she'd come. I didn't know if it would be any minute.

As the evening grew cooler, I no longer feared she was dead. I feared I might kill her myself. When she finally pulled up, I'd shriek at her for leaving me like that.

She'd tell me all the things she had done that day, and with a lilting sadness she'd say, "I'm doing the best I can," but this would throw me into full fury because now I felt guilty and *what kind of thing is that to say?*

"You treat me like dirt," was what she'd say after I yelled, which seemed true, but also, unfair. It seemed unfair to pick up your child late, then say "I try the best I can," as if that were some sort of excuse, and then say I was mean to *her*. I wished she knew how I sat in school daydreaming about her.

She was always *trying*, but never *changing*, and at some point one gets sick of the "trying" and wants the "doing," and also: *Why are we feeling sorry for you? You are the mother.*

And so I raged, because I was tired.

I was worn out by all the talking, the worries, the desire to trust, to know when my people were going to show up, so I transformed into a ball of red, to get some power. To get some control. To get some peace.

"Tell Margaret to go home," she'd say, and I'd hate her to my bones.

Later, though, in bed, I'd open my journal and write detailed updates of her marriage, and how much I loved her, and how much I wished she could hear me, and I'd wonder if she'd remembered to lock all our doors so we'd all be safe.

Maybe I was born without a moral compass. Maybe I'm sober, and I'm still without a moral compass.

An image I'd seen on social media by the editor of one of those eternally peaceful parenting magazines popped into my mind. It said: "Your words become the voices in your children's heads." My God.

The thought *they would be better off without me* skipped across my mind, and then, *I should drink again just to relieve my children of me.*

As soon as the thought came, I knew it was not true. I knew it was the sweet whisper of alcoholism, the disease getting tougher every day, and wilier as it waited for the moment I agreed to believe it again.

The next day, when I told Jack about my yelling, he said, "You're a bully. You're a bully and you're trying to control everyone. You have power over those kids and you abuse it." *A bully, huh?* Once again, I wanted to suggest he walk away from me at a fast pace for a very long time, but I was still desperate, perhaps more so, because I knew alcohol didn't work, and would never work again. To drink was to die, but there would be no relief before the passing. I could die of alcoholism or learn to live sober.

Why is this fuckin' guy always right? The bully charge was true, though nobody had ever urged the sick reality up to the surface of my brain: that I felt I owned my kids, that I could treat them how I damn well pleased. In fact, I possibly felt that way about the rest of the world as well.

"Well, Jack, what do I do about it?" I was actually spellbound at this point.

"Pray for help. Figure out why you love anger." So I tried what he said, meditating and praying in the morning, but mostly, I returned to therapy.

●　●　●

"I'm sober and still raging," I said, sitting on the wicker chair next to the window and a sprawling ficus tree. The therapist paused and asked, "What do you mean, 'raging'?"

"Anger. Raging in anger. I feel borderline again, only without the other fifteen symptoms, which I guess makes me no longer borderline. Is that possible? Can people become un-borderline? Maybe within the borders?" I was speaking like a fool because I was nervous, and it was hard to explain that my rage was like a rotten old friend I couldn't imagine my life without, or a sibling I bickered with constantly but missed as soon as she was gone.

"What are you getting from your anger?" the therapist asked, and I thought, *Holy mother of God, they're all in cahoots with one another.*

"You know that's the same thing the ex-refrigerator-box dweller asked me?" She looked confused, so I explained he was a friend, a sort of crank spiritual guide.

"When did you start raging?" She had her pen at the ready.

I contemplated not going down the whole road of my past with her, but I did. I told the truth. The alternative was too exhausting. I had lied and polished the truth for too long. Jack used to tell me I spent my life "polishing the same old turd and selling it like it was new." I didn't want to tell better-polished lies. I wanted turd truth.

But I knew that once I started she would look at me with eyes that said, "Wow, you really made it!" and I'd feel like a fraud again, because she was praising my stunning turnaround, and I knew I looked so "fine," like a good and loving mother. When I shared my ideas about parenting, she'd say, "Yes, that's right!" because I talk well, and she would be impressed with my devotion to family, especially after "such a past!" *But what would she think if she saw our house when nobody was there but us?*

What would she think if she heard the things I say?

I am a fraud. I will be found out.

We had purchased a house. I re-enrolled in the English master's program I had quit. I shared pictures of my family on Facebook, and friends rejoiced at our little family—how far we had come. We should be so proud. We are goddamn miracles.

But what if they knew? I wondered, fully and finally, if I would ever change. If I would ever be worthy of the glittering life around me.

I should not have been surprised to find my inner life unmanageable. Good News Jack always said, "Alcohol was never your problem, it was your solution.

"If alcohol were the problem," he'd say, "rehab would be churning out winners. And yet, people like us always drink again. Every relapse starts with a sober brain. So where's your problem? In sobriety." It was tough to argue with logic like that, but still I maintained a small, buried belief that once alcohol was gone, I would become the most benign version of myself. Perhaps some sort of B-level saint.

But after getting sober, I realized I was still an asshole.

In softer moments, when feeling generous, Jack would tell me, "You are a human, Janelle. What's fucking with you is that you're human."

This seemed insufficient. This seemed profoundly oversimplified. So, that's it? We harm people because we're human? Do other mothers do this? If so, why aren't they talking about it? And why, if this is how it is, if we are flawed and broken and somehow unsuccessful at snapping ourselves out of it even when kids are involved, why do we write things like, "You become the voice in your children's heads"? Do they bestow this responsibility on the heads of fathers? Why is it my job to become my kid's inner voice? Because the kid came out of my vagina? Those seem unrelated.

"You are only human," he said, and yet it feels infinitely not enough. *If this is human, if this is my best shot at life, I am not enough. Do I make peace with that now? I am not failing in cute ways. I am failing in big, big ways.*

But then I would think of the inhumanity of my former life, of the morning I woke up and realized I could not exist among humankind, of the day I couldn't use a restroom properly, of the day I woke up alone in a hospital bed, and the day I spoke in the cracked dialects of the wholly insane, and then I'd think, *I am only human*, and that is precisely the miracle.

14

THE CHILDHOOD I COULD NO LONGER BLAME

When I was a kid and circumstances turned questionable, my mother would take us to the beach. We would walk in the front door, and she would announce, "Change your clothes, kids. I have to get to the ocean!" We'd pack sweatshirts and a Smokey Joe barbeque into the back of our white Ford Taurus station wagon and head to Morro Bay or Pismo Beach. My mother would cook hot dogs in the warm blanket fog while my brother boogie-boarded and I hid in little caves and forts under the cypress trees, talking to myself in imagined worlds. I'd roll up my pant legs and flip the clean sand around my toes, chasing waves and tumbling down dunes as the sun fell into the roaring blue.

On our way home, with salt still clinging to the ringlets around my face and my pants wet and itchy, my mother and I would analyze whatever worry had nudged her to the beach. Usually it was a lack of funds, or another disappointment involving my stepfather, Keith.

When things got really bad, we'd head out on a road trip somewhere without any particular money or plan, sometimes traveling all the way to British Columbia. On these trips, in the late afternoon when it became apparent we needed to sleep somewhere, my brother and I would start looking for camping spots on a huge Rand McNally map we kept wadded up under the front seat.

One summer afternoon when I was ten, my brother and I walked in the door after playing outside to find our mother stacking food and towels and sleeping bags in the living room. "What's going on, Mom?" I asked.

She grinned. "We're going to Yosemite!"

We jumped up and down. *Wheeee! A random adventure!* It was summer, so the plan to "leave today" made more sense than her usual announcements on school nights that we were going to "see the redwoods" or "hang out at the stock car races in Laguna Niguel." If I protested, she'd say, "You'll learn way more camping than you ever will at school." This, of course, was unequivocally true.

But my jumping ceased when I remembered my mother was in charge.

"Do we have a campsite reservation, Mom?" I raised my eyebrows as she folded a giant tarp she referred to as "the blue deal." She wore stonewashed tapered jeans and a purple T-shirt that said Yosemite on it, which was quite possibly the impetus for the entire trip. Perhaps she had seen it that morning, sitting in the drawer, and thought, *I had better get to Bridal Veil Falls.*

"Of course not," she answered slyly. "How could I? I just decided to go! We'll find something."

"What do you mean, 'We'll find something'? We will not.

It's summer. It's been booked for three years." I was ten, but I knew these things because I was a tiny Republican who *loved rules.*

"Go pack!" She was grabbing pillows from around the house and stacking them by the front door.

"What about money, Mom? Do we have any?" I hadn't budged from my platform of inquiry. There were *questions that needed answering, people.*

"We have enough. I sold some new advertising." She yelled to my brother to get ready. I wanted to yell, "Let's slow down and assess the particulars of the situation!"

"What about the electricity bill?" I dropped one hip and put a hand out, as if to say, *Did ya think of that one, Mother?*

"It just came. We're fine, Janelle. We are fine."

"How much money do we have exactly?" I wanted data. Numbers. I wanted to know if we were spending the last of it.

Our money came and went so quickly. A tax return arrived and we were flush. The heater broke and we were broke. But when the money was gone, my mother's spirit went with it. We went to the beach and she drove along, defeated, and I thought for sure we'd never be flush again. I wanted to save us both from that moment.

"Janelle, go pack!" She was laughing, and I couldn't fight it anymore. The sound of her excitement—the tune of carefree—was sweet mountain air. I breathed it in and I was with her. *Let's go, Mom. Let's go adventuring.*

I walked to my room thinking of waterfalls and Ansel Adams, glaciers and granite and bears. I packed, and we piled into our wagon and drove.

An hour later, I was sent into a Carl's Jr. to gather some mayonnaise packets (we had forgotten the mayonnaise) so we could stop in the parking lot of a liquor store to eat lunch.

I was sitting on the back of our car and swinging my legs under the hatchback, while my mother made tuna sandwiches and apparently spotted a homeless woman sitting in front of the liquor store.

"Janelle, go give that lady a sandwich," my mother said, extending a sandwich my way.

"What? No." I widened my eyes and pulled my body back from the sandwich, repelled by its very association with her idea. "Absolutely not."

"Give her some chips, too," she said, packing Doritos into a baggie.

"No. Why, Mom?" I was already desperate.

"Because maybe she's hungry." I flinched in restrained rage at my mother's incessant weirdness. *Where does she come up with these ideas? Why can't we just fade back into our Ford like normal people? I already stole mayo packets from Carl's Jr. Is that not enough for one day?*

I whined, "No way," as if that had ever worked once with my mother, but I soon gave up the battle I knew I'd lose, grabbed the food, and walked across the infinite lot, cursing my mother under my breath in Mormon-approved swear words. I approached the woman and sheepishly held out the food as she squinted at me through sun-cracked skin and watery eyes. She accepted it silently as I smiled and mumbled, "Hi. Here. Okay, bye. Thanks." I walked immediately away.

Crouched in the sunshine under a pile of evidently unnecessary clothing, she had not looked at me like I was Jesus, as I had assumed she would, but rather as if I were a cow invading her afternoon—and not even a cute cow. Still, I was impressed with myself—*quite a Good Samaritan, you'll notice*—and saw my mother watching me with equal pride in her eyes as I strolled back to the car. When I was about halfway across the parking lot, the lady chucked the tuna sandwich at me, skimming the side of my head and distributing tuna and mayonnaise across my scalp. I dared not look back at her, but the shock spun through my legs as I ran to my mother, my eyes locked with hers, burning in humiliation, screaming, *What the frick were you thinking, Mom?*

"Why did you make me do that?" I was furious with the betrayal.

"I had no idea she'd throw it at you, honey," she said calmly as she pulled the tuna out of my hair with paper towels.

"This is not the first time this has happened! Remember when we picked up that hitchhiker and she pulled a knife on you? What about that?" We now had evidence of two crazy homeless people in our lives, which I figured was plenty of data to swear off homeless people forever.

"She was mentally ill, Janelle."

My eyes widened. "Then why was she in our car?"

"She needed a ride," she said, packing the remains of our lunch in the ice chest.

"Mom! That is not an answer!"

"Well I didn't know she was mentally ill. You can't tell by looking at somebody, you know? We always end up alright." She laughed again.

"Oh, you mean like when our car broke down in Las Vegas and we survived for two days playing nickel slot machines and sneaking into buffets?" *Plus,* I thought, *you can kind of tell by looking at somebody, Mother.*

"Keith should have sent us some money to pay for the car. That was a terrible thing he did, leaving us like that." My mother shook her head in disbelief as she reflected on Keith's bad choices.

"Mom, we went to Vegas to see the Hoover Dam with two hundred dollars and a nearly broken car. That is not how people do things!"

"This is a great car! And I got us a VIP tour of the dam, didn't I? Remember that? We met that security guy just when they were closing. That was the opportunity of a lifetime." She was growing tired of my inability to recognize educational opportunities.

"We also got kicked out of a buffet by a different security guy." I hated that moment. I had to leave half a Las Vegas casino buffet shrimp plate.

"And yet, here we are!" She threw her hands up. "Still okay!"

"And now we're going to Yosemite in June without a reservation. There will not be a spot, Mom. I do not want to go without a spot." I was afraid again.

"We'll get a spot."

"But how do you *know*?"

She leaned toward me. "You have to think good thoughts. You just have to *know* you're going to get a spot. Just believe it. Assume there is no other option. It's how I always get great parking spots right in the front. I drive right to the front knowing I'll get a spot, and I always do."

"You do not *always*. That is a lie."

"Well, I usually do." That was true.

My mother's life plan was: "We'll figure it out." And the method to carry out the plan was: "Think positively."

I hated that philosophy. I would think positively when I was looking at my damn campsite reservation. Why couldn't we call ahead? Why couldn't my mother *believe* the "No Vacancy" signs when we were on the prowl for a motel room? She invariably stopped the car to check anyway. "Oh, they always have extra rooms. They just put that sign out to deter people." Occasionally, she'd walk triumphantly out of the motel office with a key in her hand, announcing, "I even got us a free upgrade!"

Her eyes would say, "See, Janelle? I told you." And I would smile, because she really did pull some shit off.

•   •   •

Back in "Mudhole," which is the translation of Atascadero, our town in Central California, we pulled into the driveway of Keith's house, and I felt the weight of our lives return.

By the time we walked into the living room, my mother had already disappeared. Not in body—she was right there— but the woman I knew, the one who suggested I break into the ranger station to pilfer a reservation form, was gone. She was busy watching her husband now, with eager eyes, anticipating his needs, dangling from every barely perceptible shift in his mood, shuffling around to repair and preserve his desires. I sighed and went into my room to unpack and try to finish that Steinbeck chapter about the turtle.

We had been in Atascadero since I was seven, moving there after a dreamy stint in Calistoga, an adorable little town full of wine and wildflowers. We lived in a trailer park across the street from a hot springs pool. My brother, mother, and I had moved there after my parents divorced. My brother and I swam so often my hair turned white from the sun and green from the minerals. We rinsed it in lemon juice. It turned whiter and greener.

We had moved to Calistoga from Clearlake, where my father grew up, and where my whole family lived when it was together. The wine country town was only twenty-six miles from Clearlake, but it felt like a new country. Clearlake was in Lake County, an impoverished, rural swath of land boasting the highest number of multigenerational welfare recipients of any county in the state (according to family lore), a raging meth problem, and a lake named "Clearlake" even though it was often rimmed by a twenty-foot wall of algae one could avoid only by boat or dock. Grandma Bonny lived in Lower Lake. Grandma Joan and Grandpa Bob lived in Lakeport. And scattered between them were my aunts, uncles, and cousins.

But my mother needed a new life, and Keith, a high school friend of my father's, offered to lease her some office space. So we sold the motor home and drove a few hours south in the Ford wagon to Atascadero, every mile carrying us farther away from the unclear lake. When we arrived, we rented a tiny pink house with red shag carpet as a temporary pad until my mother's new business took off.

Her plan was to start a tourist magazine, and around the dinner table she would talk of her vision, the well-connected person she met, the special information she had that nobody else had—a unique opportunity, no other travel magazines, all very promising! For eighteen years, she helped my grandparents and father (and aunts and uncle) publish the weekly newspaper in Clearlake, which Grandma Bonny owned, so she knew weeklies. This would be a monthly, and it would be hugely successful because there was nothing like it, even though we were in the *world-renowned, tourist-packed Central California coast.*

I loved imagining with her all the ways we would spend the money, the house we would live in, the places we'd visit, the way our problems would pass into nothing. We would get a big house. We would buy a new van. At seven and eight and nine and ten, I believed these schemes and plans and dreams. With all my heart, actually. *This one is going to work.*

So let's go, Mom. Let's go to Mudhole and do amazing things.

• • •

In the bathroom of the pink house is where I first remember clinging to my mother's legs and begging her not to leave. I slid on the floor, gripping her calf pathetically, pleading with her to stay—bartering, discussing details I thought might be up for negotiation—staring at the brown cabinets and gold handles at my eye level while she sprayed her 1986 perm with Aquanet and assured me she was "only going out for a couple of hours."

This, I knew, was a lie, because she was going to die. So I'd deeply inhale the scent of her Jergens lotion and hairspray, thinking, *This is it. This is the last time I'll smell my mother.*

My brother, immune to the horrors of the world, would play Tetris on Nintendo and then go to bed as if our mother were *not* going to die, while I kept watch on the couch, rocking back and forth and crying at the *M*A*S*H* theme song (my mother's favorite) and waiting for the phone to ring. It would be the police and they would say, "Super sorry, but your mother veered into a telephone pole." I would imagine my screams upon hearing the news, my flailing on the floor, visualizing the body viewing and every word I'd say at her funeral. I saw myself crying out like they do in the movies, and my couch-crying would turn into numb shaking as I thought of the heartfelt things I'd say behind the funeral podium.

I lived and relived my mother's death until I was so desperate I'd resort to prayer. I'd get on my knees and bargain with the God I had just recently met in church: *If you bring her home, Heavenly Father, I will never scream again.*

Since there was no way that was going to work, I would begin making new housing plans. I'd remember it was just my brother, mother, and me, and *since she's dead now, would I live at my father's house?* We did not know him well enough for that. I loved him, but saw him so infrequently I still behaved around him. Nobody can endure such conditions long term.

Would I stay with my sleeping brother? Probably not, since he was only two and a half years older than me and obviously had no idea how to handle danger. *Perhaps I will be sent to live with that woman who helps my mother at her magazine—the one whose daughter had a kid at fifteen and who attempted to superglue her teeth back in?* She babysat for us a few times. Her pit bull tried to eat us and we smelled like cigarettes for nine days. *I'd rather be homeless.*

Eventually, as I sat immobile on the couch, too afraid to move, waiting for my mother or the police, my terror shape-shifted into a formless mass that usurped the body of my mother. I forgot about her specific dying, or it was overtaken by a crushing terror of something to come, or something to be removed, which I could not identify. It felt like waiting and powerlessness.

But in one glorious moment, I'd hear the garage door go up, or a rustle on the porch, and it would be her. I could not believe my good fortune. I'd hug her and she'd let me curl against her in "the big bed." She always let me in, and the warmth was always as perfect as I knew it could be. As long as she was with me, I was alright.

• • •

It turned out Keith had more than office space to offer my mother, and when I was eight, my brother, mother, and I joined Keith and his two teenaged sons on a cruise to Mexico. Keith and my mother married on the mainland in a ceremony none of us children witnessed. When we returned, we moved into his house, and I suddenly had two stepbrothers. The older one was a warm and handsome young man with a gorgeous girlfriend. The younger was a short, reserved, rat-faced human who scurried about looking like he was about to gnaw your face off. As far as I could tell, he was not to be trusted, but as luck would have it, he was the one who would babysit my brother and me in the red-shag-carpet house.

One night in that house, some older neighborhood boys came over and convinced me to spread the lips of my vagina while I sat on a couch, so they could all see. I did it, which was the horror that never left me.

I had shaken my head in protest. I had mumbled *no*. But something about them all gathered around the couch, something about them urging me on, something about them *demanding*—I found myself pulling down my own underwear.

Later, I wondered why I didn't simply walk away, lock myself in my room, staunchly refuse with a big, strong voice. I wondered why I participated in my own degradation, my own humiliation, without a soul touching me. I didn't know why I

did it, not understanding at that young age how children are manipulated. I wrote about it in my diary, a blue one with pink
pages and a white unicorn and red stars on the cover. I referred
to my vagina as my "private parts," because I was young and
mostly Mormon and that's what we called it.

When I told my mother about that and other unfortunate, related occurrences, she sent me to a therapist who explained, after
my mother left the room, that what had happened wasn't abuse
because "it wasn't done violently." That was it. No problem here.
I never saw her again, and I never told my mother what she said.

After that, I filed away in my gut the notion that I was *illegiti-
mately* tainted and evil and dirty. I thought something was wrong
with me not only because it happened, but because I was *upset* it
happened. And then everybody moved on from it but me, and
each week we went to church, where they talked about the sanc-
tity of marriage and the woman's body and how it's a temple.

Do not fuck with the temple. Mine had already been fucked
with, but we couldn't mention it, so I held a dark weird secret in
my temple like a forgotten rotting room.

I resolved I was simply garbage.

My new room in Keith's house was a loft overlooking a big
living room. Between the loft bars, when I was supposed to be
sleeping, I spied on my stepbrothers watching porn on fuzzy,
stolen channels. I hated being in the loft, where there was no
door or wall on one side. I felt exposed in the open air, like I did
that night on the couch. I'd remember the way the boys laughed
and gazed.

But I couldn't crawl into my mother's bed, because she had a
husband now.

So instead I closed the curtain to my loft room, stood in front of a little mirror next to boxes of Keith's old taxes, looked myself in the eyes, and said, out loud, "Janelle, you don't need anyone and nothing will ever break you."

I stood there in pajamas, next to a purple unicorn comforter, staring into a mirror with little ballet shoe stickers all over it, turning myself into a fortress.

• • •

I spent three months in the loft until we moved out again. During this particular separation, Keith was suddenly baptized Mormon, which I explained was a clever ruse to win my mother's affection. He kept smoking cigarettes and drinking while not actually attending church, which I gathered as evidence of the ruse theory, but my mother only agreed when she was feeling scorned.

Keith's most infuriating feature was that he was categorically delightful to me, and I fell into an immense and uncomplicated love for the man. He was my dear friend, and I suspected there had never been a stepfather who loved a stepdaughter as much as he loved me. We had a hundred traditions just between us, songs that were ours and ours alone—so many that I was never afraid of my mother and him separating. We had nothing to do with her.

She was too good for him anyway. My mother was gorgeous, with soft waves of brown and blonde hair and green-blue eyes with yellow in the centers. It's impossible to tell the color of her eyes. Ava and I have the same ones. Green? Hazel? Blue? They change according to what we're wearing, or the sky, or something inside of us perhaps.

When she put her lipstick on, she stuck her bottom lip out

too far, and I laughed and teased her, because it looked like she was sweeping pink paint on the inside of her mouth. I never understood how it didn't smear across her teeth. She explained she had to turn her lip like that because her lips were "so flat." To make me laugh harder, she exaggerated sticking her lip out, and I did it, too, as soon as I'd see the lipstick come out of her purse. The whole lipstick process seemed ridiculous to me, but her mother had taught her never to go outside without lipstick on. Grandma Joan never left the house without her "face" on, and she was strikingly beautiful even into her seventies and eighties. She had a square jaw and huge, bright green eyes. When we would go out in public, people would mistake her for my mother's sister. The family always said it was because she was half Filipino.

My mother had beauty, but she didn't have her mother's marriage, her incredible lineage of love. It must have hung over my mother's marriages like a vast and impossible utopia. With an example that solid, perhaps the only option is to blow up your own life.

We moved into Keith's house three times over the seven years we lived in Atascadero. Once we moved all the way to Round Rock, Texas, then back again seven months later, back to the same damn junior high I had tearfully abandoned mere months before, with the same horrific children, only in more solidified cliques.

I could pack my room in twenty minutes flat.

· · ·

At the end of my eighth-grade year, when my mother decided

she was unquestionably finished with Keith, we moved back to Northern California, right next to where we began, in the city where my father, stepmother, and brother lived. My brother had gone to live with our father a few months before. I believe he was tired of moving.

My mother behaved exactly as she had every other time we left: unequivocally committed to the impossibility of ever returning. By this time, at fourteen, I was not even distantly convinced, because if a Californian can move all the way to *Texas* and still not find escape, there is nowhere far enough.

That first year of high school, I ran for class president and somehow won, which I always figured was because the kids didn't know me well enough to hate me yet, but nobody cared about class president. What they cared about was the father-daughter dinner dance, the fanciest event of the year, particularly for us freshmen, who certainly weren't going to prom and probably not homecoming either.

My actual father lived five minutes from my mother and me, and Keith lived six hours away, but I invited Keith because I missed him, and I knew him better than my father. I knew he would come. He did, and we danced, and by the end of the night I was reassured that no distance or divorce could fracture us.

Three months later, I sat in a witness box in front of a courtroom describing through teary eyes in my most passionate and earnest voice the history of Keith in my family. I understood Keith was denying the legitimacy of his marriage to my mother, claiming it was done in Mexico in a fraud ceremony. My job, according to my mother's attorney, was to prove that Keith and my mother "acted married." Or, more specifically, that he acted "like my father." The situation struck me as odd, and I didn't understand *why* the debate was occurring, but I wanted to help my mother, so I listened carefully to the attorney's direction and sat ready to convince a judge.

Keith was sitting in a tweed suit coat at a table with his attorney, right across from me. I hadn't seen him since the dance. He looked weary.

I told the courtroom how we went to Magic Mountain in Valencia and to Harris Ranch on Highway 5, to Yosemite and the beach and out for hamburgers in San Luis Obispo. I told how he took me along on work trips around the county and how we listened to Rod Stewart as we wove through the fog and down Highway 1 along the coast. That was our song: "Forever Young." I told how he went to my Campfire Girl events when I was in second grade, and how he heard me read my winning D.A.R.E. essay in sixth grade, and took me to ice cream at Thrifty (where I would order mint chip and chocolate malted crunch). When I finished, I knew there could be no doubt of our love anywhere in that courtroom.

Keith's lawyer took a few steps toward me at the stand and asked, "Where is your actual father?"

I started, wiped tears from my eyes, and said, "Oh, he lives here in Santa Rosa."

The attorney raised his voice, grinned a little, filled his mouth with trash, and sneered: "So your *real dad* is not DEAD?" He chuckled after he said it. He laughed at me.

I flinched, and broke the attorney's gaze to look into the eyes of the man I thought was my closest adult friend, who loved me and watched me now and many years before, and I thought I saw tears in his eyes.

Did I? I don't think I did. Maybe I did.

It didn't matter if there were tears or not, because no matter what, I was the one sitting up there like a fool, trying to convince a court he loved me. I shuddered at the humiliation as he sat silently looking at me with the same eyes I had watched for years, eyes I thought looked right back at me and adored what they saw. I had been sold a lie, and I knew it right then, on stage, in front of battling parents and stepparents and strangers, at fifteen years old. I flinched for the first time at the pain of rejection that's unbearable in its finality.

We had nothing. Not a single thing.

Case closed.

Illegitimate. A fraud marriage. A scam love.

He won, and I never saw him again.

I went home and looked at a Norfolk pine Keith had given me when I was nine or ten, a plant he brought home to me from Yosemite, and that I tried to keep alive, water just right, position perfectly next to the sunlight. It never thrived, but I moved it all over with me, through every move, to Texas and back, and then to our apartment in Northern California. That day after court, I moved the plant onto the patio, though I kept watering it occasionally for reasons I'll never fully understand.

A year later, when I tried smoking weed for the first time, the pine wilted on the porch. By the time I had moved on to acid, it was nearly dead in the rain. On drunken evenings in that room when my mother was out of town, it was a few sticks and some dirt, a tiny sprig of green here and there out of dumb luck.

By the time I showed up on my father's doorstep at seventeen years old, announcing myself with the words, "I only have two years left and I want to get to know you. Will you turn me away?" I swear that pine was dead. It appeared completely dead.

I even *thought* it was dead but moved it anyway, because by that point I simply *brought the damn Norfolk pine with me when I moved*.

My father and stepmother did not turn me away, so I took over my brother's old room—he had left for his mission for the Mormon church—and set out to get to know my father. If he didn't want me, fine, but I wanted to know. I wanted lived experience. Case closed.

I'm not sure what my father did when I was seventeen and eighteen while I drove around and went to work as a lifeguard and waitress and sometimes went to school. I'm not sure what he did while I left the house to drink and do cocaine or mushrooms and hang with my new boyfriend who I was sure would become my husband. I'm not sure what he did with that pine while I got angry and raged at my mother and past, at the broken-down minivan and the church, or while I planted my roots as an alcoholic, wrote furiously in my journal, and had sex for the first time.

I don't know what he did, but suddenly I looked at that fucking pine tree and it was brilliant green and giant and bursting. There was no brown left.

It had grown so huge I couldn't recognize it.

Dad and I named it "Norfy," because it was so alive and part of the family it needed a name. It lived in the living room by the back door, where I guess the lighting was just right.

Keith died when I was nineteen. I didn't attend the funeral because I wasn't invited. I heard he died in a chair at his desk, slumped over, below the loft where I used to sleep. Sometimes I wonder where he's buried. If I went, I don't know what I'd say, but it would probably be something like, "You are such a fucking piece of shit. Burn in hell. Also though, how the hell are you, man?"

By then Norfy had grown so big we had to take it to my father's office where he and Grandma Bonny and my aunts ran their newspaper, where the ceiling was higher and the walls didn't confine the sprawling green branches. It seemed like something out of a book, some magical creature that refused to stop growing.

We didn't trim it. We just moved it where it could grow without reason, for as long as it wanted, and eventually it was so huge we couldn't move it at all. For years when I visited, I'd look at that plant and remember when it was a few dead sticks, and how my real father brought it back to life.

•   •   •

"I married another asshole." My mother said it with hopelessness, an almost furious fear. "I married another asshole." I looked at her shape-shifting eyes.

I was a freshman in college when she said it. She was speaking of her third husband, Albert, a man she had met at the little art gallery she owned in Bodega Bay when I was in high school—her second or third, or perhaps tenth, promising entrepreneurial endeavor.

He was an eccentric man who smoked more weed than I'd ever seen anybody smoke in my life, but my mother seemed happy and stable living in his enormous home in the Berkeley Hills. He had money through inheritance, hadn't worked in years, and owned a mind-boggling collection of rock-and-roll concert posters from the 1960s—Stanley Mouse and Rick Griffin, all the gurus—piles of them from when he worked for Bill Graham at the Fillmore. Albert was a fascinating, generous creature, but unfathomably weird. During conversations, he would flip his mouth around and randomly quote poets while gesticulating wildly, then he'd be on the ground straightening the fringe on his Turkish rugs while smoking a joint. This concerned me, but it wasn't my business. I was in college, and my mother was not alone.

I had hated thinking of her alone in her house in Bodega Bay before she met Albert. Past Bodega Bay, actually, miles outside of town. It was just her in a little two-bedroom house on a coastal hillside.

Perhaps we're supposed to outgrow such things, but during my entire first year of college, I would lie in my dorm room nearly every night wondering if my mother had locked the window over her bed. She was always hot and repeatedly failed to shut and lock that damn window. I would imagine a man crawling in and hurting her. I would hear her cries and convince myself she was trying to tell me through my thoughts that she was in danger, because we were *that* deeply connected, mother and daughter, and I would look at the clock—one a.m., two a.m., three a.m.—and wonder if she'd answer my call. I'd pray again. Within a short time, I would be sure she was dead. By the morning, I would have forgotten, and the next time I heard her voice I would laugh at my ridiculousness and remind myself never to do that weird shit again.

I was visiting her and Albert at their vacation rental in Mendocino. My mother and I had just come inside after soaking in a hot tub beneath Mendocino's magnificent fog. I sat down on a bed and feared asking her how married life was going, but I asked anyway because I feared not knowing more.

She was standing in front of a closet, drying her hair with

a towel. She wrapped it around her head and turned toward me. "I married another asshole, Janelle." That was how she answered.

It was the way she said my name. It was the way she said my name as if she were pleading, as if she were reaching out, as if she were looking to me to help her or fix it or even just be the ear to listen and care. I felt my stomach turn in a feeling that was like air in its familiarity.

I was a kid again, driving in our station wagon or minivan while she told me how she suffered, and I told her he would never change, and I felt her pain in my body until I no longer questioned if it was mine.

"I married another asshole."

I wanted to punch her in the face, hold her in my arms— scream, weep, and run. I wanted to wrap her in protection I didn't have. I wanted to leave and never see her again. I wanted to hold her in arms too weak to support anything. *She never listens. Why can't she see? These stories. Her pain. I'll kill him. Another man not nice to her.*

But I watched her marry him. I was in the damn wedding, wearing purple chiffon and smiling. I watched how weird he was and she married him anyway. I suspected she didn't want to be alone.

I hated her for doing it again.

I hated myself more for my inability to change it.

• • •

Driving home from Mendocino the next morning, I rolled the windows down as I passed beneath the redwoods and through the meadows from Fort Bragg to Willits. I opened the sunroof to see the tops of the trees and turned the heater up. The air warmed as I drove farther inland, and as I had a smoke, or five, and listened to the Dead sing of the four winds blowing you safely home, I heard her words again. I heard her call my name, the lilt and appeal and plea, and I saw my blonde head, eight or nine years old and lying in a bed, or sitting in a chair, devastated. *She never listens, but she promises, and I'm sure she'll be okay this time. God, please just let her be okay.*

But she was not, again.

I screamed and couldn't stop screaming. I screamed as loud and hard as my voice would let me. I screamed the scream of a kid who wanted her mother to not suffer anymore. It was the scream of defeat. It was the scream of surrender and a fight abandoned. The scream of finish.

I heard the noise coming out of me and it was strange, but I didn't stop. I let my face contort, and my eyes squint, and I just drove and screamed and hated her. No, I hated powerlessness. It felt the same as it had all my life.

I screamed until I thought my voice would die, but maybe it was already dead. Had been for years. Old air passing through the Mendocino redwoods and Camel Light smoke drifting to the sweet tune of Jerry. There was never a word for her to hear. Never a word worth speaking. I knew it in the freedom of shade and sunlight as I rolled on.

•   •   •

Two years later, I woke to Albert's voice one summer morning as he stood in the doorway of the room in their home where I was staying for the summer before heading to Spain. "You need to go get your mother. She took the gun down to the beach, and she said she's going to kill herself."

Without a word I rolled out of bed and walked barefoot down the trail to the sand on the Mendocino coastline, and without a thought my feet trod methodically, numbly, my heart beating blood of rage and clarity into my green-blue eyes that look like hers. When I saw her standing by the water with a .45 in her hand, I walked straight up to her and looked in those eyes that held oceans for me and said, "Just fucking do it, Mom, if you're going to do it. DO IT," I yelled, and I meant it, unable to face one more attempt to keep her safe or sound.

I turned and walked away, and I held my breath waiting for the boom I knew would shatter both our lives, but I could not scream.

It had all been said.

• • •

The blast never came, but many years later I still felt the metal in her hands. I used to tell Jack about it, and that therapist I saw about my raging, about how it felt to walk in slow motion away from her, each step a long drag through terror. *What would I have done if she had pulled the trigger?* The therapist led me in circles through and in and around it all, to deconstruct and analyze my pain, to heal the young woman who snapped that day, but I always seemed to end up where I had begun. Jack spoke words I had never heard before.

"Your mother, you know, was doing the best she could with what she had at the time." He took a deep drag of his Marlboro and looked at me from behind his glasses, his bright blue eyes terminally serious.

"But what she did was *wrong*, Jack."

"Alright. But do you want to be right or do you want to be free?"

He had a way of unraveling in a single sentence knots I had spent my entire life tying. With every replaying of that scene, every therapeutic conversation about it, every Jungian analysis, I wove a thread back through the center. *I was wronged. She failed me.* And maybe that was true. Jack wasn't arguing otherwise, but something about the way he said those words in that moment transformed my mother into a human. I never saw *her* before Jack spoke those words.

How many years had I spent blaming my failure on my parents? Blaming my brokenness on theirs? Were their sins even about me? Were they ever mine to hold? Everybody wants to blame alcoholics like me on "broken childhoods and bad parenting," but Jack said, "There's no power there, Janelle. There's no power in being angry over the past. You weren't responsible for what happened, but you're responsible for what you do with it now."

My parents were broke-down humans just like me. My mother wanted to not mess up her kids the way her parents messed her up, and she wanted to grow into a better version of herself, too, thinking *surely love will be enough.* She wanted to shove twenty or thirty years of life and disorder into a reliable and shapely parental version of herself, to not be the woman on the beach with a .45, or the loser on the balcony.

I didn't want it to be true either—that what we bring to this newborn is nothing beyond the years of mistakes we've got stacked in our souls, and that what we'll teach is not much more than the lessons we've learned through years of things we probably should have already known, and even love isn't enough to polish us up into something more presentable. Even love isn't enough to make us good enough for the tiny creature in the fuzzy pink bear suit, sleeping on the chest of a mama who's read all the books, nurses with devotion, checks her breathing five times an hour, and asks only once, a bit too seriously, if beer is allowed in birthing centers.

They were doing the best they could with what they had at the time. And so was I. We are the goddamn same.

That was when I knew. You can build a life on rosemary carrots. You can head out without a plan. You can remember an outline, and it may be enough to bring the most hideous, wilted pine into glittering life.

· · ·

We didn't find our own campsite that night in Yosemite. We circled all the campgrounds, and as I had predicted, each site was reserved. We ended up in the overflow area, where, much to my horror, you walk in, choose a spot, and share it with strangers.

The men at our site were mountain climbers from Germany, and that night around the campfire, I watched firelight swirl around their faces while they described nailing their cots into the granite face of Half Dome and sleeping perpendicular to it, suspended, hovering in the cosmos.

"But what if you roll over?" I asked, aghast.

"Well, you don't!" They guffawed, and I thought, *Well, that sounds like a plan my mother would come up with.* They prepared their food like that, too, floating over death, peeing and pooping into cans, and as I sat there, I realized I was meeting the most insane and gorgeous human beings I had ever seen in my life.

"Kid, do have any idea what the stars look like from the face of Half Dome?" The taller hiker looked right at me when he said it, but I couldn't speak, so I handed him another hot dog. He did not throw it at my head.

They explained that after some hiking the next day, they planned on hitchhiking up the coast of California and Oregon. I looked at my mother and smiled, thinking, *God, I hope we pick them up someday.*

Twenty years later, sitting next to Jack after telling him my childhood story, I realized I had never stopped looking for the hitchhikers who climbed the face of Half Dome. Even though there was no chance of happening upon them, I believed they were out there, if I kept searching. Even when I could barely open my eyes, I knew they were out there, and I wanted to meet them. I wanted to find them again—beautiful humanity met by happy accident, to show me what the world looks like beneath the Yosemite stars, from the face of a granite rock I could never scale myself.

My mother kept me looking. Her wild brokenness somehow forced me to remember humanity is mine, and I will find it, even if there is no plan, no reason to believe, and all the signs say "occupied."

15

WHAT THE HELL IS "SOUL WORK"?

If I thought I would be gentler after getting sober, I *really* thought I would round the bend into sainthood after *overcoming my childhood issues.* I thought the intermittent, insidious boredom and confusion of my inner life would disappear like hangovers. I thought the parts of my personality that repelled and repulsed would fade like chain-smoked cigarettes. I thought meaning would beckon at every turn.

And yet, I still raged, fell into caverns of malaise—a sense of godless vacuity—that seemed to live in my blood. Even when it was all "perfect." Even alongside all that fucking gratitude. It almost made it worse. *Here I am sober—a new lease on life!—and I just spent twenty minutes staring at a wall wondering if this is* really *all there is.*

I wanted to discuss Edward Said and do a Marxist reading of nineteenth-century American literature. I wanted to deconstruct dime novels and other "lowbrow" cultural products to study emergent art as resistance. I wanted to set my cubicle on fire. I wanted to get out of my house to hear myself think. I wanted a PhD. I wanted to write. I wanted to read Zizek and Gramsci and Butler and wonder what the hell they were talking about.

I wanted one to three more children. I wanted newborn breath. I wanted midwives to take care of me with their weathered hands. I wanted the moment the baby is placed on my chest. I wanted my milk trickling out of pink petal mouths. I wanted baby thighs and toddler mispronunciations.

While I wanted, I changed diapers and got myself dressed and the kids dressed, and cleaned and studied and drove and drove and drove. Everywhere and nowhere. I woke and did it again. We were down to nickels before every payday, and Mac worked two hours away in San Francisco as an ironworker. My life became five days a week of career work and two days a week of all the housework I didn't do because of the career work. In between, I went to grad school.

I went to grad school and felt embarrassed by my home life, wrestling always with some peculiar shame. *If I were a real intellectual I'd stop housing babies in my womb.* I went to mom groups and felt embarrassed by my career. *If I were a real mother I wouldn't drop my baby at daycare every day.*

• • •

On one particularly dark day, when I must have been channeling my mother's optimism, I admitted to some other mothers how my life felt monotonous and seemed to make me dumber by the day, and how I was having *a bit* of trouble finding meaning in the endless beats of working motherhood. One of the mothers suggested I read the latest feel-good story involving an existentially lost white woman "finding" herself. "Changed my life!" the mother said, and all the women cooed in agreement, glancing at me as we stood around the play structure waiting for our children to get out of class.

I smiled vaguely, thinking, *How? How the fuck did it change your life?*

"Oh, it's amazing," she continued. "She loses everything and cannot find herself—you know, *who she is as a woman*—so she starts traveling. Total spiritual quest. Can you imagine her bravery?"

"She was probably paid a fat book advance to do that," I said, regretting it immediately and thinking, *This is why nobody likes you, Janelle.*

"Well, still. It's really *inspiring*, and it sounds like you need some inspiration!" Her tone reminded me of my uncle patting me on the head at Christmas while saying, "You're doing great, kid!"

It was a familiar feeling—standing in a group of women wondering what the hell was wrong with me. I have always been plagued by the suspicion that I am defective because I don't like things I am supposed to like, that everyone else seems to like, that I would probably like were I a better American. For example: joyful white women telling me how to improve myself.

If I had been ready to face full banishment, I would have told the women around me how I really feel about the self-help soul-journeying brigade. I would have explained my full-blown disdain on a visceral level. But then they would have asked me why, and I would have struggled to articulate what, exactly, is so revolting about put-together, well-meaning women armed with expressions like "soul work."

All I can think when I hear that is, *What the hell is "soul work"?*

These women are adorable, and they say adorable heartfelt things, but when I listen to them, my face contorts in pain. Still, after the world is done acclaiming the latest disaster-to-inspiration miracle story, I give it a listen or read, to join the party, or at least discover what everybody is so enamored with. But after experiencing it, I usually think:

What is this shit?

How do people like this?

What is wrong with humanity?

I hate everything.

I shall move to a yurt on a New Mexican hillside. No. One of those off-grid houses in the Mojave made out of tires. Wait. The Mojave? Fuck deserts.

Where's my James Baldwin?

Okay, but maybe there's something wrong with you, Janelle. DO YOU HAVE NO SOUL?

Maybe. But we have to turn this crap off.

Oh, their stories of recovery after divorce, after drug addiction, after hitting that arctic ontological bottom.

That's my story, too!

Except it isn't. Because they say they were hopelessly lost in addiction but got sober the day they gazed at those sweet newborn toes. They say they beat their addiction by hiking through pine trees on ancestral trails. They overcame their soul-sucking cubicle death job by joining an ashram. They say they were hopeless addicts but still earned PhDs.

I shit in a bag and kept it. Nobody's talking about shitting in bags on *Oprah*. I was at the bottom too—*I feel ya there, ladies!*—but I didn't get a PhD. I got Ancient Age whiskey, laid off, and seven years between the day I enrolled in a two-year MA program and the day I held the actual degree.

And then, most disturbing of all, I got sober and realized I was still an asshole. I got sober and realized I still hurt people. *I even resolved my childhood issues, and I'm still fucking bored.*

Wake up. Hurry. Kiss kids. Step on Legos. Regret life. Say goodbye. Coffee. Car. Cubicle. Censor mouth. Suppress true self. Get paid. Watch it all go to mortgage and pressboard Ikea furniture and student loans. Come home. Yell. Clean. Fight. Laugh. Cuddle. Read inspirational soul travels. Throw book. Sleep. Do it again.

They say "find your passion" and "find the treasure within." And I loved that idea when I got sober, but mostly I hated the way when I lay down, my belly rested on the bed like a bag full of water because I couldn't stop eating sugar.

Even if everything they said was true, and I was simply a walking bad attitude, their polished words ultimately *felt* like lies. They felt like a well-choreographed dance around the truth. It made me uneasy because it was almost believable, all that gentle talk. It almost felt real. But my bullshit detectors blared whenever I read their words, and they wouldn't shut off until I got back to words that grapple in the center, where the ambiguity lies—where a lack of answers *is* the endpoint.

I wondered why we couldn't be real with ourselves: "We are going to die someday. We are going to rot in a coffin with motherfucking maggots. Isn't it insane that we waste our time staring at smartphones and working at desk jobs we hate while accumulating shit we can't take with us? Isn't it ridiculous that we've created this material fortress of meaning in our lives when we're all just mindless mechanics working for a giant capitalist daddy?"

Now leave me alone while I check my newsfeed.

And yet, the years mocked me with their passing. Sometimes I would imagine myself on my deathbed, looking back on my life, and I would feel—I mean *really feel*—that this life is all we get. These years, one shot, ninety years if we're lucky. And I'd grow so terrified of *just not doing anything* that I would grow almost frantic.

And yes, standing among those women, I was searching for meaning, even when nobody was looking—for connection, purpose, color—some taste of recklessness in a neighborhood of neutral tones. I've always been looking for Barcelona. *Perhaps I should eat, pray, and love it into existence?*

• • •

When I was three months sober, I sat in a conference room waiting for my first performance review since I'd cleaned up my act. I had shown up every day for ninety full days, clear-headed and ready to work, engaged in my job and no longer saying "cunt" at random. I had no doubt my bosses would offer nothing but praise for my dazzling performance.

Instead, they drew line by line the full picture of my mediocrity. I do not remember their specific concerns, but there were many. I only remember how we were sitting at the table and how it felt. They spoke clearly, professionally, and correctly.

I was decidedly standard. Even sober.

The shock drove tears from my eyes, and I did not try to stop them. They were pouring, and no amount of tough-broad bravado would have saved me. The horror was not failing to earn a glowing review. It was that I had been so sure of myself. These same bosses had once laid me off for talking to myself incoherently in a hallway. *I had come so fucking far.*

I thought they looked at me with pity. I could have sworn it was pity. It probably was. How could they not? When the review was over, I walked straight to the top floor of the parking garage to hide and smoke a cigarette and call Good News Jack. I told him all of it. I wasn't angry. I was devastated.

"I just feel pathetic, Jack. I was sitting there like a mother-fucking loser, and I just feel pathetic."

Against all evidence of my time working with him, I still expected words of encouragement, words like, "Oh you're not pathetic. Look at all you've done, Janelle! You're a shining star!"

But after a pause, he asked, "Wouldn't it be great if you could be okay with being pathetic?"

His question entered my consciousness one word at a time in neon lights. I stared at the cars around me, all lined up, the sun hitting them from the side, casting deep four-o'clock shadows. I took a drag of my smoke.

Well I'll be damned, I thought. *The problem is not that I'm pathetic, the problem is* I think I shouldn't be pathetic. *What if I am? What if I let that be?*

I smiled. *I'm pathetic.* I got sober and managed to have the worst performance review I'd ever had. *What now, Janelle?*

"Ah, shit, Jack." I couldn't think of more to say. I hung up, and pathetic settled into my bones. It ran to my skin and brain and toes. Through my whole heart.

What now? I looked around again.

I'm still here.

I dropped my cigarette onto the concrete and crushed it before picking it up and throwing it away (because *I don't litter*). Then I walked back into the building.

Back in my cubicle, I remembered what Jack had told me in

my earliest days of sobriety: "If you're sitting in the living room but want to be in the kitchen, the first thing you have to do is realize you're in the fucking living room." *Oh God,* I thought. *Good News Jack is speaking in metaphor again.* I nodded, following the concept thus far.

"Otherwise," he said, "you'll never know to get up and walk into the kitchen."

I stared at him with my mouth open. *We can't get someplace new until we're honest about where we are.*

I had spent so much time gazing at the kitchen, longing for the kitchen, crafting visions of what it would be like to be in the kitchen, that I never took the time to look down, right there, at my ass on the couch. I was so busy yearning for Spanish cobblestone, I missed the concrete beneath my own damn feet.

Not a single thing changed about my life after that day. I was still a butler and reluctant homemaker and administrative assistant craving *one iota of critical thinking.* And I still often hated it. I simply stopped fighting that I hated it. It felt like a pause, a deep breath, a long inhale of the facts. *Okay,* I thought. *So this is my life.*

I'm the motherfucking butler. What now?

And I got back to work. Because from there, there's nothing left to do.

• • •

Maybe if I had listened to the inspiration brigade—maybe if I were a different person with a different past and a more positive, reasonable outlook—writing would have been gentle, a sweet release, instead of a roaring beast that snatched me for hours after the kids went to bed, and took me away on Saturday afternoons, and locked me in my bedroom after telling my children, "If you knock on my door and you aren't bleeding, I will ruin you."

Maybe I would have continued folding the laundry and placing it in drawers rather than depositing baskets of unfolded clean clothes in front of each kid's dresser. Surely I would have written fewer expletives had I been swimming laps every day instead of fortifying myself with 70 percent cacao bars, coffee, and sarcasm.

But I didn't, and I'm not somebody else, and I didn't start writing to change lives or make money or even "fulfill" myself. I started writing because nobody was writing the life I was living. Nobody was saying a damn word about what I saw each day. *And yet, I exist. Don't I?* Nearly two years later, I was *still* looking around at the "categories" of mothers and realizing I fit nowhere. Meanwhile, the world told me to "explore creative endeavors like a hummingbird."

I would look around at the disorder of my life, the chaos and ambiguity—emptiness and servitude alongside exquisite beauty—and I'd think, *Somebody else must feel this way too.* Because I knew I was grateful. I knew I was so happy to be here I sometimes felt the hand of God himself had spread across my broken shoulders. And yet, *maybe I hate motherhood.*

"Why can't both exist, Mac? Why can't it be *this good* and *this bad?*

"I don't know, Janelle. Why don't you stop reading that crap?" he'd say.

I'd continue blathering on about whatever "sleep training" article I had read, or yet another "women should cover up when they nurse" manifesto. I'd read *one more* handy guide about how to "balance" your forty-hour workweek, spice up your sex life, speak in gentle tones to our butterfly babies, and lose twenty pounds—*in a month!* Everybody seemed to agree on a few basic tenets of motherhood—that it was precious and sacred, and that saying otherwise was Satanic.

I'd squint and curse under my breath and read more books and magazines and blogs. I'd read Twitter and Facebook and Instagram. The more I read, the more alienated I felt until I simply had to know: *Is the rest of the mothering world crazy, or am I?*

The thought *fuck these people* drove me to the keyboard. One of us was definitely lying. Words flooded my brain while I showered or drove. I'd miss the exit on my way to work and not realize it for a full five minutes. My kids' voices became white noise behind the deafening cadence of sentences I had not yet written. When I couldn't stand the beating any more, I sat down one day in my cubicle, signed up for a free blog, named it "Renegade Mothering," and wrote eight hundred words in fifteen minutes. The last of them said this:

What about those of us who love our children as much as the well-adjusted knowledgeable stable enlightened types but just can't seem to get it right? What about those of us who just aren't cut out for this shit but are doing it anyway?

I am proof that not every woman enters motherhood in some gentle, planned, ribbon-and-ruffles way. Not every woman likes this crap. Not every woman fits neatly into the mold created and reinforced by irrelevant books like "What to Expect…"

I usually look around the child-rearing world and see a bunch of crap I don't need, hear a bunch of advice I can't use—encounter a bunch of people I only partially understand.

I go home and I see a thrashed house with kids everywhere and overgrown lawns, dirty cloth diapers and books I want to read but don't and toys and dishes and sometimes I demand that my kids just sit down be quiet and watch Netflix because I can't stand one more moment of noise or movement. And if one more person says "Mama" I am going to take a bat to the windows.

And a few hours later I walk into her room after she's gone to sleep and I see my firstborn baby, nine years old. I stroke her frizzy unkempt hair and listen to her soft snores. I touch her cheek and my eyes burn in palpable adoration. I feel it surge up my body from my toes into my fingers—thick, fierce infinite expanding mama love. And I beg the universe in that moment to give her everything she will ever need and please God keep her safe and how is it that I am so lucky to have this child, right here. The one who robbed me of my great ass and flat belly and turned me into the mother I wasn't ready to become.

I lie down exhausted and think of all the ways I could be a better mom. Of the days I've missed through my own selfishness. Of the years racing by, teasing me with the illusion that this will never end, that they'll always be little. And I wish I didn't yell so much.

And so it goes on like this. Back and forth. All the time. Here's to the trip.

Someday I shall write my own book called: "What to Expect When You're [a Jackass and] Expecting." Until then, I'll write this blog.

•   •   •

It was a small, silly act. A dumb nudge in a great void. *A "mommy blog?" Bah!*

"Nobody will read you, Janelle. Nobody cares," my brain told me.

"That's okay," I answered back. "I'm okay with being pathetic."

I had forty readers, and twenty of them were my cousins. After I wrote a post—usually when I was supposed to be working—I would wait seven minutes and call my mother. "Did you read it?" I'd ask.

"Yes!" she'd say, and tell me she was crying or that I was "hilarious." And I'd think, *Nice. My mom thinks I'm funny.* Then I'd go back to my soulless work.

When I got home, I'd ask Mac if he had read it, and he'd say, "You're such a good writer, Janelle." I didn't believe him, but kept writing anyway because I'd remember the duck and the fire hydrant.

• • •

Two years later, three years sober, I sat in my advising professor's office and told her I had changed my mind about pursuing a PhD, so we need not continue drafting our article together. "Because, you see, Professor, I've had a few posts get kind of big—and I know it's stupid—blogging? How pathetic, right? But I have to try. I have to see if I can write."

"Janelle," she said. "For God's sake, do that. We will always be here."

And when I finished graduate school armed with a credential "proving" I could write, I asked Bea at the law firm to expand my responsibilities beyond pushing paper around for a dull, misogynistic new guy who demonstrated what truly unfortunate bosses act like. (I would never, ever complain about Brian and his color coding again.)

She answered, "We continue to look for opportunities to use your talents and skills in the firm."

I smiled, thanked her, and walked out of her office knowing the next time we spoke, I would be handing her my resignation. It had been nine years, an excellent run. I wasn't resentful. I was indebted. They had kept me around through the roughest years of my life, helped me fail, helped me get sober. But I didn't belong there anymore.

Possibly, I never had.

When I quit, it merely felt correct. It felt *true.* I did not have a plan in mind beyond "get some gig at a junior college teaching composition and keep writing," nor did I have money if my plan fell through, but I knew in my guts it was time to go. I knew it was time to take a step toward the kitchen. My ten-year-old self would have been appalled at my lack of planning.

• • •

And one day, a few years later, I found myself writing, and teaching some college classes, but with four children now. My days had not changed. They were frantic and they were uninspired— monotonous and heavy and rather butler-like—kid chatter and nursing and back pain and the mess. My God, the mess. Laundry and dishes and parent-teacher conferences and *I still didn't read past email number nine.*

They erase me, I'd think, until night, after they went to bed, and I'd sit down at the computer and write some words to some strangers, some other mothers. To say something that was mine. I defended that time. I blocked everyone who tried to enter it. *You can have everything, kids, but you can't have this.*

At work, I served my employer. At home, my kids. But there, on that page, I served nobody. I was in the kitchen, but not that of my grandmothers, or even my mother, but mine—my own place, if only for a few hours a week. When I got there, people asked, "My God, how brave of you to just get up and do it! I wish I could. How did you do it?" But I didn't know how to respond, because the only thing I did was get really tired of my-self, look down, and take a few steps. Then I was in the kitchen, kinda eyein' the bedroom, thinking, *It will all be amazing if I could only get there.*

It's okay, though. I see now it keeps me moving.

I didn't overcome my fear. My fear lives always like a low hum in the back of my mind. I simply lost faith in it. *Okay, fear, hi.* Maybe the man under the bed is still there. Maybe I should check the closets. But if all that searching and scrambling for safety results in nothing but the same old fear, what's the point of wasting my time? What's the point of remaining silent? *The maggots are going to come either way.*

I had nothing to prove when I sat down to write that first post. Nothing left to defend. What was the Internet going to say to me? "You are a bad mother?" *Oh! You think? I had no idea.*

There was nothing the world could throw at me I hadn't al-ready caught, no place they could illuminate in the recesses of my being that would surprise me. I had walked them all, visited each one with my whole body and bones and blood. Two inches from my eyes I studied each line, every letter my baby sent me to come home, and every time I didn't, and everything I missed, and every tear my mama shed, and every rush of hope when I seemed to *really be coming around this time.*

I guess I found my soul work, but I found it at the bottom, right there with the kid who chased with knives, the woman on her unmade bed, stepping on Legos, washing jam off the linoleum. I found it in the mess I was running from, in the life I deemed lacking, in the fingers never blessed enough.

•   •   •

I suppose some of us don't have the luxury of neatly wrapped truth, of affirmations that rest on our tongues like peppermints. Some of us need to be doused in gasoline and set aflame, until the truth consumes us, and we have no choice but to recreate ourselves. A collision, as Baldwin says, when one must choose to live or die.

I didn't want to feel better. I wanted to live.

I didn't want the pain gone. I wanted it to mean something.

When I found my voice, I didn't find answers—I found a purpose for every moment I had lived. I found power in every blackened room in my mind, every fear, every sad parent, every futile word and nightmare memory.

Because it led me to you, to the place where we are the same, to the place where words draw a line from my bones to yours, and you look at me and say, "I know," and I look back at you, thinking, *Well I'll be damned. I guess we've been here together all along.*

16

IN THE BLOOD OF OUR MOTHERS

My Grandma Bonny was a writer, too, though I barely noticed when she was alive. From age fourteen to eighteen, I pulled away from my church, father, and mother, but stayed near Grandma Bonny, and I was never sure why. Nobody in my family was interesting or smart enough for my teenaged standards, and she wasn't either, really, but I was drawn to her anyway. I admired her intellect, her power. She was deeply flawed, too—a little cold, a little prone to rage, a little irrational when it came to, say, healthcare for her five children. That was the Mary Baker Eddy in her.

By the time I was in high school, and she was in her seventies, she had been a widow for ten years but continued living as she always had, rising early each morning and putting on a pantsuit, a brooch, and heading to "the shop," where she would write at a big wooden desk in the back of the office behind a nameplate from the 1960s that said *Bonny Jean Hanchett: Editor*.

She always, for as long as I can remember, drove a Ford Taurus, along with nearly my entire family, because my father's cousin worked at the local Ford dealership. Every two or three years, she'd get a new Taurus, and every Wednesday she'd pick me up from school. I loved the smell of her car. The air that came out of the vents was musty and clean, just the same as when she'd drive me around Clearlake and to her church when I was a little girl. It smelled like Grandma Bonny.

She would wear her pantsuit even in the dead of summer, with her smooth white hair in a bob, and she'd accessorize with gold and diamond rings. Her nails were always neatly manicured, sometimes polished a sensible pink. While we drove to her town of Cloverdale, which was about thirty minutes from my high school, I would ask her astute questions like "Why is there no 'white club' at school if there's a Mexican club?" (I had a long way to go before learning of my ignorance.) But I don't remember her answers, because I was more interested in my own voice prattling on about so-and-so at school and how he was teaching a faulty curriculum.

She'd often turn on political talk radio while I stared out the window and counted trees. Even if I tried to listen, I couldn't follow for more than a few seconds because the radio hosts sounded drab and monotone, discussing topics that didn't matter to me at all, like California legislation or international diplomacy.

Occasionally, she'd yell back at the radio, which I took as a desire to engage me. So I would ask a question, but again didn't absorb her answers, because I knew nothing of international politics—or politics at all. But she talked as if I should know, so I didn't ask. I pretended to understand so she would think I was an informed and intellectually advanced teenager.

In hindsight I realize she did not expect me to know about these things. She was simply refusing to talk down to me. She talked down to nobody, except any waiter who made a mistake on our order. *God help you then, kid.*

When we'd arrive at "the shop," I'd drop my Jansport backpack at one of the empty desks and kill time by spinning around in an empty office chair. My aunts would come over to say hello and ask me how my mother was and how school was going, usually with X-acto knives in their hands, but my grandmother went immediately to her desk, and I knew not to disturb her. *She would ruin me.*

When I was a little girl in the shop, I would draw pictures or play school, make books out of paper and ad scraps, and write notes to my father. Twenty years later, when my father and aunts sold the newspaper, the notes were still hanging on the wall, although they belonged in the trash. They had faded into little wisps of orange or purple or red. Norfy, though, the massive pine, still occupied the entire front office with its sci-fi branches.

When she finished her work, Grandma Bonny and I would head back to her house, and she would make me a dinner that somehow always incorporated mayonnaise or the microwave. While she cooked, I would walk around and look at all the Madame Alexander dolls, Beatrix Potter figurines, plates with kittens, and books I had examined since I was a toddler. I wondered why she lived in a mobile home. She could afford more, but after my grandfather died, and she sold the newspaper they had run for thirty years in Clearlake and bought this one, she insisted on living in a mobile home in the little retirement park. I loved how everything had a place in it, though. I loved how I had a place, with her, in all that history.

When I was old enough to drive myself to her house on Wednesdays, I would walk in and she'd be reading *Democracy in America* or Proust or Dickens, or embroidering while hollering at politicians on TV. I'd scour the freezer for ice cream without a layer of crystals, and instead find Bon Bons. I'd eat the whole package while she made me a chicken sandwich with canned chicken, mayonnaise, and walnuts.

I've never seen anybody eat chicken sandwiches like that since, but that's still what I make when I want to remember.

• • •

If it was October or November she would tell me it was time to start wrapping gifts for Christmas, and that she was going to pay me for my work. I would say, "You don't have to pay me, Grandma."

She'd shake her hand at me and say, "No, you're good at it, and I hate wrapping, so you'll earn it."

I knew she was telling me the truth.

I'd begin by laying out the paper choices. I needed plenty of options to balance the landscape under the tree. Then I would set out the tape, making sure it was in an upright metal dispenser, so I could rip the tape pieces off with one hand. Next, I would set out the scissors, tags, and a pen. Just one pen. A ballpoint that wouldn't smear on the labels. Finally, I would stack the gift bags and boxes and tissue paper.

After it was all set up, we would move into the guest room and open the bottom drawer of the dresser, which would be stuffed with tiny gifts she had been buying all year. She would remember who almost every single one was for. All year, every year, she bought gifts for her five children and six grandchildren and two great-grandchildren and all the family members who weren't *actually* family members but really, at that point, *were*— plus everybody's boyfriends or girlfriends or spouses.

She bought the tiny porcelain tea set for Aunt June in London because Aunt June loves England, and she bought the horse figurine for Aunt Caroline because she loves horses. Some gifts were catchall gifts. These she would often hold up in the air, resting one finger on the side of her mouth in the classic thinking pose, contemplating who would be the perfect recipient. She looked so tender and affectionate in those moments. She might put the gift back, or she might make a decision. Sometimes I found the gift in the drawer long after Christmas had passed. *Guess she never decided on that one*, I'd think.

After I gathered my stack of gifts from the drawers and closets, I would begin wrapping. I loved the boxes the most because I could wrap the corners tight and clean, and easily center the bow. When I was done, they felt perfect. I'd wrap for hours while she'd listen to talk radio, occasionally walking by in her long robe that zipped up the front, patting my back.

"I don't know what I'd do without you!" she'd say. The finished products were spectacular.

I felt I made Christmas with her. I felt it was us doing it together. I wrapped for her when I was nine, ten, eleven, and twelve. I kept showing up when I was thirteen, fourteen, fifteen, sixteen, seventeen, and eighteen. *Grandma Bonny needs me. I am the one who wraps the gifts.* I was thorough. We had a system.

My first year of college, in 1997, I made sure to come back at Christmas to wrap with my grandmother, but after that, I didn't come again. My stepmother took over the wrapping.

• • •

When Ava came in 2001, I had grown impatient with Grandma Bonny's phone calls, because she spoke slowly and quietly, and there was rarely time to listen to old women talk about the British Parliament. I saw her at Christmas, and every year at the Cloverdale Citrus Fair, and I never failed to stop at the shop when we drove out to Mendocino, because it was right on the way. But I had grown busy.

My father told me in 2008, the last year of my drinking, not to come visit her, even though it was the last year of her life. If I were in my right mind, I would have gone immediately anyway. I would have sat by her side and touched her if she would let me, and I would have studied her eyes to remember. He said not to come because of her dementia, because she wouldn't remember me, but I wonder if it was because of the state I was in, and maybe they didn't want her to see me like that. I was the sickest I had ever been.

We were both, I suppose, the sickest we had ever been.

So I cannot remember the last time I saw her, what we talked about, or how. I have one vision of her standing in the doorway of her last home, the bigger home she told me "the children" had convinced her to buy after the mobile home. She was wearing a pink fleece robe, and she was waving to me as I drove away. She seemed to wave an extra long time, and I noticed.

"One of these times will be the last time I see her," I said to Mac.

But I don't think that was the time. That day, we kissed and hugged in the doorway and I said goodbye, but I don't think that was *the* goodbye.

In the end, there was no goodbye, and I was still a loser when she died.

• • •

She once told me while I sat across from her on the couch that she wore red velvet to her wedding in 1943. She said, "They weren't going to turn me into some blushing bride!" When she said "blushing bride" she put her hands up under her chin, wagged her fingers up and down, and flitted her lashes to make me laugh. That was not the last time we talked, but it was the conversation I have chosen as the last, because it was my favorite, and I can't bear to think of what our actual last conversation would have been. If I could see her with the mind I have now, I would tell her how much fun I had with her, and how I always felt a strange, superhuman connection to her, because we are similar women, skeptical and "offending" and "just too much," with tiny rage problems and loads of children, but an inability to accept them as the full definition of our selves. I would thank her for reading me Beatrix Potter and letting me eat three Danish pastries with butter on top and showing me how intellectual mothers can be and that some of us will simply never fit.

"You know? We just don't, Grandma," That's what I would say.

I would record her talking about her life, so I could hold it and hear it and learn it, because there were a thousand stories beyond the ones she told me and I forgot, and a thousand more she never told me, about growing up behind the stage, becoming the first woman editor of the University of Washington's newspaper, about World War II and a veteran husband who sometimes woke up sweating from nightmares, about the time she crawled onto the couch and refused to move, and nursed herself back to sanity by doing paint-by-numbers her friend had brought her. About the day Uncle John died of alcoholism, and she said simply, "A parent should never outlive her children," and it was the only time I saw her drink a glass of wine.

Oh, I want to hear about writing, Grandma, about people who hated you, about journalism and female editors in the 1950s, the Mafia men you fought with about the resort on your lake—the algae lake with the rough water that lulled me to sleep on those hot-cold sunburned evenings, the one I drove by and remembered, and wondered when it was that we last spoke, and if she wondered the same as she drifted on, or if the dementia took that away, and I had become nothing but a speck of curled ribbon in the recesses of a fading mind.

Part of me wished that were true. Part of me wept at the thought.

On the day my father called to tell me she had died, I was sitting in a bar that smelled like urine and bottom-shelf bourbon. I notified the man sitting next to me of the passing of my grandmother, and he felt very sad for me. Surely he would have bought me a round had he a few extra bucks. I remember feeling almost nothing, and wanting to, but I had passed the moment when feelings came the way they should and I lived like a real human on a real earth.

Six months later, I left myself in a bed, maybe the way Bonny Jean left herself in hers.

• • •

When I was a month sober, my bedroom door opened suddenly in the middle of the night while I was in a dead sleep. I startled and sat up in bed in time to see the door open, rest for a second or two, and then shut again. My dog jumped out of his bed and barked at the door.

I thought it was my mother, the only other person in the house, but I needed to make sure, so I said her name and opened the door. But I saw only an empty hallway. I walked across the hall to her bedroom, and from the doorway I saw her sleeping and heard her snoring.

As I sat on the edge of my bed considering what had just happened, I was overwhelmed with a feeling that Bonny Jean had visited me. Out of nowhere, a feeling of her presence overtook me, as if she were standing right there, and I could smell the scent of her car, see her wrinkled hands as they clasped in delight at my wrapping or in rage at the audacity of Fox News.

It was as if she had opened the door and looked in, saw me sleeping there, and moved on. As if she had opened the door, looked in, and said, "Oh, finally, you're okay."

Perhaps that is the last time we met; though we didn't say goodbye, we were both in our right minds, and that's saying something, I guess.

•   •   •

Seven years later, when my maternal grandfather, Bob, was dying in October 2016, I was there, because I knew what it meant to miss a grandparent's final days. When I walked into his hospital room, I leaned over the foot of the bed, and he grabbed my hands and said, "It's time." And I said, "Yes, it is," and made my bravest face for him, because I saw fear in his eyes. He wanted to die at home, but Grandma Joan wasn't ready to accept his death, not quite yet. But by the time she stopped demanding more pills and doctors and possible new medical advances, he had mere hours to live, and they couldn't arrange hospice in time. He passed away in the night surrounded by his daughters and wife, by a window overlooking the maternity ward.

He and Joan Lila had four daughters, twenty grandchildren, and forty-four great-grandchildren. Many of us passed through his hospital room, taking turns sitting by the bed and leaning against the walls. We cried and laughed as we had done our whole lives together in the basement of their home two miles from that sterile room. Occasionally, Grandpa Bob would wake and lift his head, startled and sudden, and look slowly and deliberately around the room at each one of us, from behind the oxygen mask he kept yanking off, and I wanted to beg my family to just let him take it off. *Let him be comfortable. He clearly hates that thing. What does it matter now? What are we hoping for? An extra hour?*

Then I realized we were keeping him alive for us, for Joan Lila.

He would lock eyes with one of us, hold our gaze for a few seconds, and fall back asleep. When he locked eyes with me, I did my best to send him strength, to see the part of him that knew he was stepping into the great journey and didn't want to go. I wished something could soothe him.

Grandma Joan refused to leave his side. She rubbed his arm where there were no IVs and fixed the tape around their entry points. She brushed wisps of hair from his forehead and said, "Oh Bob, we had a good life together, didn't we?" She told him story after story, of their friends and daughters, and boating on Clearlake, and he watched and dozed and nodded in recognition. His eyes held hers desperately. Once, he pulled his oxygen mask off and they had one big, last smooch, and it made a nurse kneeling next to them drop her head and cry. Their hands entwined and he pressed himself against the side of the bed, his face as close as he could get to hers. To watch them felt like watching the perfect end to the love story we all wish we could have, the piercing agony we all strive for.

When it was bedtime that night, and all of us grandchildren were heading out for sleep, we said, "We'll see you in the morning, Grandpa," but we knew that was unlikely, so we said longer goodbyes than usual. Mostly, though, we relied on the thousand goodbyes we had tossed over our shoulders as we left their home of forty years. *Until next time. Love you.* There was no way we could say enough, so we simply said one more goodbye— lingered longer, grasped his hand, let go, and forced the turn to walk away.

When I was standing in the doorway looking into his room, aware that I was probably looking at my living grandfather for the last time, a new nurse came in to help settle him and check his gear. The air hung heavy with nearing death, and my grandfather was restless. So when the nurse walked by the television, she said to nobody in particular, "We have a special channel for moments just like this," and flipped to a station with soothing music and goldfish swimming around against a blue background.

It was a fake fishbowl television death station.

During moments like this I feel like I am on the edge of the world, looking on, a hundred miles from whatever land the rest of you are inhabiting, wondering how nobody sees the tragedy of that gesture, how infinitely weird and empty we are. I studied the scene: my grandmother staring into his face, my mother and aunts bustling or sitting, eighty-seven years of life and love circling to its close in mere hours, and here, on the night before us—the last night—all we have to offer are motherfucking TV goldfish to see him into the abyss.

Hey man, sorry you're dying. Here are some goldfish.

I took a hard look at his big, calloused hands that he used to sweep over his mouth after he cracked a joke or teased my grandmother, and I walked out the automatic doors.

• • •

Five weeks after we buried my grandfather, on the morning of November 10, 2016, I was pulling out of my children's school parking lot after dropping them off when my phone rang, and I thought, *Oh, good, it's my mom telling me she's forgiven me for being an asshole last night.* Donald Trump had just been elected President, and I had taken my shock out on my mother. But as soon as I clicked "answer," I only heard her screaming.

At first I thought my mother was getting stabbed because I heard "knife" and "stabbed" and "killed," so I screamed at her to leave her house. But through more chopped screams I realized it was my grandmother who was being stabbed.

Then I learned she had already been stabbed, and was in fact dead, and my cousin was the one who did it. My own cousin, the one who sat with me in my grandfather's hospital room but registered no emotion, no affect, no nothing. I noticed, and I asked about it. I was told he was suffering from depression. I said I thought he needed help, that he was perhaps suicidal.

I was twenty minutes away from my mother when I picked up the phone, and I knew she was alone in her house, so I drove and wailed and tried to breathe while telling Arlo—our fourth child, two years old, the beautiful completion of our family— that I was okay, even as the air I breathed felt like fire and the air moving out felt like drowning, my terror a thousand shards of glass tearing through me, slamming the outside of my body.

I drove to her while my baby looked at me wide-eyed and silent from his car seat. I called Mac and screamed to him. He thought one of our children had been killed. Hysterics, actual hysterics, are virtually impossible to comprehend. I tried so hard to pull enough air to speak sentences, but all that happened were quick bursts of guttural wails and broken words through burning breath.

When I got to the intersection two streets away from my mother, a wooden arm came down in front of me and a huge cargo train rolled in. The train stopped entirely, and I couldn't get to her. I was the first in line in the intersection, and I couldn't get to her, so I yelled "No no no no" while immobile in the car and shook my head and sweated and screamed and looked at my boy who sat silent, until I could get to her. When I did, she was half-dressed, doubled over in a chair and shrieking with the shock of a terrified child, "My beautiful mother! He killed my mother!" When she said "mother," she rose and spun around and ran across the room, and sat and rose again and cried out again, "He killed my mother!"—over and over, while I watched with eyes wide, fighting wild, insane panic and sorrow.

An old woman murdered by her grandson. My grandmother. My mother's mother. Joan Lila.

My mother fell against the walls, and I held her up while my little boy stood looking out the front door I had forgotten to shut, holding his monkey lunch box in front of him with both hands, as if he were waiting for a ride on a train that had just departed.

In those early hours we knew no details of the crime, so I imagined my grandmother suffering, slowly bleeding to death in pain and isolation. But it turns out that after eating Chinese takeout with her and his mother, my thirty-five-year-old cousin went upstairs to the bathroom, and when he came out, went into his bedroom, where he unsheathed a Kershaw hunting knife, stuck it up his shirtsleeve, came downstairs, and stabbed my grandmother in the neck, once, from behind.

This I found to be a significant relief.

After spending a day envisioning her body mutilated and writhing, I felt relief that she hadn't seen him coming. I felt relief that it was instantaneous. I felt relief that her last thought was not, *My grandson is about to kill me.* I felt relief her final moments were not terror and betrayal and the watching of a hand raised to annihilate her, defenseless and yet fighting anyway—the instinctual shriek and cowering—and the subsequent fall, bleeding, and extinguished light, with not even a goldfish to comfort her.

•   •   •

Grandma Joan and I had not spoken in almost a year before my grandfather's death because I was angry with her, and had convinced myself we need not speak again, ever. She had sent Mac a message online asking why our daughter Georgia was "shorn like a boy" and inquiring if her mother was using her as a political project. You know, a sort of "girls can have short hair" poster child to further my liberal agenda.

But when my mother told me my grandfather was dying, I was reminded of the eternal backdrop of impending death, and my charge grew petty and damn near shameful. I left for the hospital immediately. As soon as I turned the corner in the hospital hallway, Grandma Joan came running to me and grabbed my face, saying, "I'm sorry, I'm sorry. Do you forgive me?" Of course I did, and had for many months, but was still clinging to the self-righteous indignation that always failed me. I took special care to focus mostly on my grandmother, to pat her back, bring her water, and hold her hand. She was dizzy with confusion and exhaustion and helplessness, watching her love travel on without her, and I wanted to fix what I had done, because she was eighty-five and didn't understand little girls with mohawks. Do we hate them for that? Our mothers and grandmothers? Do we hate them for roles they've internalized and been forced to play? Or do we simply love them as they pass into the gray?

Joan Lila was told she couldn't go to college because she was a girl, and my grandfather preferred she not work, but she did anyway, and perhaps she had some ideas and hopes for herself that simply were not viable on account of her gender. So when she came to my house a week before she was slaughtered, and then again two days before she was slaughtered, I felt a rush of joy that I had a grandmother again—to be near, to be with, to maybe wrap presents with. I thought, *Oh, we can do so many things together. I'm going to take her everywhere.* Because there was a part of her that had come alive, maybe the part of her that had wanted to go to college at eighteen, and even though she loved my grandfather with a fantastical-type unicorn love, there was a brightness in her step as she told us of her plans.

Oh, her plans. She was going to buy a little place closer to the city, closer to where we lived, and she was going to visit each grandchild to get to know each great-grandchild "really well." On the last day she visited, she wore makeup that matched her blouse and a vibrant red scarf around her neck as we perused the books at Costco—her tiny, wrinkled fingers stretching over the embossed covers—with more places to visit now, at eighty-six, than perhaps in the entirety of her life.

Instead she was eliminated at 7:30 p.m. on Wednesday, November 9, 2016, by a grandchild she loved with the fullness of her heart, a grandchild who had ceased taking medications for a psychiatric condition nobody told us he had.

●   ●   ●

Within a few hours of arriving at my mother's house, after a friend had picked up Arlo, and Mac and my brother had come to help hold my mother's trembling body, I realized she was living the fear that had been pulsing through me since I was a little girl. Somebody had hurt her mother. Somebody had taken her mother. Somebody had caused indescribable suffering to the woman who held her as a newborn, whose existence was a blanket around shivering shoulders. And my mother, my mother got the phone call I was always waiting for, for years, rocking on a couch as a child, wide awake in college, imagining an intruder. *Here it is, Janelle. This is what it looks like. This is the horror you built in your imagination.*

"Maybe she is not actually dead. We haven't heard from anybody who saw her body. Maybe she's just sick at the hospital," my mother said, getting up and packing a suitcase. "I have to be with her."

Mac rose silently, called the police in the city where the crime occurred, and spoke softly with the detective. We watched him taking notes while my mother ran around the house packing, and I searched for the power to say, "Mom, she's dead."

When Mac hung up the phone, my mother cried, "Where is she?"

Mac looked at her with the same kind brown eyes I knew from that first night sixteen years before, the eyes that caught me in the flurry of my life and held me near him, with him, if only to discover how deep the kindness goes. He nearly whispered, "She's at the coroner's" and grabbed her as she collapsed again against him, her legs too weak to support the truth.

That night, as I slept next to my mother like she had always done for me, as I pulled the blankets up under her chin and tucked her hair behind her ear, I wondered if all the agony and all the terror of my life—of the surety that my mother would die one night in some horrific way, and I would be left motherless and powerless—had been leading only to this very moment.

Maybe I knew. Maybe I knew somewhere in my bones that a mother would die, and that her daughter would mourn, and though it would be my blood, it would not be my body.

Maybe I knew it would be so close I could touch it, but it wouldn't quite be mine.

I rolled toward her and closed my eyes, thinking, *This is it. Here it is.*

I felt a silk-spun terror pulled from my body, thirty-seven years of web around my bones, lifted and carried off, as I opened my eyes again to watch her sleep—my motherless mother, my grandmothers gone, and an entire night before us.

17

IF I KNEW THE WAY

January 20, 2017

Did my aunt see him first, and gasp, causing my grandmother to turn? Just in time to see his face before the knife sunk into her neck? And if she was looking forward, no warning at all, was she speaking when the knife went in? What was she saying? Was she looking at her phone? Or doing absolutely nothing? Maybe they were talking about her flight the next day to visit her granddaughter, who was cleaning her house and preparing her guest bed at the very moment a thirty-five-year-old man we all grew up with but suddenly stood a complete stranger buried metal into her tiny neck, wrapped in her mother's pearls.

Is this how we go? Is this all there is? Is this what we're doing here? Do we live our whole lives in work and service to families only to be slaughtered? And in a kitchen, no less? The kitchen we warmed with our own love? To be slaughtered like a fucking barn animal by the very humans we devoted our lives to?

If I could, I would kill him. If I could, I would rip his fucking throat out. But I cannot. Because I am not a murderer. So I remain. We remain. In the blood of our mother.

We remain in the blood of our mother.

We remain in the blood of our mother.

•   •   •

I wrote the words "we remain in the blood of our mother" fifteen times on the page of my journal while sitting alone on a beach in Santa Cruz, and each time I wrote them, the letters were bigger and more jagged and I pressed harder and harder, just as I had my whole life, hoping the torture in me would absorb like ink.

I couldn't save her—nobody could—and nobody could save my other grandmother. That day on the beach I felt it, their absence, and how I simply remain in their blood—my grandmothers, and my mother, who seems different now, who seemed to have a light in her eyes extinguished that day, a wild light that carried her to Yosemite and back home, to me. I understand, though I fear she won't return. I fear she will remain in the blood of her mother, and not a damn one of us will be able to save her.

So I drove to the ocean as my mother had done with us. I looked to the rage of the water as it sang its roar against the rocks of my heart, and waited to be filled again.

I pulled out a fountain pen and the leather traveler's journal my brother had given me for Christmas, and found myself writing that I wanted to kill somebody. But really, I wanted relief. I felt I was drowning in the blood of my mother and her mother and my father's mother, all the mothers in my life and beyond, whose blood pulsed through me like fire but never like annihilation, until then.

I saw myself in them. I saw myself in their eyes or turn of the head or laughter, and it had always felt like connection, like life. One Christmas after Grandma Bonny died, my aunt walked up to me after I had been writing about motherhood for years, and handed me a thick plastic-bound book. On the cover it said, "*Between Us Girls*, by Bonny Jean Hanchett."

"Your grandmother wrote a column to mothers for many years. I collected them for you. Did you know that?"

I looked at my aunt. "No, I had no idea," I said.

As I thumbed through the pages, a chill ran up my body, an electric channel that opened to words and a woman who wrote them seventy years before. I understood then why I kept showing up at her house. I was to become her: in words, in rage, in broken, slightly pathetic mothering.

It was better than a ghost. She was with me. No, she was me. I am her.

We remain in the blood of our mother.

Sitting on the sand with my journal on my knees, I looked up and saw in the breakwater the shadows of my children as they played on that very beach a few months before, before my grandfather watched goldfish swim into the abyss and my grandmother bled on the linoleum, before I knew such things were even possible. The older children chased waves and explored tide pools while my mother, Mac, and I corralled the younger ones, held their tiny resistant hands, tending to the little minds who don't yet know white water can turn without warning into massive sleeper waves.

"Never turn your back to the ocean!" the older children told the younger ones, but they hadn't seen enough to listen yet.

. . .

We have always visited Santa Cruz a few times a year, but for four years in a row, Rocket wanted to go there for his birthday celebration. We often stayed in a motel in Aptos, a little town a few miles down the coast from Santa Cruz. We'd wake up on Saturday morning and walk a few blocks to the beach, then turn right and head down to the pier with the metal boat at the end, on the other side of a wood fence. It's a famous metal boat. Everybody knows about it, though nobody seems to know why it's there.

On our second trip to Aptos, we were walking to the beach when a white house with gray trim caught my attention. As we moved closer, I realized I had seen it before, many years earlier. I looked harder as the memory formed in my mind, and I realized I had actually been in that house before.

I had driven there with a boy named Evan when I was sixteen years old. The entire night rushed into my mind: sitting in his Jeep along winding roads, pulling up to the house on the corner, parking across the street, getting beer from a supermarket that sold to underage kids. The joint he smoked while I politely declined.

"No thanks, weed's not my thing," I said. He was older than me and excessively popular, and I was trying to act confident, but I was afraid.

Evan and I drank a lot of alcohol that night, took some ecstasy (which was bunk) and some cocaine, but I remembered that night in particular because it was when I smoked heroin for the first time. He and his friends had to teach me how, though I felt no resistance. I sat on a couch with people I had just met, and somebody brought out the tinfoil, lit it underneath, and showed me how to inhale the smoke through a straw.

After that, Evan and I decided to go for a walk, so we went down to the beach, turned right, and walked down to the pier. It was the middle of the night and there was nobody around. I wanted to see the metal boat at the end, but the fence was locked. I tried climbing it but couldn't get a footing on the front of the boards, so I kicked off my shoes and scaled the railing of the pier while Evan yelled at me to stop.

I did it anyway, and he joined me, probably afraid of compromising his masculinity. We were high up, and beneath us was the crashing, freezing ocean. It was two or three a.m. and black below us. The fence extended from the sides of the pier for a few feet, but if I could get around to the other side I could get on the boat. So I tiptoed along the tiny wooden lip beneath the fence, clinging to the top of the boards, all the way to the end, but then I had to swing my body around the last pillar, and that seemed particularly dangerous. Evan was with me until then. He said, "You're fucking crazy" and went back onto the pier. I looked at him and smiled, held on tight, and swung my body out over the ocean and around to the other side, not knowing if there was a footing.

I made it. I looked down at the rolling water, and it only looked lovely and soft. By the time I got to the metal boat, whatever drugs I had in my body were wearing off and I got that familiar anxiety and urge for more that made me forget everything I was doing and focus on what mattered. More. So I didn't even sit and enjoy the boat. I just yelled at Evan on the other side of the fence and told him I was there, then climbed the boards on the back of the fence and hopped down. I put on my shoes and walked back, hoping this guy wouldn't try to have sex with me and wondering how much more blow was available.

• • •

The second time I recognized the Aptos house and recalled the metal boat escapade, I was thirty-five and pushing a three-month-old baby with Mac and our three other children. I felt fat and frumpy with my gray roots showing, and was hit with a blast of shame and sadness because back then I had been young and beautiful and hopeful about what life would become. Life was really going to be something, and when Evan was gone, I thought someday I would find another man who loved me even more, and I would have reached that potential everybody had been talking about since I was a kid in the "Gifted and Talented" program.

This whole cocaine booze sex cigarette jumping-over-fence thing is merely a phase. It's a silly one-time, maybe few-year, young-person phase, and the metal boat is just around the corner, I tell you. The thing I'm risking it all for is just right there.

I believed it.

As Mac and I walked with our children, we had Styrofoam cups of motel coffee in our hands. It was nowhere near strong or plentiful enough. Georgia was throwing a tantrum because she wanted to push the stroller and we wouldn't let her. Ava was complaining about the flies. I told her it was from the seaweed. Rocket wondered about the driftwood scattered across the sand. Mac told him there must have been storms recently.

I watched the joggers in awe, as usual. *Look at them out here running at nine a.m. on a Saturday.* The fog was perfection. People were already arriving to set up birthday parties in the barbeque areas. I saw them and I saw us and I saw the ocean. And in flashes, when I had a second or two in silence, I saw me—sixteen years old, spinning over oceans and piers and men like straws over heroin.

I wasn't going to fall. I could not. I was holding on and too young to die.

I walked along this road at sixteen, high. I walked it again at thirty-five. I walked it at thirty-one, too, but somehow failed to notice.

•   •   •

Perhaps it took a few years for my mind to accept the memory of that white and gray house. Perhaps the brain blocks us from what's too strong, too soon. After eight years of sobriety, I've grown better at it, better at encountering places that bump me into history, into living for a moment a tiny irreconcilable truth.

At first, I couldn't look at the places at all. I couldn't look the first time I drove by the motel where Mac and I stayed because there were "people" in our house. When I think about that time in the motel, the pier and metal boat seem less appealing, and even though I'm older and more tired now, I am freer, because I don't need to throw myself over a cold dark ocean to get to where I'm going.

At first, I couldn't look at the craft store in my town either, because I once drove Ava to preschool after taking drugs, and I couldn't make it back in time because those lines wear off quickly, so I stopped behind that craft store and did another line, right there in the car off the back of a binder. Many years after that, I bought material there for the Harry Potter costume my mother was sewing for Ava. Now, I buy felt and poster board there for school projects, and clay for Ava to shape into little animals for gifts at Christmastime, and mini hay bales to decorate our porch in the fall.

The liquor store down the road was *my liquor store*, where they knew me by name, and I was sure nobody from my family would see me. I could hide there. I could buy my bottles in peace. Once, Mac saw me driving out of that liquor store parking lot and followed me in his car. He was irate and wanted to know who I was with. I couldn't stop because I was drunk and thought he would kill me, though that was my imagination. Mac is a gentle man, but it was a dangerous time for both of us. I was absent and loose, insane and drunk, and he was sober but miserable and insane, and losing his wife.

I wanted to be as good as him but I didn't know how. I wanted to be his wife but could not. I felt sorry for myself and ordered another whiskey. But after that run-in, I was very particular about where I went. I found a new liquor store. Now I buy milk at that liquor store when I don't have time to make it to the market.

●　●　●

I don't shake my head anymore to get rid of the memories. I take a deep breath, look at each line of the picture in my mind, and get as close as I possibly can to the image and the pain it causes. I say "thank you" sometimes, in moments when I'm sitting at some horribly boring back-to-school night or student pick-up line, or working at my child's preschool, or doing some other motherly thing. Because on the surface, I fit in now.

But I have a secret that's not really a secret, and I hang out with many alcoholic mothers, trying to make those years worth living. When they tell me the horrendous and disgusting things they've done, I flinch and think, "What kind of fucking dirtbag...," but then I remember my own damn story, and that I, in fact, was that dirtbag. So I nod, and tell what I did, and how I recovered, because I want them to see that the water they need to wash themselves clean flows always and immediately to the lowest possible places. And I know that God, to me, is that kind of love.

I always thought I had to get holy before some Power would help me, if there was one. Now I see that it is when we are our most vile that help comes pouring in, meeting us where we are at the bottom, where all the humans refuse to go anymore, because it's dark and reeks of the dying. Maybe they've forgotten that from their sunlit vistas, that some of us are broken enough to believe we need rebuilding, and that lifting us is worth their time. Or maybe they never knew.

I know, though, and I'm here with them still, though I'm walking around a life that isn't my life or wasn't my life once, and the two seem wholly incompatible, impossible even, and yet this is the same body that inhaled and spun around the pillar over the ocean, and now I'm making semi-forced small talk with you in your yoga pants and Honda Pilot because we're both mothers picking up our kids and it's hard and thankless and perfect. The only indicator of those years are my ill-timed swear words and the slash marks on my arm, which you probably can't see now anyway, as the years have faded them into almost nothing. (You can see them if you really look.)

You can't even get to the metal boat anymore. It sank down farther into the ocean and now it's completely removed from the fence. Even if you jump the fence you can't get to the boat. Now it's only a place for the seagulls to shit and the tourists to wonder what it was like to sit on its hull or walk along its sides. It looks creepy and broken and rusty now, half submerged in murky blue.

I knew it when it still seemed like a boat. I knew it during its better days. It never saw me during mine.

•   •   •

I didn't reread what I wrote on that journal page, not on that January day, though I noticed how my handwriting got big and jagged and crooked as I fought and scribbled "blood of our mother" the last few times, my hand growing tired and unhinged from confusion and pressing so hard. I looked up at the waves and remembered one particular birthday trip to Santa Cruz—the worst one. The best one.

Mac and I had woken up in the mood preceding a day trip to the beach, chatting for a few minutes while still in bed. I told him a friend was really interested in a woman she'd been dating.

"Is she down like four flats on a dump truck?" Mac smirked, cracking a dubious smile.

I raised my eyebrows, "I have no idea what that means."

"Flats," he said, lifting his hand in the air and flipping out his fingers. "On a dump truck... Wait. Are you serious?"

"Of course I'm serious. I do not understand your construction talk." I said this in my bitchiest, most pretentious voice, knowing he'd play, knowing we were on the frequency of old friends.

"This is not construction, Janelle. This is about trucks." He tilted his head forward toward me and looked at me side-eyed, as if that face was going to help me understand the simile.

I stared at him.

"What do you think it means?" he asked, almost hesitantly.

"I have no idea," I said. "Something about flatbeds? Flats? The back of trucks?"

He shook his head and with a quick flash in his eye, said, "You know what? The next time you say something about Baldwin or Foucault I'm not even going to try to understand what you're saying. I'm just going to say whatever stupid shit first comes to my mind, like you do."

I roared in laughter. It was perfection, because that was exactly what I had done, and he saw it, and knew it, and yet I really had no idea what he was talking about, because so often, the obvious answer is lost on me. It's right in front of my face, but I'm staring left, or right, or over in some dark minuscule corner, where vague metaphor and "deep meaning" lie.

I spent the first ten years of our marriage like that, trying to change Mac, trying to mold him into the man I thought he needed to be, the kind of man who could "fulfill me," a better version of himself that only I could see, of course.

But it never worked. He never got better at organizing linen closets or finishing projects he started. He never got better at budgeting or perfect at anticipating family needs or articulating his deep emotional development. He never talked as I talked at him. He never got better at realizing my vision of "wedded bliss." But during a particularly difficult moment at around marriage year ten, when I was four minutes away from divorce, Good News Jack asked, "Janelle, where did you get your ideas about marriage?"

"What do you mean?" I asked, frowning through the phone.

"Where did you get your ideas of romance, of what it's all supposed to be?"

I traced my concepts of "marriage" all the way back to the beginning, all the way back to the magazine wedding dress shoved in my journal, to the yachts in the San Francisco Bay, to the love songs and teenaged daydreams.

I realized then it was Hallmark cards and Meg Ryan movies.

And I was wrong again.

"For people like us," Jack said, "life is a series of discovering all the things we've been wrong about."

That morning, the day we were heading to Santa Cruz, I stood cooking some bacon at the stove, and Mac sat in the dining room adjacent, and for some reason Georgia asked about our wedding photos, which I had burned, one by one, in the little apartment where I had lived alone, desperate and sure I would never need them again. The ones that showed us beneath the trees at the courthouse. The ones with Ava in a carrier on my mother. The ones of Mac and me holding hands and looking at one another with tears in our eyes.

I told Georgia, "Well, we don't have any because your dad got upset one day and destroyed them all."

I threw Mac a knowing smile.

Georgia asked, "Why did you do that, Daddy?"

I was about to own up to my lie, but before I could, Mac answered, "Because I was very sad, and I thought getting rid of those photos would make me feel better."

After he said it, he looked up at me straight into my shame, with a love and compassion and forgiveness that now, sixteen years after that courthouse wedding, takes my breath away, as if I were standing in a white gown in a castle in France, or on a yacht in the San Francisco Bay. I held his eyes again, as I had done the night we met, and I couldn't believe that love was mine.

But I had no evidence of the things to come back then. I wish I could elbow myself as I stood there. I'd say, "Hey, Janelle. Just wait. There's some big love coming your way. The wedding doesn't matter, kid."

I never would have believed me, though. That's for sure.

We were friends. We were always good friends. And mine were tears of joy after all.

As soon as we pulled into our parking spot at the Boardwalk in Santa Cruz, a beachfront amusement park, Mac jumped out through the passenger door and vomited on the asphalt. I figured that was an ominous sign. He spent the next five hours in the car, green-faced and sweating, while I tried not to lose four kids in the endless crowds and sweltering heat that is Santa Cruz in September. It was Rocket's tenth birthday, after all, and I tried to make it great. I never forgot his first one, and I'll never give up trying to repair it.

I was convinced Mac's sickness was my fault on account of my bad behavior at Starbucks a couple of hours before. I had been flippant and rude to one of the baristas because they charged us extra for a dash of soy milk as cream, even though I explained that Mac can't drink milk and "nobody ever charges us for a little bit for his coffee." I was thus convinced they had poisoned him with spoiled soymilk. I vowed once again never to snap at the people preparing my food.

By the end of the day, it was clear Mac wouldn't make the three-hour drive home, so we paid $300 for a last-minute motel room that should have cost $100, and piled our children into the tiny rectangle. After dinner, Ava started feeling sick. And then Rocket. I began to think perhaps my bad behavior had not caused the illness. By two a.m., everyone was sick except me, so I passed the night rotating around the bathroom and beds, and I thought, *Well, obviously I am in hell.* As the only well person, I cleaned vomit and changed Arlo's diarrhea diapers, unpacked the car and helped the kids wash their faces and sip water and change out of puke clothes.

I woke up the next morning after one hour of sleep, facing a three-hour car ride over winding roads with four sick children and a barely recovering husband. We had to get home. Mac had to work the next day, and staying would cost too much money anyway. I loaded everyone into the car and drove straight to a liquor store, where I knew they'd sell those red party cups, which would be perfect vomit cups.

It was a beautiful day, but my eyes ached in the sun, my bones heavy from exhaustion. I had spent the whole day before in the relentless heat, and in crowds, *my God, the fucking crowds. And now I'm standing here in a liquor store buying bottles of water and red party cups.* I gathered it all into my arms and walked to the checkout line, where I saw a woman who swept my mind immediately, erasing every thought and filling every crevice.

It was twelve p.m. on a Sunday. She stood in front of me in a ruffled skirt and combat boots and tights. It was too hot for such a get-up, and she'd probably been wearing it since Friday, when things were better. Her hair was sticking out and frizzy around a few-day-old braid. When she turned, I saw tattoos along the side of her face, which was swollen and pale with bloodshot eyes. The alcohol radiated off her body, and the smell smacked me into eight, nine, ten years ago.

That sweet-stale reek. Cigarettes and sweat.

"Can you give me a deal on a pint?" she asked the cashier.

He had already put her pint on the counter, grabbing it before she asked. He knew what she wanted. I looked down at the bottle. Rot-gut whiskey.

My kind of girl.

"No, sorry," he said, offering a vague smile. He didn't have to say it, though. We both knew what his face meant: "It's been too many times."

I considered setting my stuff down on the counter, because my arms were achy against the cold drinks, but I didn't want her to feel rushed. She had enough stress.

"It's cool, man, give me a minute," she said. "You know I'm good for it, though." She set some change and a couple of dollar bills on the counter.

"How much do I owe you?" she asked, and her feigned cheerfulness made my heart damn near crack.

One dollar and seven cents more for the rot-gut pint.

She dug in her bag and in the folds of her green canvas jacket, pulling a nickel or two from the plastic penny holder on the left.

I used to do that. Saved me a few times, too.

She remained seven cents short. I opened my purse to grab a dime when she said, "Hold on!" and ran to the back of the store, where I watched her grab a dime off the floor. She placed it on the counter triumphantly.

"We're good today, man!"

I was happy she didn't have to take money from me. I was

happy she got her pint without a front or a handout, and I was happy she could kill the shakes. I knew she was thinking, *I'll be okay today,* and I was glad that moment was happening for her, though it wouldn't be enough.

It will never be enough.

There will never be enough.

She grabbed her whiskey and turned around, wafting that smell again, but as she faced me, she stopped, and looked me right in the eyes. She paused, and looked harder with her chin high and proud.

"Any day now I'll be back to my normal self," she said.

I held her gaze. I couldn't speak. Her words seemed to knock the breath out of me. I smiled a little and nodded, seeing her as best I could. She probably didn't notice my nod, or my smile, but I watched her walk outside and get on her bike. I watched her ride away in the clear sunlight.

God dammit, why did you say that to me? Why? Of all the people and things and moments in the world, I stood behind you on just another alcoholic day in a liquor store and smelled your smell, my old smell, and you spoke the saddest words maybe I've ever heard in my life, and your watery eyes were mine again, yet they were not. Because I'm free now.

Why?

I'm a stranger to you. A nobody. A nothing.

When I was you I would have turned away from a woman like me, all clear-eyed in the midday with kids and shit.

"Oh, fuck you, lady. Fuck you and your decent life." That's what I would have thought.

(And then, in the throes of the morning, I would have begged God to join you.)

I knew her. The pain. The hope. The energy in the unopened bottle. The strength pulsing through the walls of the glass in my hand. *Just this last pint. Just this one. I'm okay today. It's okay.*

Tomorrow I'll pull it together.

And tomorrow, tomorrow I'll be me again.

Any day now. Any day now I'll be back to my normal self.

I wanted to stare at where she last stood, to stay with her. I wanted to chase after her. I wanted to say something. Instead I met eyes with the man behind the counter. It was time to pay, time to go on. It felt weird, once again, to be on this side of normalcy.

Me and this dude at work at the liquor store. Me, buying water and red cups because my kids are sick and we have to drive home. Me, tired from being up all night in a motel room during a trip gone awry. Me, frustrated with the day, but, well, lost in the web of the normal life.

You buying a pint with scavenged change at noon, looking to tomorrow. You telling me you're okay while you stink and waste away. You riding away in hope, until the shakes come again.

Me pulling out my debit card and spending nine dollars.

I used to grab pennies out of the plastic container to buy pints. Ancient Age whiskey, a pack of Pall Malls, and a Coke if I had extra money. If I think really hard, maybe I can remember the exact amount of those three items. The cost of okay. The cost of the day. I'd dig in the folds of my car, under rugs and in deeper and deeper spots as if I hadn't looked there already.

Sometimes he'd give me a pint on credit. But never the Pall Malls. He knew I'd be fine without those. I always paid him back as soon as I could because I knew I'd need his help again. After the first pull hit my gut I'd feel hope, and the shakes would quiet, and I'd know just like her that tomorrow would be different.

Tomorrow I'll call my mom and get sober. I'll get with Ava and Rocket and work. I'll call my dad. I'll tell him everything. I'll eat some good food and clean my car and above all I'll never drink again.

Any day now I'll be back to my normal self.

Any moment. Maybe this moment.

I wanted to tell that lady that the most important word in that strange sentence was "self." The word she can't forget. The word she can't let go of. She has one. It's there. Buried beneath a few thousand years of separation and pain, or so it feels, but it's still intact, on fire, alive, pulsing through the reek of shame and humiliation, the part of her who looked at the woman behind her in line and knew they were the same.

I was still thinking of her as I got in my car and passed out the red cups. *I wish I would have bought you the pint. I wish I would have handed it to you and said, before you could speak, "I see you."*

I wished I had told her I saw God in her cracked eyes—that it's been years, but I still love her.

Instead, I got in the car and threw it in reverse and turned on "Ripple" because I needed to hear Jerry sing it: "If I knew the way, I would take you home"—because that's what I wanted to tell that lady, really, and that's where I was headed.

Home.

Ava saw me staring, and asked me what was wrong.

"Nothing, baby," I said, and squeezed her wrist, so just for a moment I could feel our pulse.

ACKNOWLEDGMENTS

A massive thank you to my manager, Jermaine Johnson, for seeing something in my work that was worth pursuing, for that eight p.m. email that changed my life, and for the direction and brilliance and humor of our every call. And to my agent, Richard Abate, for teaching me what the hell a book proposal is and giving me more essential writing guidance in five-minute phone calls than I got in the entirety of my college career. Working with 3 Arts is probably the greatest honor of my life. Don't tell my kids.

To Lauren Hummel at Hachette, thank you for your editorial clarity, insight, and tireless work, and for seeing this book always as what I hoped it would be. You know how I feel about "magic," but the intersection of our lives was, well, you know.

Michael Barrs and Michelle Aielli, thank you for your incredible work on marketing and publicity. Thank you also to Mauro DiPreta, Mike Olivo, Sean Ford, and Marisol Salaman. The Hachette team was better than I ever could have imagined.

To the readers of Renegade Mothering, where do I fucking begin? Thank you for reading all these years, for every comment and email, for not getting too angry when I crossed that line, or maybe for sticking around *because* I crossed that line. In absolutely unequivocal terms: THIS BOOK IS BECAUSE OF YOU. You became my people when I was sure I had no people.

To the Sauce Tank for handling my exquisite insecurity, my Pescadero renegades for writing anyway, and to you, Dave E., for sticking around and delivering the truth, thank you.

Sarah, my dear friend, from that bastard red tree to you in my kitchen after Joan died, you live the art I'm trying to write.

Skyler Paul, I could not have written a single sentence as clean as a bone without you, soul friend. Let's hum those radio songs.

Dad, thank you for watching kids and supporting cabin trips, for our conversations and the pride in your voice, but mostly for teaching me how to spot bullshit from a very young age. And Neena, thank you for loving me even when you didn't have to, and for giving me Jerry.

And, you, mama, whom I couldn't possibly thank sufficiently, I'll just say thank you for the billion moments of help, now and before, for posting my writing on the refrigerator when I was ten, and for always leading me home.

Ava, Rocket, Georgia, and Arlo: *You are my best.*

Mac, you are the reason I kept writing when I was sure it was pointless and you were right, my love. You saw what I could not with those kindest brown eyes. I love you terribly.

And finally, to the alcoholic who still suffers, and the children of alcoholics, with every word I typed, you were never far from my mind.